AIDING AND ABETTING

AIDING AND ABETTING

U.S. FOREIGN ASSISTANCE
AND STATE VIOLENCE

Jessica Trisko Darden

STANFORD UNIVERSITY PRESS
Stanford, California

Stanford University Press
Stanford, California

Printed in the United States of America on acid-free, archival-quality paper

Library of Congress Cataloging-in-Publication Data
Names: Trisko Darden, Jessica, author.
Title: Aiding and abetting : U.S. foreign assistance and state violence /
    Jessica Trisko Darden.
Description: Stanford, California : Stanford University Press, 2020. |
    Includes bibliographical references and index.
Identifiers: LCCN 2019019672 (print) | LCCN 2019022027 (ebook) |
    ISBN 9781503611009 (electronic) | ISBN 9781503610231 (cloth :alk. paper) |
    ISBN 9781503610996(pbk. :alk. paper)
Subjects: LCSH: Human rights—Developing countries. | Political
    persecution—Developing countries. | State-sponsored terrorism—
    Developing countries. | Military assistance, American—Developing
    countries. | Economic assistance, American—Developing countries.
Classification: LCC JC599.D44 (ebook) | LCC JC599.D44 T75 2020 (print) |
    DDC 323/.044—dc23
LC record available at https://lccn.loc.gov/2019019672

Cover design: Olivier Ballou

Typeset by Westchester Publishing Services in Garamond Pro.

Contents

Preface

ON OCTOBER 26, 1973, a family huddled on the tarmac of Manila International Airport, waiting to board a plane that would take them to an unknown future. My mother, her five siblings, and her parents were leaving for San Francisco. The eight tickets cost the equivalent of about $14,000 today. They sold everything they had— car, house, furniture—to buy them. In order to leave the country, each family member had to get clearance from the National Bureau of Investigation, the police, and the tax authorities; they had to endure interrogations and medical screenings. They left behind family, friends, and, in my mother's case, a sweetheart.

When the plane took off, the family said goodbye to the only country they had ever known—a place where my grandparents had survived a brutal Japanese occupation and tasted the beginnings of a country at peace, and eventually enjoyed a happy and comfortable life. They would never again call the Philippines home.

After a brief stop in San Francisco, my family arrived on October 30, 1973, in Vancouver, Canada—where I was later born and grew up. Like many immigrants, the eight of them lived together in a family member's basement until they could afford a home of their own. My grandmother, forty-four at the time, tried her hand at a number of jobs—as a cashier, as a mail clerk at the post office—and was eventually able to get a data entry position at a state-run insurance company. In the Philippines, she had been a college graduate with a well-paying job. But both of my grandparents settled for jobs far less prestigious than the ones they once had. That's the typical immigration story: the older generation makes sacrifices for the opportunities of the next generation. But my family had not longed to immigrate to a new land. They had a comfortable and even privileged life in the Philippines. They were forced to leave, largely because of the influence of Western powers on their country, and the fate of President Ferdinand Marcos.

A lawyer and career politician, Marcos was democratically elected as president of the Philippine Republic in 1965, and in 1969 he was the first leader ever to be elected to a second term. But on September 21, 1972, as leftist demonstrations and a communist insurgency roiled the country, Marcos declared martial law. A nation-wide curfew was immediately imposed. Press freedoms declined overnight. A total of 292 radio stations were closed throughout the country. Seven television stations were shut down, as were sixteen dailies published in Filipino, Chinese, English, and Spanish. Key opposition figures including the former governor and senator Benigno "Ninoy" Aquino Jr. were accused of murder, illegal possession of firearms, and subversion, and placed under military arrest. After Ninoy had endured a hunger strike and two years of detention, a military tribunal sentenced him to death (although the execution was never carried out).

Student activists and media personalities critical of Marcos were also detained. Congress was shut down and, the following year, a new constitution was declared that extended Marcos's rule. My mother—herself a student activist—and her family were among a fortunate few who sold what they could and fled to Australia, Canada, or the United States.

Amnesty International claims that 70,000 Filipinos were imprisoned and 34,000 tortured during the almost ten-year period of martial law (September 1971 to January 1981). A total of 3,257 people are thought to have been killed by the military under the Marcos dictatorship, though many families will never know what happened to loved ones who simply disappeared. Lurid stories drifted out of the Philippines: imprisonments and repeated rapes; American priests arrested and deported. When finally given the opportunity to air their grievances in 2013, Filipinos alleged 75,730 claims of human rights violations against the Marcos regime.

Yet, despite all of this, Marcos was considered a friend of the United States. A history of American imperialism, liberation from Japanese occupation, and the 1951 Mutual Defense Treaty bound together the security of the Philippines and the United States, committing them to mutual aid in the face of an aggressor in the Pacific. The long-standing presence of U.S. military bases throughout the country gave the United States access to the region, but also meant that it had to maintain amicable relations with the Philippines. That was relatively easy because Marcos's struggle against an insurgency led by the Chinese Communist-leaning New People's Army made him, like General Suharto in Indonesia, a key figure in the fight against communism in Asia.

The United States did not want to see the Philippines fall to communism, and, in that sense, America's Cold War policy clearly succeeded there. But by assuming responsibility for the Philippines' defense and training its military, the United States allowed the leaders of the Philippines to focus on internal threats—to their power, to their wealth, and to their continued rule. The foreign assistance provided to the Philippines during the Marcos era also undermined the broader development goals that the United States had for the country. During the decade of martial law, U.S. military assistance to the Philippines totaled the equivalent of about $1.16 billion, while overall foreign aid from the United States exceeded $3.5 billion. No matter what Marcos did, American aid dollars flowed. But even as aid kept coming, the Philippines—which had been one of the most prosperous countries in Asia—became one of the poorest. A system of crony capitalism enriched Marcos's friends and allies; corruption reached far into the judiciary and police forces. Shortly after the declaration of martial law, the state took ownership of Philippine Airlines and forced foreign companies to give up their stakes in the Philippines National Oil Company. The military bought private steel mills to form the National Steel Corporation. And while the elite pillaged the economy, the percentage of Filipinos living in poverty grew.

But eventually, the Filipino people fought back. Twenty years after the People Power Revolution toppled the Marcos regime and he fled with his family to Hawaiʻi, my mother returned to the Philippines. I sat beside her as our plane landed at Manila Ninoy Aquino International Airport. In the years between my mother's departure and her return in 2005, Ninoy Aquino had become the face of Philippine democracy. He was released from a military prison and allowed to travel with his family to the United States for medical treatment. After a brief stint lecturing at Harvard and MIT, Ninoy left to return to the Philippines and lead the opposition to Marcos's rule. He was assassinated, with a single gunshot wound to the head, when he landed in Manila—at that same airport—in August 1983. Although sixteen servicemen, including a general, were eventually convicted in 1990 for his murder, conspiracy theories and allegations of the Marcos family's direct involvement persist.

Ninoy's death marked the beginning of the end of the Marcos regime. Millions of Filipinos took to the streets and the United States finally began to press Marcos for meaningful political reform. Ninoy's wife, Corazon Aquino, would challenge Marcos in elections and ultimately become the first woman president of the Philippines, following Marcos's resignation. Their son, Benigno Aquino III, would become president in June 2010 and sign into law the Human Rights Victims Reparation and Recognition Act. The act acknowledged the victims of human rights violations during the Marcos regime and offered them financial compensation for their suffering. *Yo so Ninoy.* I am Ninoy.

Only two months after my mother's return to the Philippines, President Gloria Macapagal Arroyo—herself the daughter of a former president—declared a national state of emergency after an attempted military coup against her, the second attempt in less than three years. In the months and years that followed, opposition journalists continued to be arrested and murdered. The Philippines was ranked alongside Russia in freedom of the press. Democracy is a fragile thing.

Some members of Congress urged the United States to make military assistance to the Arroyo government dependent on the end of extrajudicial killings. Little came of their efforts. And although Arroyo and other former politicians have since done prison time for corruption, none have been held to account for the human rights abuses that occurred under their watch.

What exactly, then, was the United States buying with decades of foreign aid to my mother's country, the Philippines? After the closure of American military bases in the country in 1992, U.S. military assistance dropped by 84 percent. Over the course of four years, military aid to the Philippines went from $316 million to $1.3 million. Clearly, the continuing threat of communism in the Philippines, seen in attacks by the New People's Army, wasn't enough to sustain America's attention once its military bases were gone. Nor was an Islamist insurgency in the country's south. Economic aid fell as well, while millions of Filipinos (roughly 20 percent of the population) were left to live in extreme poverty. Democracy held, but when looking at the Philippines now, the clearest outcomes of decades of U.S. support appear to be endemic corruption, a preference for justice outside of the courts, and a shocking naiveté about the risks of authoritarian rule.

Today, the Philippines is experiencing renewed violence and movement toward autocracy. Rodrigo Duterte's election as president in May 2016 in many ways demonstrates the long-term consequences of foreign intervention in the Philippines. Long associated with "death squads" in his home city of Davao, Duterte launched a national War on Drugs that claimed over 7,000 lives in its first nine months. President Donald J. Trump praised him for doing an "unbelievable job on the drug problem." On May 23, 2017, Duterte declared martial law in the southern province of Mindanao and later threatened to expand it throughout the country. Unsurprisingly, he supported the reburial of Marcos in the country's Cemetery for Heroes (Libingan ng mga Bayani), an honor reserved for former presidents and distinguished military officers but formerly denied to the dictator. Duterte also supported Marcos's son in his quest for the independently elected role of vice president (Bongbong, as Ferdinand Marcos Jr. is known, came a close second). The possibility of a new era of human rights abuses in the Philippines feels more real than ever.

This book examines how U.S. foreign assistance policy has shaped state violence throughout the developing world, from its inception in 1949 to the present day. America's ability to influence violence abroad is not simply some long-gone Cold War phenomenon. I illustrate how foreign assistance, even when given for benign or altruistic purposes, can be diverted by recipient governments to support their continued hold on power through violence. Simply put, foreign aid can do as much harm as it can good.

I dedicate this book to those who lost their lives or left their homes because of violence and unrest that, in a different sort of world, might not have occurred. In his "Message to the Twenty-First Century," Isaiah Berlin said of the atrocities of the Russian Revolution, the Second World War, and the postwar revolutions that tore through the developing world: "They were not natural disasters, but preventable human crimes, and whatever those who believe in historical determinism may think, they could have been averted."[1] The story of the Philippines could have been different if the United States had used its foreign aid more judiciously. Policies, well-intentioned or not, well-devised or not, have very real consequences.

AIDING AND ABETTING

Introduction

Aiding Freedom: Human Rights and U.S. Foreign Assistance

WHETHER FOREIGN INTERVENTION in the affairs of a sovereign state is justified is at once a practical and a moral question—a question which is often raised in
regard to so-called humanitarian interventions, economic sanctions, and international financial institutions such as the World Bank. The study of foreign intervention
has ranged from analyses of covert operations during the Cold War to investigations
of American efforts to promote democracy abroad and U.S. support for state and
nonstate actors during civil wars. Although it is broadly accepted that such interventions are not neutral, it is less often acknowledged that they can both inadvertently and intentionally contribute to the very dynamics they seek to disrupt.

In the study of foreign intervention, foreign assistance has rarely been a focus.[1]
This is surprising because since its inception in 1949 the United States' foreign assistance program has been seen by policymakers in Washington, D.C. as one of the
country's primary means for influencing the political and economic orientations of
other countries, and as a powerful tool for encouraging higher human rights standards.[2] Many believe that it is possible for the international community and individual donor nations such as the United States to use foreign aid to buy better
behavior from aid recipients, or at least to raise the costs of human rights violations.
The rationale underlying such beliefs is that once countries have become dependent
on foreign assistance, they won't risk upsetting the aid donor because that could
lead to a reduction or curtailment of aid. In this view, aid recipients are treated much
like a child given an iPad as a gift; it becomes something that concerned parents
can threaten to take away whenever the child's behavior becomes unruly.

But international politics is not that simple. Foreign donors such as the United States often face scenarios in which a government receiving aid violates the very rights they are tasked to protect. More important, foreign aid may be a contributing factor to human rights violations in the first place. In this book, I examine how U.S. foreign assistance policy contributes to state violence and government repression in countries receiving American aid. State violence—the use of force by state agents against civilians in ways that violate fundamental human rights—and government repression—the actual or threatened use of physical sanctions (including both violent and nonviolent means) against an individual or organization—are both ways in which state agents seek to control and constrain the behavior and beliefs of citizens in the interest of the state and its institutions. My focus is therefore on how foreign aid can undermine individual freedoms and embolden repressive rulers. Sometimes this is an unintended or secondary effect of U.S. foreign assistance; other times, it is an explicit goal. While foreign assistance has undoubtedly had positive effects globally—ranging from improved infant mortality rates and control of infectious diseases to increased literacy—it is crucial to know when, where, and how aid harms more than it helps.

Foreign Aid: The American Way

On January 20, 1949, President Harry S. Truman stood in front of the Capitol and declared, "It may be our lot to experience, and in a large measure bring about, a major turning point in the long history of the human race."[3] His second inaugural address laid out four courses of action for the pursuit of peace and freedom. The first was unfaltering support for the United Nations (UN). The second promised what would become the Marshall Plan—a massive aid program to bring about economic recovery and stave off the advance of communism, named after Secretary of State George Marshall. The third course of action would lead to the establishment of NATO, arguably the world's most important military alliance. The fourth course of action, what came to be known as Truman's "Fourth Point" or "Point Four," aimed to reshape the developing world: "More than half the people of the world are living in conditions approaching misery. Their food is inadequate. They are victims of disease. Their economic life is primitive and stagnant. Their poverty is a handicap and a threat both to them and to more prosperous areas. For the first time in history, humanity possesses the knowledge and skill to relieve the suffering of these people."[4] As historian Amanda Kay McVety notes, "It was the perfect foreign policy program: morally good, economically feasible, and, most importantly, diplomatically strategic, all of which made it palatable to the American public."[5]

Under Truman, the U.S. foreign assistance program would not be simply a handout, but neither would it be the predatory system established by imperial powers. Its aim would be to help the free peoples of the world—through their own efforts—to grow more, to produce more, to build more, and ultimately to lighten their burdens. Unlike the Marshall Plan, the Point Four program was based on the concept of long-term aid to nations that had never industrialized or been connected to the global economy. The Point Four program would help the United States achieve existing policy objectives, including increased national economic productivity, a more balanced world economic structure, peace, and the wider spread of democracy abroad.[6] Its ability to do good seemed boundless.

It took time to translate Truman's vision into practice. The Act for International Development was signed into law on June 5, 1950. Later that year, the Technical Cooperation Administration was established within the State Department to administer the Point Four program. David Ekbladh writes that "while various bodies had been responsible for 'uplift' or 'civilizing' efforts that were development programs in all but name in the Philippines or during the extended U.S. military occupation of Haiti, these had never been given a perennial, global mission."[7] The Point Four program was fundamentally different. The global scope of Truman's vision was reflected in the initial agreements signed, first with Iran on October 19, 1950, followed by Liberia, Brazil, Chile, El Salvador, Afghanistan, Indonesia, and Pakistan.[8]

The United States' vision of foreign aid shifted somewhat toward greater security concerns in October 1951 with the passage of the Mutual Security Act. The Mutual Security Act was a response to communist gains following the 1949 revolution in China and the invasion of South Korea by North Korea in June 1950. It explicitly harnessed U.S. foreign aid in service of the Cold War, a policy that continued as Soviet aid to the "Third World" also expanded throughout the 1950s and 1960s. During this period, the United States developed new instruments for providing military assistance—including Military Assistance Program (MAP) grants and Foreign Military Financing (FMF)—that enabled partner governments to receive equipment and training from the United States or access equipment through American commercial channels by funding military spending and subsidizing military equipment purchases. International Military Education and Training (IMET) funds permitted foreign military officer and personnel training to take place abroad, as well as at U.S. staff colleges, on a grant basis. Over the past fifty years, roughly half a million foreigners have been trained in U.S. military institutions thanks to American taxpayers.[9]

Other foreign aid tools were soon developed. Under President Dwight Eisenhower, the Food for Peace program (Public Law or PL 480) was established. This marked the beginning of America's food aid program, which continues today. Through subsidized sales of grain, cotton, and other agricultural products, PL 480 helps transfer excess American farm production to the developing world. The

Food for Peace program established by Eisenhower was, and still is, strongly backed by a domestic constituency—American farm organizations—who directly benefit from the government purchases that make food aid possible. The American shipping industry benefits as well. Less than two months after PL 480 was signed, a requirement was added that at least 50 percent of all U.S. government food aid shipments must be carried overseas by U.S.-flagged vessels. This requirement has made its way into newer American food aid programs as well, including the Food for Progress Program and the McGovern-Dole International Food for Education and Child Nutrition Program.[10]

As early as the 1950s, the tensions in U.S. foreign aid policy were apparent. Humanitarian, national security, and commercial interests all shaped how American aid was distributed. Then, as now, U.S. foreign assistance was not driven by a single, consistent vision of what it could or should achieve. Yet, few politicians openly acknowledged these tensions. Instead, moral imperatives were often evoked as a justification for continued aid. In his inaugural address, President John F. Kennedy promised "to those people in the huts and villages of half the globe struggling to break the bonds of mass misery, we pledge our best efforts to help them help themselves, for whatever period is required—not because the communists may be doing it, not because we seek their votes, but because it is right."[11] Only a decade after formal foreign aid institutions were created, providing foreign assistance had become simply what America did.

The passage of the Foreign Assistance Act in 1961, arguably the definitive innovation in U.S. foreign aid policy, did little to resolve the tensions. The Foreign Assistance Act defines U.S. foreign assistance as

> any tangible or intangible item provided by the United States Government [including by means of gift, loan, sale, credit or guaranty] to a foreign country or international organization under this or any other Act, including but not limited to any training, service, or technical advice, any item of real, personal, or mixed property, any agricultural commodity, United States dollars, and any currencies of any foreign country government which are owned by the United States Government.[12]

As a result, the United States has a much more expansive understanding of what constitutes foreign assistance than most other countries. Indeed, what many countries count as their foreign aid—official development assistance as defined by the Organisation for Economic Co-operation and Development (OECD)—covers a relatively narrow slice of America's foreign assistance efforts.[13]

Given the scope of America's foreign assistance, Kennedy created the United States Agency for International Development (USAID) as the main administrative body.[14] USAID administers bilateral (country-to-country) development assistance—

for example, funds for building schools in rural areas, or new farming initiatives—in individual countries. With a staff of more than 9,500, the agency is responsible for overseeing the implementation of projects by thousands of contractors, consultants, and nongovernmental organizations (NGOs) and tracking and administering aid from a variety of U.S. government agencies. For example, the State Department provides economic aid to support initiatives in areas including global health and child survival, narcotics control, migration and refugee assistance, and nonproliferation and terrorism-related programs, among others. The Department of Agriculture largely funds PL 480 food aid programs in addition to other health and agricultural services, whereas the Centers for Disease Control and Prevention provide assistance for global health programs including malaria and pandemics prevention. USAID's original emphasis was on solving long-term development problems, but as soon as a year after its creation, critics complained that USAID was too slow and showed too few results.[15] Such criticism persists.

U.S. foreign aid policy has consistently been torn between supporting the common good, realized through economic development, and furthering America's own security and diplomatic interests. These conflicting priorities and policies have produced what is at once the world's largest foreign aid program and also one of the most incoherent.

As political theorist Hans Morgenthau noted more than fifty years ago, the provision of resources to other states has historically been used by dominant powers to create and maintain ties with countries in order to shape their political and economic orientations.[16] During the Cold War, the United States consistently increased the level of aid it provided to states under the threat of Soviet subversion or the actions of Soviet client states.[17] In signing the Foreign Assistance Act, Kennedy noted that the bill "provides military assistance to countries which are on the rim of the Communist world and under direct attack. It provides economic assistance to those governments which are under attack from widespread misery and social discontent which are exploited by our adversaries."[18] But under President Lyndon Baines Johnson, aid became explicitly strategic.

Foreign aid was used as a carrot to entice recipients to support U.S. policy objectives, while the possibility of withholding aid could be used as a stick to punish movement away from those same objectives. Secretary of State Dean Rusk argued, "A properly directed foreign assistance program is a vital instrument of United States foreign policy. Economic and military assistance remain far and away the most powerful means at our command to influence the massive forces at work in the less developed nations. They are our primary source of influence on the economic and military evolution of most of the countries of the non-communist world."[19]

Diplomatically or strategically important countries received high levels of U.S. aid, often with little consideration of whether the aid would have any effect on their economic development. Rather, foreign aid helped strengthen regimes such as that of Zaire's Mobutu Sese Seko, which received American aid from 1960 to 1990 in order to prevent a communist-leaning ruler from coming to power. The strategic use of foreign aid became so integral to U.S. foreign policy that Carol Lancaster, a former deputy director of USAID, argued that "foreign aid as we know it began as an instrument of Cold War diplomacy."[20]

In the mid-1970s, U.S. foreign aid policy shifted as Congress passed a series of amendments introducing human rights conditionality. The Harkin amendment (named after Tom Harkin, D-IA) to the International Development and Food Assistance Act of 1975 reads:

> No assistance may be provided under this part to the government of any country which engages in a consistent pattern of gross violations of internationally recognized human rights, including torture or cruel, inhuman, or degrading treatment or punishment, prolonged detention without charges, or other flagrant denial of the right to life, liberty, and the security of person, unless such assistance will directly benefit the needy people in such country.[21]

An amendment to Section 502B of the Foreign Assistance Act spearheaded by Donald Fraser (D-MN) adopted similar language requiring that "except in extraordinary circumstances, the President shall substantially reduce or terminate security assistance to any government which engages in a consistent pattern of gross violations of internationally recognized human rights."[22] Further amendments specified that it is a policy of the United States to promote and encourage increased respect for human rights and fundamental freedoms. Together, this legislation codified human rights as a consideration in U.S. foreign aid policy. Congress began receiving annual human rights reports on foreign countries from the executive branch as part of new reporting requirements.

The impact of this congressionally imposed human rights conditionality remains disputed. Analyses of decades of State Department Reports on Human Rights show that State Department criticism of governments for human rights abuses, considered by Congress in its annual allocation of foreign aid, was strongly influenced by broader Cold War political dynamics.[23] The United States was less likely to criticize the human rights practices of its Cold War allies.[24] In particular, there is strong evidence that the State Department's initial human rights reports to Congress were designed to have as little a disruptive effect as possible on bilateral relations.[25]

To strengthen the responsiveness of U.S. foreign aid to human rights conditions overseas, Senator Patrick Leahy (D-VT) sponsored a series of amendments in the late 1990s that came to be known as the "Leahy Laws."[26] Initially motivated by concerns about human rights abuses by the Colombian and other Latin American militaries, which were receiving aid as part of the United States' War on Drugs, the first Leahy amendment to the Foreign Operations Appropriation Act (Public Law 104–208) was passed in 1997. It prohibited U.S. counternarcotics assistance to foreign military units facing credible allegations of abuses, unless the partner government was taking effective measures to address the allegations. The requirement was later extended to any foreign security force unit through Section 620M of the Foreign Assistance Act. A similar condition is present in Section 362 of Title 10 of the United States Code, which prohibits the Department of Defense from using appropriated funds for "any training, equipment, or other assistance for a unit of a foreign security force if the Secretary of Defense has credible information that the unit has committed a gross violation of human rights." The United States has restricted military assistance to armed forces units in Bangladesh, Colombia, Ethiopia, Egypt, Indonesia, Iraq, Mexico, Nigeria, Pakistan, the Philippines, and Turkey, among others.

Although the Leahy Laws were intended to make the recipients of foreign assistance more accountable to their own people by using the power of America's purse, the impact of these restrictions is not clear-cut. In Indonesia, the United States cut off all military aid in response to widespread human rights abuses in East Timor (now Timor-Leste) in 1999. In particular, Indonesia's army special forces command, known as Kopassus, was singled out for egregious human rights violations including extrajudicial killings. In 2010 the Obama administration chose to resume most Department of Defense cooperation with Kopassus. Three years later, the Indonesian army determined that members of Kopassus were guilty of the extrajudicial killings of four prisoners in retribution for the murder of a fellow soldier.[27]

Other cases demonstrate how the Leahy Laws can be easily circumvented. The Obama administration cut military aid to several Pakistani military units in 2010 as punishment for human rights abuses, including at least 300 extrajudicial executions in the Swat Valley.[28] But the restrictions imposed on Pakistan occurred while a $2 billion counterterrorism assistance package was being negotiated. Mexico stands as another example. Only 15 percent of the total U.S. funds supporting the Mexican police and military are conditional on human rights abuses. This meant that in 2015, only $5 million in aid was withheld from Mexico because of human rights abuses in the country's drug war.[29]

Potentially worse, imposing these restrictions can undermine American influence with and oversight of abusive foreign security forces. A 2013 investigation found that in some cases, the State and Defense Departments had cut off funds to the wrong units.[30] Once units were barred from receiving U.S. funding, resuming cooperation became exceedingly difficult even if partner governments had taken remedial actions. Policy associated with the Leahy Laws has yet to adequately address the question of when a unit is determined to be free of human rights abusers. For example, should restrictions be lifted from a unit when none of its current members had been members when violations took place, or should the entire chain of command for the unit be distanced from prior human rights violations?[31] The actual process for human rights vetting also remains unevenly implemented.[32] An investigation by the State Department's Office of the Inspector General recently found that the Bureau of African Affairs continued payments to Somali National Army units despite a lapse in Leahy human rights vetting approvals.[33] Overall, although human rights vetting of security forces is now a prerequisite for receiving U.S. foreign assistance, the process remains flawed. The implementation of penalties can mean that military-to-military ties are often strained in countries that have the most to gain from U.S. military training and cooperation.

With the end of the Cold War, a significant part of U.S. foreign aid policy lost its underlying logic. The threat of communism, which had shaped American foreign policy for more than four decades, rapidly lost its salience. Under President Bill Clinton, foreign aid policy lacked much direction beyond his strong support for the successor states of the Soviet Union and countries emerging from communism in Eastern Europe. Although U.S. foreign aid was used to secure cooperation in nuclear nonproliferation initiatives in post-Soviet states such as Ukraine and Kazakhstan, overall foreign aid levels declined throughout Clinton's first term and eventually reached a historic low in 1997. Even so, aid continued to be used as a diplomatic tool. Congress approved $400 million in grants for Palestinians, $300 million for Jordan, and $1.2 billion for Israel to fund the implementation in 2000 of the Wye River Agreement, which laid out steps to complete the Oslo peace process. The use of foreign assistance in grand diplomatic bargains continued under the George W. Bush administration: the Six-Party Talks (2003–2007) promised economic and food aid for North Korea in exchange for the suspension of nuclear tests and greater access for international weapons inspectors.

The aftermath of the September 11, 2001 (9/11) attacks brought a significant shift in the distribution of U.S. foreign aid and a reaffirmation of aid's strategic value. As part of the rapid expansion of America's military footprint, military assistance took on quasi-development functions, and development assistance served national security goals. The Commander's Emergency Response Program originated in Iraq as a way for U.S. military commanders to use funds seized from Saddam Hussein's regime to benefit the Iraqi people by funding emergency relief and reconstruction projects.

Projects funded through this program, which was later expanded to include U.S. government funds, included school refurbishments, water- and sewage-related repairs, road and bridge reconstruction projects, and logistical support for the distribution of humanitarian assistance.[34]

Bush reversed the cuts to aid under Clinton and led the largest expansion of U.S. foreign assistance to date. Much of this expansion took place under the auspices of the Global War on Terror, as foreign assistance was recast as a counterterrorism tool. But Bush was also motivated by a deeply held belief that providing foreign aid is in the United States' moral and national interest, once stating that the generosity of the American people "reflects the view that all lives are precious, and to whom much is given, much is required."[35]

Under the George W. Bush administration, foreign aid resumed its early role as an instrument for promoting democracy overseas. The Millennium Challenge Corporation (MCC), an independent aid institution supporting countries that exhibit good governance, economic freedom, and investments in their citizens, was created. The MCC provides aid to countries that meet preset standards in three general areas: rule of law, anticorruption measures, and respect for human rights; social investment in areas such as health care and education; and the promotion of open markets and sustainable government spending. The idea behind the MCC is that countries will willingly make improvements in these areas in order to qualify for and receive MCC funding.

Equally enduring is Bush's other signature foreign assistance program, the United States President's Emergency Plan for AIDS Relief, or PEPFAR. PEPFAR is the largest commitment in history by any country to address a specific disease. It currently provides antiretroviral support to more than fourteen million people. The program's budget has expanded from $2.27 billion in 2004 to $6.75 billion in 2017, and it retains strong bipartisan support.[36]

That the George W. Bush administration managed both the militarization of aid and the world's largest global public health program speaks to the historical tension in U.S. foreign aid policy between humanitarian and strategic objectives. This tension persisted under the administration of Barack Obama, who maintained high levels of foreign aid to strategic allies and to countries with wars that he could not end. The securitization of economic aid expanded under the auspices of countering violent extremism in terrorism-prone countries.[37] Yet, at the same time, President Obama called development a core pillar of American foreign policy. Harkening back to the early expansive vision of U.S. foreign aid, the 2010 National Security Strategy argued that "our diplomacy and development capabilities must help prevent conflict, spur economic growth, strengthen weak and failing states, lift people out of poverty, combat climate change and epidemic disease, and strengthen institutions of democratic governance."[38] The first Quadrennial Diplomacy and Development Review, spearheaded by Secretary of State Hillary Clinton, referred to development as "a strategic, economic, and moral imperative—as central to our foreign policy as diplomacy and defense."[39] As part of its "development diplomacy" approach, the Obama administration launched global initiatives in the areas of public health, climate change, and food security, with funding for environmental protection programs rising from $324 million in 2008 to $1.8 billion in 2016. Between 2001 and 2016, foreign aid funding for the health sector increased by more than 800 percent.[40]

The Obama administration's signature foreign assistance program, Feed the Future, was authorized by the Global Food Security Act of 2016 (Public Law 114–195) and built on the United States' existing food aid program. The law established a specific statutory foundation for global food security assistance, required the president to develop a whole-of-government strategy to promote global food security, and authorized over $1 billion in funding to support the strategy. The United States has recently provided more than 40 percent of global food aid, averaging about $2.4 billion in spending a year since 2014. When it reaches communities where food is scarce, food aid can save lives and improve children's health outcomes.[41] And yet, America's food aid program has been heavily criticized for distorting agricultural markets, failing to improve nutrition, subsidizing poorly run governments, and worsening civil wars.[42]

Policymakers have long tried to tackle the disconnect between the lofty goals of U.S. foreign aid policy and its ability to achieve those goals. To remedy the inefficient administration of foreign aid, President Richard Nixon proposed the elimination of USAID as an independent agency and the reorganization of U.S. development programs. Congress declined Nixon's suggestion, but Nixon and Hubert Humphrey pushed through the New Directions legislation, which shifted USAID from the megaprojects of the Kennedy and Johnson administrations toward a functional, sector-specific structure. In line with his belief that "no single government, no matter how wealthy or well-intentioned, can by itself hope to cope with the challenge of raising the standard of living of two-thirds of the world's people," Nixon created the Overseas Private Investment Corporation, which provides political risk insurance and loan guarantees to support American investment in the developing world as an alternative to foreign aid.[43] Under President Jimmy Carter, a proposed reorganization of USAID failed in Congress. President Clinton tried, and failed, to roll USAID into the State Department.

Although technocrats have struggled with the administration of U.S. foreign assistance for decades, the 2016 election of Donald J. Trump led to a different kind of debate about foreign aid. In response to the need for increased evaluation of the effectiveness of U.S. foreign aid policy, Congress passed the Foreign Assistance Accountability and Transparency Act in 2016.[44] The Trump administration, for its part, proposed a 2018 America First budget that featured dramatic cuts to overall State Department and USAID spending. The response was a seemingly unprecedented bipartisan effort by the foreign policy community to rally together in defense of foreign aid. Although many acknowledge that the structure of the U.S. foreign aid system is in desperate need of reform, few in the policy world seriously considered the proposed cuts. Congress agreed. The Senate Appropriations Committee voted to secure $51 billion in funding for the State Department and related programs, an amount almost $11 billion above the Trump administration's request. Undeterred, subsequent Trump administration budgets featured similar cuts. The administration also proved adept at circumventing Congress by cutting voluntary U.S. contributions to multiple UN agencies.[45] The struggle over the direction of U.S. foreign assistance policy continues unabated.

How Foreign Aid Succeeds or Fails

To understand the impact of foreign aid on human rights, it helps to turn to other forms of foreign intervention—international condemnation, economic liberalization, sanctions, democracy promotion, and military intervention—which may offer clues about how foreign aid similarly succeeds or fails in changing states' behavior. In recent years, for example, the UN Security Council has condemned human rights abuses in Syria, the International Monetary Fund (IMF) has championed economic liberalization in Central Africa, and the United States has placed sanctions on Iran, promoted democracy in Jordan, and waged military intervention in Afghanistan and Iraq. All of these tools have their shortcomings when it comes to protecting and promoting human rights.

International condemnation, or "naming and shaming," usually occurs through institutions such as the UN. It is based on the belief that international actors are able to pressure abusive countries to adopt better human rights practices.[46] This normative pressure can sometimes push states to join international human rights treaties or to allow greater international oversight.[47] The effects of human rights treaties on actual government practices, however, vary substantially. The steps from ratification of a human rights treaty to its implementation and, finally, to actual compliance are fraught with challenges.[48] Naming and shaming can pressure governments to enforce some rights, but they are likely to promote and enforce only those rights that do not threaten the state's political power and status, such as women's social or economic rights, for example.[49] Some states are able to resist normative pressure in part because they receive other signals, such as bilateral foreign aid, that suggest their existing relationships with powerful states outweigh the attention on their negative behavior.[50] Because of this, and other factors, international condemnation and pressure may fail to stop human rights abuses in a timely fashion.[51]

Normative pressure to change states' human rights behavior is appropriate only when abuses are occurring on a scale that is recognized by the international community but are not yet serious enough to warrant stronger action. Few diplomatic levers were applied to Libya prior to NATO intervention to overthrow the Muammar al-Qaddafi regime. Pressure is likely to work only where the international community has the power and interest to effect change. Despite significant media attention to Myanmar's persecution of Rohingya Muslims, there has been little concerted international effort on their behalf. Many countries are too invested in Myanmar's supposed economic and political liberalization to openly tackle this thorny issue. Indeed, the 2017 budget request for USAID included $82.7 million in economic support funds for Myanmar's transition, a more than 30 percent increase over 2015. Yet, 2017 saw growing violence in the country, including the displacement of more than 400,000 Rohingya men, women, and children from Rakhine state to neighboring Bangladesh in what the UN high commissioner for human rights called a textbook example of ethnic cleansing.[52]

The structure of international institutions can also work against their ability to promote change. Russia has protected Syria from harsher UN Security Council condemnation, including for alleged chemical weapons attacks.[53] Yet, the UN General Assembly passed ten resolutions aimed at Israel in a single day in November 2016.[54] Academic studies have largely ignored the moral ambivalence of the existing international system as one explanation for why human rights violations persist despite ongoing pressures for compliance with international legal obligations.[55] In short, international pressure may help on the margins, but the relationship between human rights rhetoric and actual human rights practices remains shaky at best.

Economic liberalization is an even more indirect way of improving human rights. Opening a country's borders to trade and financial investment can stimulate economic growth, the development of a middle class, and support an increasingly stable political environment that respects individual human rights and civil liberties.[56] The United States, in this view, works through institutions such as the World Bank, the IMF, and the World Trade Organization to promote neoliberal economic values centered on openness and free trade. It signs bilateral investment treaties and preferential trade agreements with individual countries that help tie them to the economy of the United States and by extension, to the global economy.[57] When China joined the World Trade Organization it was initially hailed as a boon to human rights because many assumed that improved labor rights and economic conditions in China would eventually lead to broader gains in individual political rights.

The empirical record on this issue is mixed.[58] On the one hand, it appears that integration into the world economy may improve respect for rights.[59] Evidence suggests that preferential trade agreements may lead to improved human rights practices because trade partners may moderate abusive behavior because they fear losing the benefits of trade.[60] On the other hand, however, IMF austerity programs and World Bank structural adjustment agreements have been found to worsen human rights conditions in developing countries, albeit sometimes after an initial period of improvement.[61] By engaging with the global economy, countries may also become more vulnerable to global economic shocks and capital flight, which may contribute to escalating opposition to the government and trigger a repressive response by the state.[62]

Economic sanctions impose restrictions on trade or financial transactions to punish a state—for violating international law, for instance—by hurting its economy. Occasionally, specific individuals are targeted through the freezing or seizure of their overseas assets, or through travel bans. Sanctioning is a two-pronged approach to behavioral change. States can threaten sanctions to affect another state's behavior, and they can implement the sanctions if the threat does not get results.[63] Like international condemnation, sanctions are often ineffective because they are imposed on countries that already have poor relationships with the country or countries threatening action.

In May 2017 the House of Representatives voted to place expanded sanctions on North Korea that prohibit goods produced by North Korean forced labor, and to sanction employers in places such as Russia, Qatar, and Kuwait that use North Korean forced labor. Given the already limited economic relationship between the United States and North Korea and the worsening relations with Russia and Qatar, the sanctions cost the United States very little—but they also had little impact on North Korea. Following a North Korean intercontinental ballistic missile test, the UN imposed new sanctions. But even the threat of further trade restrictions and the possibility of North Korea being excluded from the U.S.-led international financial system did not deter its leadership from conducting another nuclear test or launching ballistic missiles over Japan in September 2017. After two summits with President Trump failed to bring about denuclearization, North Korea's dictator Kim Jong Un oversaw another tactical guided weapons test in April 2019.

Even when targeting pariah regimes such as North Korea's, advocates of sanctions as a tool for promoting human rights need to be careful. Research suggests that both unilateral and multilateral economic sanctions worsen human rights conditions by damaging the economy and increasing popular opposition to the governing regime, which increases the likelihood of repression.[64] In some cases, sanctions may also strengthen the targeted regime; sanctions have bolstered support for Russian president Vladimir Putin by fomenting anti-Western sentiment. Furthermore, the ultimate value of sanctions is questionable, considering their negative impact on civilian livelihoods. Despite the attempts to craft "smart sanctions" that target the state's leadership, sanctions create scarcity, which allows governments to control the distribution of essential goods.[65] This means that governments can more easily distribute resources to supporters and withhold them from opponents. In Syria, Bashar al-Assad's regime has controlled the flow of humanitarian assistance into the country and restricted access to besieged and opposition-held areas, prompting accusations that humanitarian assistance provided through the UN and other aid agencies is effectively subsidizing Assad's hold on power.[66]

Perhaps the most controversial way of improving human rights behavior has been through democracy promotion. Democracy promotion is a broad term that covers any attempt by a state or states to encourage another country to democratize, either via a transition from autocracy or the consolidation of a new or unstable democracy.[67] Expanding individual freedoms through the spread of democracy has been a long-standing tenet of American foreign policy. On April 2, 1917, President Woodrow Wilson stood in front of Congress and declared:

> The world must be made safe for democracy. Its peace must be planted upon the tested foundations of political liberty. We have no selfish ends to serve. We desire no conquest, no dominion. . . . We are but one of the champions of the rights of mankind. We shall be satisfied when those rights have been made as secure as the faith and the freedom of nations can make them.[68]

Seventy years later, President Ronald Reagan bluntly stated, "We want to promote democracy, because it is right, and because democratic governments are less likely to become involved in wars of aggression."[69] In acknowledging the importance of democracy to U.S. foreign policy, President Clinton more eloquently argued, "Our hopes, our hearts, our hands are with those on every continent who are building democracy and freedom. Their cause is America's cause."[70] Across administrations and parties, support for democracy and the human freedoms it entails has been a core component of U.S. foreign policy. In one of its more moving articulations, democracy promotion as foreign policy contends that "it is true that as much as America invented 'human rights,' conceptions of liberty invented America. It follows that 'human rights' isn't something we add on to our foreign policy, but is its very purpose: the defense and promotion of liberty in the world."[71]

Democracy promotion takes many forms, including the provision of foreign aid, election monitoring, support for civil society groups and opposition media in nondemocracies, the strengthening of legal institutions in democratizing countries, and nation-building through military occupation.[72] Overall, the main objective of democracy promotion is to expand the number of democracies worldwide. This is driven by the belief that democracies have greater respect for human rights, maintain greater economic openness, and are less likely to engage in wars with each other.[73] In the wake of the American-led invasion of Iraq, political scientist (and former U.S. ambassador to Russia) Michael McFaul argued that "although Western democracies historically have a mixed record of exporting various forms of democracy, the legitimacy and practice of external actors promoting democracy—be they states, NGOs, or international institutions—has grown in the last two decades as the idea that people have a right to democracy has gained support."[74]

Despite a deeply held bipartisan belief in the value of spreading democracy abroad, the effectiveness of democracy promotion in improving human rights remains unclear. More than one-third of the world's population lives in countries that are both democratic and abusive of human rights.[75] In India, the world's largest democracy, government-supported groups have stepped up attacks on religious minorities. Of even greater concern is the impunity of the country's security forces, which, in one episode in July 2016, caused ninety deaths and hundreds of injuries while responding to a protest in the contested province of Jammu and Kashmir.[76] The same holds true for democracies such as Indonesia and the Philippines, home to a combined 360 million people, which struggle with the legacies of military dictatorships and where minorities, journalists, and opposition politicians are regularly targeted by the state.

At the same time, the absence of democracy does not necessarily mean that all human rights are destined to be violated. In countries such as Singapore, where political rights are severely restricted, episodes of outright violence by the state can be exceedingly rare. But in countries with some political freedoms, the heavy emphasis of democracy promotion activities on stimulating political participation at the local level may antagonize governments, leading to restrictions such as those imposed on foreign NGOs in Egypt, Hungary, India, and Russia.[77] Human rights organizations can provide resources and catalyze action, increasing the levels of protest against a state.[78] But as Sarah Sunn Bush points out, democracy promotion has also bred a "democracy establishment" in which many groups have a vested interest in continued funding from foreign donors.[79] This creates a perverse incentive for such groups to refrain from seriously challenging the power of authoritarian governments because a transition to democracy would undercut the rationale for their existence. The potential results of democracy promotion, then, include accepting more opposition activity within a nondemocratic system, which makes the country appear more open to dissent without creating actual political change. An alternative outcome is more repression, which fuels international support for opposition groups. Neither outcome necessarily leads to any significant change in a state's human rights behavior or democratic orientation.

The most extreme and direct form of human rights promotion is military intervention, which may occur under the mantle of humanitarian intervention or nation-building.[80] The elimination of a particular dictator is often the main goal of this type of military intervention, with improved human rights conditions as a potential positive outcome of this change. American intervention in Haiti to overthrow the Duvalier regime and attempts to unseat Mohammed Farrah Aidid in Somalia are examples of this type of military intervention. Under the George W. Bush administration, military intervention was used to achieve regime change in Afghanistan and Iraq. NATO intervention in Libya under the Obama administration overthrew Qaddafi and established a parliamentary system. Three relatively free elections occurred in Libya before the terrorist group calling itself the Islamic State gained a foothold in the city of Sirte in 2016.[81] Although it is always difficult to judge whether conditions would have been worse had these dictators remained in power, the limited scholarship in this area suggests that human rights improvements after a dictator is deposed are highly contingent on the political stability of the subsequent government.[82]

Improving human rights through military intervention has been most successful in the context of a civil war, where the reduction or elimination of violence against civilians by one or both parties is often a direct result of the conflict's resolution. NATO intervention in Kosovo in 1999 played an important role in ending Slobodan Milošević's violence against Kosovar Albanians, and eventually helped to establish Kosovo's contested statehood. Naming and shaming by international organizations can make such interventions more likely.[83] However, military intervention is by far the costliest foreign policy tool for promoting human rights, based on almost all imaginable measures—with real economic, political, and social costs. The potential devastation caused by military interventions in the name of human rights or humanitarianism suggests they should be executed sparingly and where local conditions favor the long-term success of regime change.

It is clear that all of these foreign policy tools for encouraging improvements in human rights have grave shortcomings. But unlike these examples, one tool—foreign aid—has largely gone unexplored.[84] This omission is likely due to the lofty goals that foreign aid seeks to achieve: the elimination of poverty, the expansion of industry, and improvements in health and education, among others. With goals such as these, how could foreign aid do wrong?

Aiding and Abetting: The Argument

The conventional view of foreign aid is that at its best, foreign aid helps lift people out of poverty, and at its worst, foreign aid is simply wasted. Foreign aid proponents argue that aid promotes political and economic stability by supporting economic growth and public services.[85] Yet, a growing body of research suggests that foreign aid contributes to the deterioration of political institutions and to the likelihood of civil war.[86] Because foreign aid is rarely completely cut off or even substantially reduced to strategically important countries, I focus on the ways foreign aid influences a state's coercive behavior—or its tendency to use violence or commit human rights abuses against its own citizens—while aid is being provided. In other words, I focus on whether and how foreign aid can actually *facilitate* state violence against civilians.

State violence refers to the use of force by the state or its agents against civilians in ways that result in human rights violations, and in particular, in the violation of personal (or physical) integrity rights. Personal integrity rights are concerned with individual survival and security and include freedom from torture, disappearance, imprisonment, extrajudicial execution, and mass killing. In focusing on state violence as the violation of personal integrity rights, I do not consider the effect of foreign assistance on other types of human rights (typically referred to as second- or third-generation rights) addressed by the International Covenant on Economic, Social and Cultural Rights (1966), such as the right to an adequate standard of living or the right to form trade unions. I do, however, focus on government repression. As Christian Davenport notes, government repression involves the actual or threatened use of physical sanctions against an individual or organization within the territorial jurisdiction of the state.[87] The purpose of government repression is to impose a cost on the targeted individual or group and/or to deter specific activities or beliefs perceived to be challenging to the government. Government repression does not necessarily imply the use of outright violence by the state, because it includes suppression of the freedoms of speech, assembly, and movement through violent and nonviolent means. By looking at both state violence and government repression, I can identify nuanced variations in coercive state behaviors.

Although some studies have examined how human rights abuses affect the amount of foreign aid money countries receive, relatively little work has been done to demonstrate the opposite: how foreign aid affects human rights.[88] As a result, we have only a limited understanding of how foreign aid affects a state's ability to use violence and repression against its own citizens. Yet, from Made in America tear gas canisters lobbed by Egyptian police against anti-Mubarak protestors in Tahrir Square to U.S.-trained counterinsurgency units charged with crimes against humanity in Indonesia and El Salvador, evidence of the ways that foreign assistance can undermine basic human freedoms, such as the right to life or freedom from torture, is right in front of us.

By focusing on how the very provision of foreign aid can influence a state's human rights practices, I challenge the long-standing notion that aid does no harm to individuals. Recipient countries can harness the foreign assistance given by developed donor countries such as the United States to increase the coercive capacity of the state *irrespective of the intended purposes* of the aid. By acting as nontax revenue to the state, bilateral foreign aid is not tied to any popular expectations of government behavior. This renders governments unaccountable and enables them to use foreign aid to support spending in a variety of areas—sometimes improving or increasing government services such as health care and education, and at other times increasing military spending or arms purchases. Donors ultimately have only limited control over what their aid dollars are spent on.

Although some countries are largely immune to the dynamics that lead to state violence and repression, in other countries foreign aid may help tip the balance and enable unstable regimes to use violence against their citizens as a way to ensure their continued survival. For nondemocratic regimes, the state's coercive capacity—the strength and preparedness of its military, police, and other security forces—is often a vital resource for political leaders who are intent on maintaining their hold on power. This is especially true in the context of an ongoing threat such as an organized political opposition or civil war. Foreign aid is unlikely to make a peaceful democratic state repressive, but foreign aid to nondemocratic states or those characterized by weak institutions can be harnessed to increase the likelihood and/or intensity of government abuse, with significant consequences for human rights. In short, foreign aid can exacerbate what could be thought of as preexisting risk factors for human rights abuses.

Using statistical analyses of four decades of U.S. bilateral foreign aid flows and detailed country case studies, I identify two pathways—capacity-building and an income effect—for the coercive effect of foreign aid and illustrate how aid contributed to violent outcomes in recipient countries. In some cases, U.S. policymakers turned a blind eye to human rights violations; in others, members of the U.S. government intentionally manipulated foreign aid to achieve their policy objectives, irrespective of the human rights consequences. I also provide evidence that the coercive effect of foreign aid has endured well beyond the end of the Cold War.

Following the Money Trail

The next chapter develops a theory of the coercive effect of foreign aid. To provide the foundations of the theory, I first turn to the question of why states repress their citizens. I then examine how foreign aid, as an external resource to the state, can be used by governments to expand the state's coercive capacity. This expanded coercive capacity can be harnessed by governments to ensure their continued rule through indiscriminate state-led violence and repression. I contend that, counterintuitively, economic aid can be as harmful for human rights as military aid is often thought to be.

The theory's plausibility is tested through a series of statistical analyses presented in Chapter 2. I analyze data on 142 countries over a forty-year period to identify broad trends in the relationship between U.S. bilateral foreign aid and various forms of state violence, including state-led killings, torture, and government repression. Other potentially relevant influences such as the country's political regime type, natural resource wealth, level of government service provision, armed forces size, and past history of conflict are taken into account. The results show that foreign aid is in fact associated with negative changes in a range of human rights–related behaviors.

Next is a deep historical case study of American and, to a lesser degree, Soviet foreign assistance to Indonesia from its independence in 1949 to the present. Chapter 3 draws heavily on archival documents from the State Department and the Central Intelligence Agency (CIA) as well as reports from international and Indonesian human rights groups. The analysis shows that foreign aid played a direct role in building up Indonesia's military strength under President Sukarno through a capacity-building mechanism. This resulted in waves of repression by the domestically oriented military as Sukarno attempted to consolidate control over the Indonesian archipelago. After Sukarno was ousted, President Suharto and members of his administration used the threat of diverting resources from economic development to the military to ensure continued foreign assistance from the United States. Economic aid from the United States, as well as U.S. Export-Import Bank loans, supported the military through an income effect. The U.S. government intended economic aid, and in particular PL 480 food aid, to provide general budgetary support for Suharto's government to use to fund the military. Indonesia also shows how improvements in military capabilities brought about through foreign aid can withstand temporary reductions or cutoffs of aid.

Chapters 4 and 5 test the generalizability of my findings through case studies of El Salvador and South Korea, respectively. Whereas Indonesia represents a case where the United States initially competed with the Soviet Union for influence, the United States had no notable interests in El Salvador until a communist government came to power in neighboring Nicaragua. In El Salvador, both economic and military assistance from the United States proved to be highly fungible—as documented in multiple U.S. government investigations. The amount of food aid and cash transfers (which constituted more than 60 percent of U.S. economic assistance) not only staved off the country's economic collapse, it also underwrote the entirety of El

Salvador's military budget. Although many have pointed to U.S. military assistance to El Salvador as a factor that prolonged the country's bloody civil war, my analysis demonstrates that damage was also done by economic aid.

South Korea is a case where the United States had strong security and development interests as a legacy of the Second World War and the Korean War. In South Korea, more so than any other case, the United States was directly involved in developing the state's security apparatus through foreign assistance. The decades of essentially military rule that followed the end of the Korean War resulted in significant government repression but few episodes of outright state violence, in spite of sustained high levels of U.S. foreign aid and, in particular, military assistance. The presence of U.S. troops in South Korea, the threat posed by North Korea, and the noncommunist orientation of the country's political opposition tempered but did not completely eliminate the coercive effect of foreign aid there.

Chapter 6 returns to statistical analysis to better understand whether the coercive effect of foreign aid was simply an outcome of Cold War geopolitics and whether it persists today. By examining differences between the Cold War and post–Cold War eras, as well as the impact of the 9/11 attacks and the subsequent wars in Afghanistan and Iraq, I find evidence that the coercive effect of foreign aid continues and is driven by economic aid. These findings should serve as a caution to those who argue that high levels of military aid drove government repression in the developing world during the Cold War and that a retrenchment in military aid (to most countries) and/or congressional restrictions on military aid have solved the problem. Notwithstanding such restrictions, the provision of economic aid poses a continuing human rights concern, as seen in South Sudan and elsewhere.

The concluding chapter tackles tough questions for foreign aid policy, including whether donor countries such as the United States can responsibly provide foreign aid. It lays out the current debate over the future of U.S. foreign assistance policy, which is shaped by low levels of public support for foreign aid and years of the highest foreign assistance budget since the Marshall Plan. To effectively counter the coercive effect of foreign aid, policy should target countries that rank low on risk factors for state coercion—that is, countries with little or no history of civil conflict, countries that feature open and democratic political regimes, and countries that do not use their national militaries for internal security purposes.

Ultimately, this book tries to determine whether the United States' financial support of governments abroad has ever *truly* fulfilled its purported principles. The many billions of foreign aid dollars funded by American taxpayers have not translated into improved human rights conditions in much of the developing world. This book helps us understand why.

1

Abetting Violence

The Coercive Effect of Foreign Aid

THE USE OF FORCE IS AN ESSENTIAL PART of the modern state. States are defined by their ability to monopolize the use of violence within their borders.[1] States and their governments typically use violence legitimately, for example in responding to an armed robbery or terrorist attack, and ensure that the use of violence by non-state actors is prevented or punished. But not all use of force by the state is legitimate. We trust the police because we believe the police are an appropriate extension of the state's authority. But when the state uses force in ways that are seen as illegitimate by the population, those very acts of violence can undermine the state's authority. When citizens doubt whether police forces exist to protect and serve or to prey and extort, their value as an extension of the state is diminished. Since the illegitimate use of violence can erode or undermine support for the state, the state has a strategic interest in using violence against the population only when absolutely necessary.

This book focuses on the illegitimate use of *state violence* or *state coercion*. State violence is illegitimate if it is extralegal or indiscriminate. Extralegal state violence, such as torture or extrajudicial killings, occurs when the state uses violence in ways that go beyond the use of force as established by domestic or international law. Indiscriminate state violence occurs when the state uses violence against a segment of the population in ways that may be classified as legal by the state, but when the targets of that violence are defined only on the basis of some shared attribute, such as their geographic location or ethnicity, and/or the scale of the violence is arbitrary or disproportionate.[2]

Practically, this includes a range of human rights violations, including state-led killings, government repression, and torture. Torture is a specific form of extralegal state violence: the intentional infliction of severe pain or suffering, whether physical or mental, on a person by a government agent. State-led killings are the direct and intentional use of armed force against civilians by a government or government-affiliated group that results in civilian deaths. They can range in severity from targeted assassinations to genocide. Although it can be difficult to differentiate between civilians and combatants in the context of a civil war, and civilians are often inadvertently killed as collateral damage during the course of military operations, civilians can also be *intentionally* victimized by the state as part of a war effort. It is the latter phenomenon that I am most concerned with. Government repression, in contrast, is used by state agents with the intention of controlling individuals' political behavior and can include interrogations and arrests, as well as activities aimed at breaking up demonstrations, strikes, or riots.[3] Although civilian deaths may result from repressive acts, directly causing such deaths is not necessarily the primary goal of government repression. Instead, the objective is to create a generalized sense of fear and intimidation to silence and suppress opponents. All of these behaviors constitute human rights abuses under the Universal Declaration of Human Rights.[4]

Many factors can influence whether governments resort to the illegitimate use of state violence against their citizens, as well as the likelihood that citizens will take up arms against the state. State violence may be adopted in response to a conflict between the government and opposition.[5] In one possible sequence, a government responds to a protest with repression—arresting protestors en masse or firing into an unarmed crowd. If this proves ineffective in suppressing unrest, it can provoke an escalation in protest behavior. In response, the state may engage with the opposition even more forcefully, and the two sides can become locked in a cycle of action and response—a tit-for-tat strategy where repression is met with increased dissent which is then countered with greater violence by the state.[6] Countries with a history of civil war may be more likely to experience the cycle of opposition dissent and government repression, in part because countries that have faced rebellion in the past have individuals with the organizational strategies and experience to engage in further violent dissent. This lowers the cost for opposition groups to adopt violent tactics.[7]

Ted Robert Gurr's groundbreaking work *Why Men Rebel* argues that relative deprivation—defined as a discrepancy between what one expects to receive in life and what one can actually achieve based on existing socioeconomic conditions—affects the level of political violence in a country.[8] Studies have found that countries with higher levels of income inequality tend to have slightly higher levels of political violence.[9] The incentives for rebellion, including the ability of groups to capture resources from the state, can also influence the likelihood of state violence.[10] Countries with abundant natural resources may have a higher risk of conflict as rebel groups compete with each other and with the state to control resources. For example, research on Indonesia suggests that the discovery of natural resource wealth in Aceh province was directly linked to an escalation of separatist demands there.[11] Today, rebel groups successfully control gold mines in the Democratic Republic of Congo, Côte d'Ivoire, and the Central African Republic and use these resources to operate independent of the state. However, this argument has its limits. Countries with a very high dependence on natural resources, such as Saudi Arabia on oil, may have a relatively lower risk of political violence because these resources provide the government with substantial revenue to spend on greater internal security (thereby staving off the threat posed by opposition or rebel groups) and/or increased public services (to buy popular support).[12]

States may also turn to violence even when opposition forces are weak or seemingly nonexistent. Hannah Arendt's work challenges the cyclical view of confrontational opposition-government interaction. She posits that the use of terror and coercion by authoritarian regimes increases as the regime gains power relative to its opponents.[13] Juan Linz relatedly argues that authoritarian governments may resort to violence as a means of policy implementation.[14] Countries may therefore feature high levels of state violence irrespective of the strength of organized opposition groups if the use of violence reinforces the state's authority over the population.

The Coercive Effect of Foreign Aid

There is no definitive theory of when or why states resort to violence against their citizens, though we have an expanding list of potentially relevant factors. One understudied factor is foreign aid. Bilateral, government-to-government foreign aid can be used by the recipient country for a variety of purposes besides what it is designated for in a budgetary spreadsheet.[15] The foreign aid that the United States provides to developing countries can be channeled as easily into state violence as into economic development. The result is that states that may have been too weak to respond to dissent with repression may, through foreign aid, come to possess the necessary resources to do so. States that already had the ability to repress may see their coercive capacity strengthened through the receipt of foreign aid, with potentially deadly consequences.

This argument rests on a mechanism—aid fungibility—that enables foreign aid to be used as a general government resource irrespective of what the donor intended it for. A substantial economic literature on the fungibility of aid suggests that whether it is provided as project-based aid (for building a school or irrigating farmland, for example) or as humanitarian assistance in the form of food aid, foreign aid can be easily diverted from its designated purposes.[16] Aid can be thought of as fungible or transferable across different "goods" that the government can "purchase" (in the same way that money given to buy college textbooks can in practice be used to buy beer). But aid is also sometimes provided with no particular project or "good" in mind. USAID's Economic Support Funds (ESF), which function as a monetary form of political support, are a case in point. Furthermore, only a small proportion of foreign aid is directly provided for programs that the local government would not otherwise undertake or provide in the absence of aid—IMET funds stand out as an example of this.

Although an aid recipient's ability to circumvent donor-imposed restrictions and spend some aid on nontargeted programs is often linked by the press to corruption and the diversion of funds for personal gain, aid fungibility occurs even in contexts where corruption is minimal.[17] For example, the Institute for Health Metrics and Evaluation found that for every dollar of foreign aid given to developing countries for health sector programming, governments decreased their own health spending by between 43 cents and $1.14.[18] Even as the United States provided billions in foreign assistance to help fight the spread of AIDS and other infectious diseases, most aid recipient governments in Africa decreased their own health spending in favor of other priorities.

The effects of aid fungibility are profound, and donors bear some responsibility. If, as Bruce Bueno de Mesquita and Alastair Smith contend, "aid giving and getting is a strategic process in which donors purchase policy support from recipients who use at least some of the assistance to ensure that they are securely ensconced in power,"[19] then donors ought to be accountable for exactly *how* recipients use the aid given to them. Donors may secretly or openly acknowledge the use of foreign aid to bolster a standing government. McVety provides a compelling example in an interview with Dennis A. Fitzgerald, a former U.S. foreign aid director in the 1950s:

> Dulles went to Ethiopia once. He told Haile Selassie or somebody—(we had what was considered a highly important communications center somewhere in the country) that the U.S. would give him nine million dollars of aid as a quid pro quo. We didn't learn about it for a couple of months. We'd get communications from our embassy over there asking "Where's this nine million dollars we promised Haile Selassie?" We replied, "What nine million dollars?" It was a hell of a mess. . . . We finally developed a program which had a price tag on it of the amount that Dulles had promised the Ethiopians, but it had no real underpinning and had a negligible effect on that country's development.[20]

Those who focus exclusively on the development impact of foreign assistance overlook the deep political implications of examples like this. The aid promised by Dulles to Selassie served two purposes: first, for the United States, this aid cemented access to a much-needed military installation; second, and central to my argument, it was also intended to support Selassie's continued hold on power—no strings attached.

The aid donor's intentions (both explicit and implicit) are particularly important to analyze when considering how aid can be used to support military spending.[21] Economists contend that if a donor country refuses to provide military aid while continuing to give economic assistance, it does not ensure that the recipient country is effectively constrained from spending that aid on its military.[22] Indeed, Daniel Kono and Gabriella Montinola find that economic assistance is routinely diverted toward military spending by autocratic governments.[23] It therefore is both possible and likely that when the provision of military aid to a particular country becomes unacceptable in the donor country, the donor may increase the amount of economic aid given to that same country with the understanding that the aid will be used for military purposes. Economic aid, because of its fungibility, can substitute for military aid. This can involve the actual monetization of foreign aid through, for example, the sale of food aid for cash, or it can occur within the budgetary process of the aid recipient country.

While fungibility is intrinsic to the very nature of foreign aid, international donors can decide whether or not to pay attention to how it impacts their intended policy outcomes. For example, a government that is pursuing bad policies may be criticized by donors for treating aid as fungible and diverting funds for less productive expenditures. Another government, pursuing good policies and trusted by donors, may be allowed to treat foreign aid as fungible, setting its own development priorities and allocating aid to the programs that it deems most beneficial to the country.[24] Either way, the overarching implication is that donors will not be able to convince governments receiving aid to implement policies that they themselves do not want to put into action. This may be attributed to the recipient government's political or institutional weakness or the inherent difficulty of monitoring by donors.[25] But in practice, aid fungibility means that donor priorities do not trump national ones when it comes to how foreign aid will be used.

Informed by what we know about why states repress, I contend that governments receiving foreign aid are likely to use it to remain in power through two mechanisms: cooption and coercion. The government can use foreign aid to buy increased support for its continued rule through cooption, usually by subsidizing key goods or improving government services. In Egypt, for instance, the state subsidizes not only fuel but also sugar, cooking oil, and other staples. These subsidies also allow Egyptians to buy multiple loaves of bread a day for only a tenth of their real cost.[26] In March 2017, hundreds of Egyptians took to the streets to protest a reduction in the state supply of bread from five to three loaves per person per day.[27] Money saved by constituents can translate into increased support for politicians—a political strategy seen across the world. But whether a particular country devotes most foreign aid to cooption as opposed to coercion is determined by structural characteristics of the state, such as its form of government, as well as government decisions about how to spend foreign aid within the context of the domestic budget.[28]

Figure 1.1 presents a theoretical model of how foreign assistance can affect the behavior of a country receiving aid. The first stage of the model begins with a donor state giving aid to a selected recipient country. In this aid allocation stage, the donor chooses whether to provide military and/or economic aid to a specific country and decides the amount of aid and any conditions placed on that aid. These funds are then provided (i.e., disbursed) to the recipient government and incorporated into the receiving

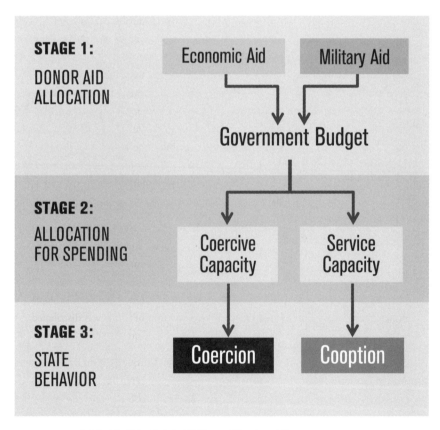

FIGURE 1.1. A Model of the Political Effects of Foreign Aid.
Source: Author's illustration.

government's budget. In the second stage, the country that has received aid decides how to spend it. In its most basic formulation, the government decides whether to spend aid on guns or butter—that is, whether to channel aid resources into building up the capacity of coercive institutions such as the national military, police, and intelligence services, or to provide public services such as education and health.[29]

Military assistance is always used to support the state's coercive capacity.[30] Theoretically, military aid could free up funds that could then be spent on other government services, but it is unlikely to be used for this purpose due to the relatively higher defense burdens of developing countries.[31] Developing countries rarely feel secure enough, and military assistance is money that can easily be used to bolster the country's security sector or feed patronage networks centered around the military.

In countries where the governments face a high level of threat or are not accountable to their populations, economic aid is unlikely to be spent on what the donor intends.[32] According to Paul Collier and Anke Hoeffler, around 40 percent of African military spending is inadvertently financed by foreign aid.[33] Even "tied" aid—which must be spent on goods or services that originate in the donor country—frees up resources that the recipient government would have otherwise devoted to providing similar goods.[34] The same holds true for nonmonetary forms of economic aid such as food aid. An egregious example of diverting economic aid for military purposes occurred in Ethiopia during the 1985 famine. Western food aid deliveries enabled Mengistu's dictatorship to divert almost all of the government's resources from feeding the starving to resettling men from the troublesome north-central highlands to other areas where the rebels waging war against Mengistu could not actively recruit them.[35] As McVety recounts,

> At the height of the famine, Mengistu Haile Mariam was spending 46 percent of the national budget on armaments and used international food aid to fill bellies in his 3-million-man army—the largest in Africa. Ethiopia's main partner, the Soviet Union, did not reduce military assistance and the United States sent a staggering $87.4 million worth of food aid through PL-480 in 1985 alone. That year, Ethiopia received 1.25 million tons of food relief, only 90,000 tons of which was distributed in the non–government-controlled regions of Tigray and Eritrea.[36]

In addition to the inadvertent security consequences of providing aid during a conflict, some economic aid actually is intended to bolster internal security by supporting civilian security institutions such as police forces. U.S. foreign assistance for counternarcotics and antitrafficking efforts currently play such a role.

It is surprising how easily governments receiving foreign aid can spend it on whatever sector they deem to be a priority. Although many point to tied aid as a factor inhibiting aid fungibility, Haley Swedlund demonstrates that foreign assistance for general budget support was a primary way for major donors to disburse aid well into the 2000s.[37] In Rwanda, 70 percent of the development aid given by the United Kingdom in 2009 went directly into the Rwandan government's budget. As a trusted aid recipient, the Rwandan government was expected to allocate that aid to the projects it deemed most appropriate, rather than having bureaucrats in London decide. Ultimately, the decision about what precisely a government will spend aid on is shaped by a number of factors, including the overall financial resources the government has at its disposal, whether the country is democratic or not (i.e., whether the public plays a meaningful role in governance), and the government's prospects for remaining in power.

In the third stage of the theoretical model, the government uses its newly increased capacity either to coopt opposition by offering public services (or by buying off the opposition in some other way) or to coerce the opposition into acquiescence. If the latter path is chosen, then directly or indirectly, the foreign aid will have contributed to the state's coercive capacity and increased the likelihood of state violence and repression—leading to what I identify as the coercive effect of foreign aid.

The coercive effect of foreign aid can be thought of as the dark underside of the traditional view of foreign assistance that sees aid as supporting the recipient government's ability to provide services to its citizens. This is one potential outcome of foreign aid, but it is not the only one. When a government receiving aid decides that relying on force will be more effective than buying support, or that it may one day need to resort to repression to maintain power, the coercive effect of foreign aid is likely to operate.

Influences on the Coercive Effect of Foreign Aid

The process described here is likely to play out differently in particular countries based on the characteristics of their political systems, the structure and strength of their state institutions, and their past experiences of conflict. Some combinations of the following factors predispose countries to the coercive effect of foreign aid, while others make them more amenable to using aid for amicable purposes.

Regime Type and Political Institutions

An extensive body of research demonstrates that democracy may reduce the likelihood of both government repression and civil war.[38] Democratic states are more internally peaceful in part because individual-centered norms regarding tolerance and deliberation pose a high barrier to the use of violence by the state. Democracies also feature institutionalized channels for grievance airing and accommodation, such as local representatives and regular elections, which reduce the likelihood of conflict.[39]

States with responsive political institutions should therefore be less likely to exhibit the coercive effect of foreign aid. Democracy is not a guarantee against the use of foreign aid to support security sector institutions. Indeed, military assistance has been given to many democracies for this explicit purpose. But in democratic countries, we are less likely to see the state's coercive capacity openly used for the purposes of societal control. Essentially, democracy limits governments' incentives to choose violence over other means of reinforcing their authority.

In authoritarian countries, where dissent is often severely limited, both violence and repression may be less likely due to the high degree of societal control exercised by the state—a characteristic referred to as "steady pressure."[40] The severe costs of rebellion in an extremely repressive political environment—in Iran, for instance— may even prevent an organized opposition from forming.[41] In such contexts, state coercion may be so deeply entrenched that fluctuations in the amount of foreign aid a country receives would have little observable impact on the extent of human rights abuses.

Because state coercion may be limited in both democracies such as Canada and Sweden and authoritarian regimes such as North Korea and Saudi Arabia, scholars have focused on understanding the sources of political violence in transitional or semiauthoritarian regimes. These include countries such as Egypt, Turkey, and Malaysia, which are neither consolidated democracies nor outright autocracies. In what is known as the "more murder in the middle" hypothesis, scholars argue that the vast majority of violent state action is perpetrated in countries with mixed political institutions.[42] Countries transitioning from one political regime type to another, for example during the first round of free elections, have been found to be highly politically unstable. Movement from one set of political institutions to another means that a government unused to strong opposition will face a decision about how to best deal with political rivals and an increasingly engaged and potentially vocal citizenry. Myanmar's political opening, which began in 2010, is an example of this type of shifting political regime. Movement from a closed to a more open political system is a risk factor for increased use of state repression and civil war.[43] At the same time, countries facing a political transition may also receive greater amounts of foreign aid for democracy promotion, creating the potential for a strong coercive effect of foreign aid.

State Strength and the Capacity for Violence

State strength has typically been conceptualized as a continuum ranging from strong states with consolidated governments to failed states that display few domestic attributes of statehood, such as secure borders or a functioning central government.[44] Strong states unquestionably control their territories and can deliver a full range of services to their citizens. They have firm control over their militaries and internal security forces but may choose not to engage in repressive behavior because they have the resources and institutional strength to accommodate dissent. Weak states, by contrast, tend to vary in their ability to command and control their armed forces. Some governments invest in large militaries to maintain their hold on power, whereas others try to extract as many resources from the state as possible while in office, undermining overall state capacity. Weak states are likely resort to violent tactics because their institutional weakness precludes less extreme responses.[45] At the extreme, failed states such as Somalia and South Sudan are unable to provide services or other economic incentives as a means of dealing with opposition and are therefore largely left with force as their only option. Even then, the governments of failed states may have only limited control over the country's coercive institutions or may be able to exert control only in certain regions, leading to the emergence of stateless areas.

These variations in state strength influence a government's ability to effectively provide services. Because of this, state strength is also an important factor that international aid donors consider when deciding how to distribute their aid. Weak states, in particular, provide a fertile environment for foreign intervention because their governments are often unable to fully project power within their national boundaries. This can allow rebel groups to gain and hold territory, as seen in the Islamic State's ability to establish enclaves in Syria, Iraq, and Libya. One purported reason why people were fleeing Syrian government-controlled areas to areas controlled by the Islamic State was the latter's greater ability to provide social services, including food, security, and transportation.[46] The creation of stateless areas beyond the central government's control may result in the continual threat of secession, civil war, and large-scale internal struggles for control that may eventually lead to state collapse.[47]

Foreign aid can, of course, directly shape state capacity. During the twin oil crises of the 1970s, poor, non–oil producing Muslim countries received a foreign aid windfall.[48] This influx of foreign aid allowed the recipient governments to become more repressive. However, when foreign aid contracted in the mid-1980s due to a fall in oil prices, the countries that had been receiving aid experienced an uptick in civil conflict. Both the provision and the contraction of foreign aid, then, can affect the state's ability to manage internal conflict.

A History of Armed Conflict

Warfighting directly shifts state resources toward the use of force. Nations engaged in armed conflict spend more on the military than they otherwise would, and once a country has participated in a war, it subsequently chooses a considerably higher level of military spending.[49] Countries at risk of war also tend to have larger armed forces. Repeated participation in conflict can also affect state institutions by raising the profile of the national military in politics. A history of armed conflict can lead to other legacies as well, including the presence of foreign military bases or the stationing of large numbers of foreign troops.

Armed conflict also affects foreign aid flows. Donors with oversight concerns can be hesitant to give aid to countries at war and are averse to high levels of military spending by potential aid recipients.[50] Yet, armed conflict can also have neighborhood effects that increase the overall flow of foreign aid into a region as donors address regional humanitarian crises and try to stem the spillover of conflict into neighboring countries.[51] As the recent wars in Afghanistan and Iraq demonstrate, conflict can also increase foreign aid levels as international donors rush to fund a country's postwar reconstruction. Such aid often fails to improve local security.[52]

A country's history of armed conflict may therefore influence the coercive effect of foreign aid by drawing aid to countries that are primed for state-led violence. Multiple studies have found that humanitarian assistance, and in particular food aid, increases the length of civil wars.[53] But other forms of aid can also prolong conflict. In Colombia, U.S. military assistance increased murders by paramilitary groups.[54] Foreign aid given in the context of civil war may also influence the opposition. For instance, large development projects have been linked to increases in insurgent attacks.[55] It is therefore likely that foreign aid may have differential effects based on the type of conflict a country has experienced. Civil wars, for instance, tend to draw a country's armed forces inward through counterinsurgency operations. Interstate wars are more likely to contribute to the development of large militaries with very specific hardware requirements, and they may be less conducive to state violence.

Conclusion

There is a long-standing belief that bilateral military assistance and economic aid are fundamentally different and therefore have distinct effects in recipient countries. Few would contest that military assistance is intended to increase the effectiveness and, by extension, the lethality of the recipient country's military. Yet, the fungibility of foreign aid means that even aid given for economic development (e.g., for the construction of roads or hospitals) or for humanitarian purposes can contribute to a country's military might. By increasing the state's coercive capacity, both forms of assistance can contribute to an increased likelihood of state violence and government repression under favorable conditions.

The coercive effect of foreign aid is most likely to occur in countries transitioning between authoritarian and democratic political regimes—where dissent and protest are possible and a government is not effectively constrained by democratic norms from using force against its citizens. Democracy helps limit the coercive effect of foreign aid because representative institutions can accommodate opposition and respond to dissent through nonviolent means. Weak states are also likely to experience the coercive effect of foreign aid because state institutions are not strong enough to effectively provide services as a form of cooption or otherwise maintain control over the population through peaceful means. The coercive effect of foreign aid is also more likely to occur in countries with a history of armed conflict. This is because war mobilizes the state for the use of violence and foreign aid given in that context can more easily be directed toward the state's coercive institutions.

2

Patterns of Foreign Aid and State Violence

LIKENED TO BRIBERY BY MORGENTHAU, foreign aid has been given to democratic and authoritarian rulers alike.[1] It has helped build dams that supply millions with electricity, and it has been spent on lavish conspicuous consumption projects that benefit few. It has saved lives by providing much-needed health care, and cost lives by purchasing military technology that has been used in conflicts, both internal and external. And although military assistance props up some governments, it also has been linked to numerous coups, including, most recently, the March 2012 coup in Mali that precipitated years of internal conflict.[2]

Empirically assessing the weight of these competing claims is a challenging task. Tracing the flow of aid dollars through government budgets rife with poor accounting and/or corruption is nearly impossible. Even more problematic is the reality that both aid donors and aid recipients often see the negative consequences of foreign aid as secondary, at best, to the political ties that bind donor and recipient. This chapter tackles this difficult challenge by using statistical analyses to assess the relationship between U.S. foreign assistance and subsequent changes in state violence and government repression in countries receiving this aid. It explores whether, on average, foreign aid is associated with improvements or declines in governments' respect for human rights. Do countries receiving U.S. foreign aid do better or worse in protecting their citizens from abuse?

Measuring Aid and State Violence

If the coercive effect of foreign aid is inherent in the very nature of aid, then we should see it across a range of countries and over an extended period of time. Based on existing theory, the coercive effect of foreign aid—when the receipt of foreign aid results in increased state violence—is more likely in (1) semiauthoritarian or politically transitioning countries; (2) countries with limited state capacity and/or weak state institutions; and (3) countries with a history of armed conflict. To test these expectations, I analyze bilateral U.S. foreign aid to 142 developing countries in the period 1976 to 2016.[3] I break down U.S. foreign aid into two categories, military aid and economic aid, to uncover potential differences in how the type of aid given by the United States may affect human rights abuses overseas.

Of the 142 countries that I examine, roughly the same number receive economic aid or military aid from the United States (139 and 137, respectively) and the proportion of economic to military aid is fairly consistent over time. Historically, the top four recipients of economic aid for the past four decades are the same countries that were the top four recipients of military aid: Israel, Egypt, Afghanistan, and Iraq. (Note that Israel is excluded from the statistical analyses that follow because it is classified by the World Bank as a high-income country and because of discrepancies in the data on state violence.) Of the countries receiving foreign assistance from the United States, democracies tend to receive more military and economic aid than nondemocracies. However, countries with transitional political regimes (anocracies) receive less economic and military aid than dictatorships.

Figure 2.1 illustrates the annual amount of U.S. military aid received by the top ten overall recipients. For the majority of these countries, U.S. military ties are longstanding. U.S. military aid has played a vital role in securing Israel's defense, and foreign aid to Egypt has been highly influenced by that country's participation in a peace process with Israel. The United States' extensive role in supporting South Korea's military is detailed in Chapter 5. Other countries, such as Greece and Turkey, were seen as bulwarks against the expansion of communism during the Cold War. Poland, for its part, received a surge in military assistance for its participation in the 2003 invasion of Iraq. As Figure 2.1 shows, military assistance to Afghanistan and Iraq is a much more recent development, as is a surge in military aid to Pakistan as a result of its participation in the Global War on Terror. However, the vast majority of countries receive significantly less U.S. military aid than these outliers. The other countries included in this study average about $17 million per year in military aid.

Annual U.S. bilateral economic aid for the top ten overall recipients is shown in Figure 2.2. It illustrates the wide variation in the amount of economic aid given over time, even among the top recipients. Notable variations include the billions in

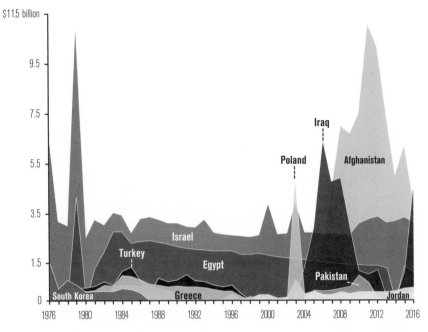

FIGURE 2.1. Top Ten U.S. Military Assistance Recipients. Note: Reported in 2016 dollars. Source: USAID, 2018.

economic aid that Russia received from the United States a few years after the breakup of the Soviet Union and again following the 1998 financial crisis. The amount of economic aid given to Afghanistan and Iraq was driven up by the United States' military engagements in those countries during the 2000s. In 2004 Iraq received the single largest allocation of U.S. economic aid to date: almost $9.5 billion. But after Afghanistan, Iraq, Turkey, and Egypt are omitted, the other countries in this study average about $78 million annually in economic aid from the United States. Even a major U.S. aid recipient such as Pakistan received only about one quarter of the total economic assistance that Afghanistan has received.

This variation in the type and amount of U.S. foreign assistance is a key explanatory factor, or independent variable, in my analysis of state violence. I am interested in its relationship with a variety of measures of state violence, including government repression, mass killings, state killings, and torture. Taken together, these outcome measures, or dependent variables, reflect important differences in the form, intensity, and purposes of state coercion that can help us better understand the coercive effect of foreign aid.

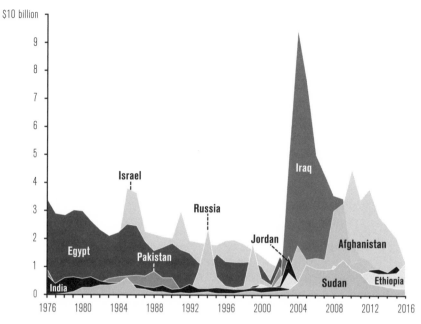

FIGURE 2.2.   Top Ten U.S. Economic Assistance Recipients. Note: Reported in 2016 dollars. Source: USAID, 2018.

Mass killings. The most explicit and controversial way to study state violence has been to focus on mass killings—episodes of state or state-sponsored violence that occur on a large scale. Research on this topic has sought to explain when and why a government resorts to genocide or the murder of large numbers of its citizens.[4] However, dealing with the magnitude of mass killing episodes is difficult.[5] Results that rely on casualty counts can be driven by a few extreme cases, such as the Rwandan genocide, and the omission of one or more of these cases can dramatically affect the results. To deal with some of these challenges while also capturing a relatively high intensity of state-led murder, I draw on a variety of data sets to create a measure of mass killing that reflects 300 or more intentional state-caused civilian deaths in a country in a given year.[6]

State killings. State killings are the direct and intentional use of armed force against civilians by a government or government-affiliated group that results in civilian fatalities. This includes extrajudicial killings. The state killings measure uses the same underlying data as the mass killings measure but has a lower threshold, indicating countries where twenty-five or more civilians were intentionally killed by the state in a given year. This allows me to capture variation in the extent of the intentional murder of civilians by the state.

Repression. Repression refers to coercive acts undertaken by state agents with the intention of controlling citizens' behavior. Specifically, state repression is defined as the direct violation of citizens' physical (or personal) integrity rights, a subset of human rights affirmed in the 1948 UN Declaration of Human Rights. Violations of physical integrity rights include the use of beatings, torture, mass arrests, disappearances, and summary executions. To measure repression, I use data from the Political Terror Scale that categorizes countries according to the extent and severity of relevant human rights abuses.[7] This approach allows me to identify significant changes in the overall conditions within a particular country.

Torture. Torture is defined under international law as "any act by which severe pain or suffering, whether physical or mental, is intentionally inflicted on a person . . . when such pain or suffering is inflicted by or at the instigation of or with the consent or acquiescence of a public official or other person acting in an official capacity."[8] I use data from the Cingranelli and Richards Human Rights Data Project, which captures the scope, intensity, and range of torture carried out by a specific country in a given year.[9]

In order to fully capture the theory outlined in Chapter 1, I also include a variety of additional explanatory and control variables that are summarized in the Appendix and discussed further below.

Does Foreign Aid Facilitate State Violence?

The analyses presented here help establish a broad association between U.S. foreign aid and state violence while accounting for other factors that are commonly used to explain why a state may resort to the use of force against its own citizens. The results of logistical regressions are presented in the form of odds ratios in Table 2.1. Values greater than one reflect an increased odds of a particular form of state violence; values of less than one mean that the variable is associated with a decreased odds of state violence in the following year. Each state violence measure that I address is indicated at the top of the column. The results for bilateral U.S. economic aid and military aid, the primary variables of interest, are listed in the first two rows. I use a one-year lag to ensure that the correlation runs in the intended direction—that is, that the analysis is capturing the relationship between foreign aid given in one year and state violence that occurs in the subsequent year. Although the type of statistical analysis I use does not establish direct causality, it is hard to imagine that the United States rewards countries engaged in mass killing by increasing foreign assistance. Indeed, this is exactly what the human rights conditionality in U.S. foreign aid legislation seeks to avoid.

TABLE 2.1. *U.S. Foreign Assistance and State Violence*

VARIABLE	MASS KILLINGS 1976–2016	STATE KILLINGS 1976–2016	REPRESSION 1976–2016	TORTURE 1981–2011
Military aid$_{t-1}$	0.961***	0.949***	0.991	0.973***
	(0.011)	(0.007)	(0.006)	(0.009)
Economic aid$_{t-1}$	1.043**	1.038***	1.021**	0.978**
	(0.022)	(0.139)	(0.010)	(0.006)
Anocracy$_{t-1}$	0.159***	0.749***	0.426***	0.816**
	(0.069)	(0.079)	(0.036)	(0.071)
Dictatorship$_{t-1}$	0.914	0.590***	2.844***	1.187
	(0.175)	(0.714)	(0.278)	(0.132)
Armed forces size$_{t-1}$	1.438***	1.112***	1.561***	1.193***
	(0.140)	(0.059)	(0.071)	(0.051)
Govt spending$_{t-1}$	0.978	0.974***	0.993**	0.987**
	(0.007)	(0.008)	(0.004)	(0.006)
Resource wealth$_{t-1}$	1.327	1.362	1.396***	0.695***
	(0.270)	(0.188)	(0.112)	(0.060)
Interstate war$_{t-1}$	0.174***	10.086***	0.321***	0.943
	(0.052)	(4.262)	(0.074)	(0.347)
Civil war$_{t-1}$	13.011***	6.089***	3.659***	2.387***
	(3.06)	(1.551)	(0.837)	(0.465)
GDP$_{t-1}$	0.915**	0.872**	0.778***	0.824***
	(0.085)	(0.049)	(0.031)	(0.036)
Population$_{t-1}$	1.119***	1.967***	1.556***	1.304***
	(0.161)	(0.134)	(0.078)	(0.066)
Observations	4064	3105	3406	3043
Pseudo R^2	0.2089	0.2214	0.1159	0.0462
Wald Chi^2	404.21	612.28	935.15	352.99
Log pseudo-likelihood	−597.546	−1310.075	−4282.443	−3070.539

NOTE: Odds ratios with bootstrapped standard errors. Cut points not reported for brevity. ***p<0.01, ** p<0.05, *p<0.10.

SOURCES: Cingranelli, Richards, and Clay, 2014; Eck and Hultman, 2007; Gibney et al., 2017; Marshall, 2017; Marshall, Gurr, and Harff, 2017; Marshall, Gurr, and Jaggers, 2017; Schrodt and Ulfelder, 2016; USAID, 2018; World Bank, 2018.

The results indicate that U.S. economic aid and military aid do have different relationships with state violence in recipient countries. As the theory suggests, economic aid is associated with an increased likelihood of mass killings, state killings, and government repression. The implication, then, is that over the past forty years, receiving U.S. economic assistance has been associated with increases in subsequent levels of state violence (with the notable exception of torture) in aid recipient countries. The findings reported here are strongly supported by an independent analysis by Faisal Z. Ahmed that examines U.S. economic aid to 150 countries from 1972 to 2008.[10] Using an instrumental variable statistical strategy and different measures of state repression, Ahmed finds that U.S. economic aid harms political rights and increases repression. It is simply not the case that economic aid only supports peaceful economic development activities. The results presented here and supported by a separate study covering roughly the same period suggest that U.S. economic aid plays a meaningful role in facilitating increased human rights abuses abroad.

Unexpectedly, U.S. military aid is associated with *decreased* levels of mass killings, state killings, and torture. It has no discernable association with government repression. There are several possible explanations for these results. As previously noted, military aid may be used to support the higher defense burdens of developing countries and be absorbed in military upkeep or personnel costs. If so, military aid does what it is supposed to do—better equip a country's military for external defense. Relatedly, it may be that the forms of military assistance that the United States provides are not conducive to the use of coercion against civilians. Certain types of technology (e.g., surface-to-air missiles) are not particularly useful in suppressing a rebellion or silencing dissidents. The same is true for much of the technical training that the United States provides. But evidence from El Salvador, presented in Chapter 4, demonstrates that military assistance is also fungible and could therefore be redirected toward internally focused coercive institutions such as the police or intelligence services.

Others argue that there is a clear and direct relationship between U.S. military assistance and improvements in human rights behavior: U.S. military assistance helps professionalize militaries and exposes them to international law and human rights norms, which make them less likely to use force against civilians. In *Aid for Elites*, Mark Moyar argues that in developing countries the military is often less prone to abuses of power than the police and other civilian security institutions.[11] He argues that the rigors of military training serve to differentiate the military from the civilian security apparatus and instill a different system of values that guards against corruption and other vices. Moyar contends that by investing in another country's military, U.S. military aid supports what is often one of the most professional and capable institutions in an overall context of state weakness. The relevant human rights problem from this perspective is not that abusive militaries receive U.S. military assistance but rather that they do not receive *enough* assistance.

Empirical assessments of related claims demonstrate that U.S. military assistance does not have a uniform impact on human rights practices. The nature of the program, the ways in which funds are allocated for their execution, and whether educational exchange or training constitutes an important element of the program can all influence the human rights effects of U.S. military assistance.[12] When military assistance is broken down into specific programs, research finds that Foreign Military Sales (FMS) and FMF funding do not lead to human rights improvements. However, IMET, both in terms of dollars spent and the number of students trained, is associated with a slight decrease in state violence (measured in terms of state-led atrocities). More specific foreign assistance programs such as the Regional Defense Combating Terrorism Fellowship Program and the Joint Combined Exchange Training Program have similar positive effects for human rights.[13]

The differences in the relationship between U.S. military assistance and various forms of state violence identified across a number of studies may ultimately come down to what *type* of military assistance a country receives from the United States. Countries receiving a high proportion of U.S.-funded professional military education may see improvements in human rights behavior due to exposure to the law of war, socialization into civil-military relations norms, or American influence over military doctrines and standard operating procedures.[14] But professionalization and socialization into human rights norms may not be the only way U.S. military assistance influences the behavior of militaries. Indeed, given significant variations in the length of U.S. government-sponsored military training and the time it takes foreign officers who have received training to make their way through the ranks of their militaries, it is difficult to identify a clear causal relationship between U.S. military training and changes in the behaviors of individuals who have undergone training. As Omelicheva and colleagues note, "U.S. military training programs have graduated some of the most notorious anti-democrats and human rights violators worldwide."[15]

Other causal pathways are possible as well. Governments that rely on U.S. military assistance may be more constrained in their use of the military as an instrument of state violence because there are relatively few alternative suppliers of military assistance. This is especially true if a country has relied on U.S. military assistance for a significant period of time and acquired military technology that requires American parts or training for upkeep. In addition, although many countries receive some military aid from the United States, aid is highly concentrated in a few countries (as shown in Figure 2.1), and a few cases may be driving this result. This issue is taken up through robustness tests.

After accounting for other factors that may influence a state's use of violence against its citizens, the observed relationship between U.S. bilateral economic aid and increased state-led killings and government repression still stands. Contrary to expectations, state violence appears to be less likely in countries undergoing political transitions (i.e., anocracies). Although dictatorships are strongly associated with government repression, they feature lower levels of state killings and are not correlated with other forms of state violence. This is consistent with the "more murder in the middle" hypothesis. The results also suggest that countries with larger militaries are more likely to engage in a variety of forms of state violence. It is possible that the size of a country's armed forces acts as a proxy for the level of threat the country faces. Combined with the finding that U.S. military aid is associated with decreases in state violence, this result suggests that we should pay close attention to the military's role in individual countries, rather than assume that it has a consistent role internally.

Countries with higher levels of government spending, measured as government consumption expenditure as a percentage of GDP, tend to have lower levels of state killings, repression, and torture, reflecting the fact that increased government spending on public services can serve to coopt opposition, lessening the state's incentive to repress.[16] Countries rich in natural resources, indicated by the resource wealth variable (where 10 percent or more of the country's GDP is derived from rents from coal, oil, or natural gas), are in general more likely to feature repression but less likely to employ torture. This could be interpreted as suggesting that high levels of government repression render torture and state-led killings unnecessary. However, for our purposes, the results suggest that when controlling for natural resource wealth, foreign aid has an impact on human rights abuses.

Turning to the relationship between armed conflict and state violence, the results indicate that civil war significantly increases the likelihood of all forms of human rights abuses examined here. This is to be expected, given that civil wars pit the government against a segment of its own population. However, even after accounting for this dynamic, U.S. economic aid is associated with state killings and government repression. By contrast, interstate war has an uncertain relationship to state violence. The results suggest that mass killings and government repression are less likely in countries that recently experienced or are currently engaged in interstate wars. However, state killings are much more likely in countries that participated in an interstate war in the previous year. This result is driven primarily by the wars in Afghanistan and Iraq (based on unreported t-tests). Both GDP and population are used as control variables.

Additional Analyses (Robustness Tests)

To assess whether the coercive effect of foreign aid is more pronounced in countries undergoing political transitions, I interacted U.S. foreign aid with the anocracy measure and reestimated the model for all forms of state violence. The results of the interaction term were not statistically significant for any of the outcome measures (results not shown). Although a country's political regime certainly influences whether it will use coercion against its citizens and what forms it will adopt, there is no meaningful difference between nondemocratic and democratic countries with regard to how foreign aid affects state violence. There is more state violence overall in nondemocratic countries, but in both democracies and nondemocracies, receiving U.S. economic aid is associated with an increase in the likelihood of various forms of state violence.

To make sure that the results presented in Table 2.1 represent general trends, I reestimated the analysis after removing the data on Afghanistan, Egypt, and Iraq, which are potential anomalies. The results for U.S. economic aid and state killings, repression, and torture remained statistically significant with very similar substantive effects. However, the association between U.S. economic aid and mass killings was no longer significant. This increases confidence that the results are not being skewed by strategically important and high-profile aid recipients or by the violence associated with the post-9/11 military occupations and government transitions in Afghanistan and Iraq.

Conclusion

The results provide initial empirical evidence of foreign aid's coercive effect. They indicate that the relationship between U.S. foreign aid and different forms of human rights abuses depends on the type of aid (military versus economic) that the United States gives to a particular country. Economic aid is associated with an increased likelihood of mass killings, state killings, and government repression. Counterintuitively, military aid is associated with a reduced likelihood of mass killings, state killings, and torture. The results also suggest that torture may be driven by factors distinct from those associated with other physical integrity rights violations, such as extrajudicial killings. As a result, the United States and other economic aid donors may need to drastically reorient their foreign aid policies to mitigate the harmful effects of economic aid.

Although the statistical analyses tell us a lot about the general relationship between foreign aid and state violence in countries receiving U.S. foreign assistance over the past four decades, they tell only one part of the story. The analyses cannot demonstrate that U.S. foreign aid directly causes human rights abuses, a claim that oversimplifies my argument. But the results do support my contention that foreign aid can provide recipient governments with resources that support their use of violence against their citizens.

The chapters that follow provide nuance and context for this important finding by examining varied cases—Indonesia, El Salvador, and South Korea—to discover where, when, and how U.S. foreign aid has played a pivotal role in facilitating human rights abuses. In particular, the case studies remedy some of the constraints of the statistical analyses. Although quantitative analyses typically assume a relatively short delay between cause and effect, the timing of aid disbursement cycles and arms procurement processes do not fit neatly into this time line.[17] Indeed, the effects of significant changes in military capacity brought about through foreign aid—such as the acquisition of new aircraft that increase surveillance capabilities or counterinsurgency training that shifts how a military engages in combat—can extend well into the future, even if aid is subsequently reduced. Similarly, because protest and opposition dynamics operate independently of donor's decisions about when and where to provide foreign aid, episodes of state violence do not necessarily occur immediately after aid-funded increases in a state's coercive capacity. Likewise, the existence of gaps between episodes of state violence does not necessarily suggest that the violence is unrelated to U.S. foreign assistance. For these reasons, I draw special attention to the sequencing and context of aid requests by the recipient governments and the specific resources offered up by the United States and other aid donors in order to trace the process through which foreign assistance shapes a state's use of violence.

3

Indonesia

Arming and Expanding

MARI ALKATIRI STOOD in front of the UN General Assembly in 1980 and pulled back the curtain on U.S. policy in Indonesia for all the world to see. The future first prime minister of an independent Timor-Leste (East Timor) stoically declared, "Although Indonesian aggression in East Timor has been dependent upon U.S. military aid, and although tens of thousands of East Timorese have been killed by weapons supplied by the U.S., we have faith in the generosity, humanity and goodness of the American people."[1]

The financial support provided by the United States, as well as other donors, funded the initial development of Indonesia's military capacity under Sukarno, the country's first president. Following an abortive coup, the transition from President Sukarno to Suharto—an anticommunist general who led a purge of Communist Party supporters that left between 200,000 and 800,000 dead[2]—ushered in a new era of U.S.-Indonesia relations.[3] U.S. foreign assistance flowed despite widespread knowledge of hundreds of thousands of killings.[4] This foreign assistance combined with the special role of the military, the Tentara Nasional Indonesia (TNI), as guarantors of the country's internal stability to create an enduring capacity for violence.[5] In the decades that followed, the Indonesian government consistently used violence as a tool of governance in areas where its control was contested. This pattern persisted even after Suharto's resignation in 1998 and the country's transition to a multiparty democracy.

Two mechanisms link foreign assistance with state-led violence in Indonesia. First, military aid directly contributed to the size and capabilities of the TNI through

a capacity-building effect. This heightened coercive capacity was then used in bel-
licose foreign policy moves to expand Indonesian territory through the occupation
and annexation of the Portuguese territory of East Timor and the Dutch colony of
West Irian. As Indonesia effectively colonized these territories, it used force to put
down any opposition that arose. The Indonesian occupation of East Timor was so
violent that experts claim it amounted to a genocide.[6] In the early 1970s, U.S. military assistance enabled Indonesia to acquire and hold territory through technologi-
cal improvements and the development of specialized human capital in the form of
counterinsurgency training. In the decades that followed, the patterns of violence
employed by the TNI in suppressing independence movements in these areas were
then transferred throughout the archipelago as troops redeployed from one hot spot
to another. In the far west of the country, the military quelled a separatist movement in the restive province of Aceh in part through episodic mass killings.

Second, U.S. economic aid, and in particular food aid, provided general budgetary support for the Indonesian central government. Economic aid from the
United States greatly exceeded military assistance to Indonesia. Food aid was sold
to generate foreign exchange. This income effect allowed economic aid to be diverted
toward increased military expenditure, regardless of the aid's intended purposes. The
budget support this aid provided helped sustain the country's high levels of military spending in the 1960s and 1970s by alleviating pressures on the government to
spend in other critical areas. The scale of U.S. economic assistance meant that it
could substitute for additional military assistance, which was constrained by
Congress.

Conditions unique to Indonesia facilitated the fungibility of economic assistance
into military expenditure. Suharto's doctrine of *dwifungsi* (dual function) established
the TNI as both the defender of the nation and the promoter of national development (including economic development). Under Suharto, military enterprises
benefitted from preferential access to credit and monopolies. More importantly, the
military dominated the country's economy. For example, Pertamina—the state-
owned oil, natural gas, and mining company—was formed in the 1950s when the
army was appointed to manage Sumatran oil fields. Pertamina was at one point
responsible for 70 percent of Indonesia's foreign exchange.[7] Economic assistance,
including millions of dollars in Export-Import Bank loans to Pertamina, enabled
the government to buy the military's continued support through an extensive
patronage network. Because the TNI was so embedded in key sectors, using foreign
aid to grow the Indonesian economy meant directly expanding financial support
for the military.

Background

Spanning 5,150 kilometers and composed of some 17,000 islands forcibly unified under Dutch colonial rule in the late 1800s, Indonesia has long been a country unified through violence. In 1926, over 13,000 Indonesians were arrested and 1,300 sent to prison camps in response to a rebellion.[8] Dutch rule was interrupted by a brief but oppressive Japanese occupation during World War II (from March 1942 until September 1945) during which existing political and social institutions were devoted to supporting Japan's war effort. By the end of the Japanese occupation, over 25,000 Indonesian youths had received basic training as Japanese auxiliary forces and 57,000 more took part in a volunteer army known as Peta (Pembela Tanah Air, or Protectors of the Fatherland), which swore to resist an invasion by the Allies.

Indonesia's eventual independence was borne of an armed struggle against the Dutch attempt at reoccupation following Japan's defeat. Four years of anticolonial guerrilla warfare followed Sukarno and Mohammad Hatta's 1945 declaration of Indonesia's independence. The TNI's origins in the war against the Dutch led to a domestically oriented command structure. Indonesia's Kodam (*komando daerah militer*), or military command areas, divide the archipelago into fifteen different operational zones. Another legacy of the war for independence is the TNI's Doctrine of Territorial Warfare, which emphasizes that the armed forces must be able to return to guerrilla warfare in response to a foreign invasion.[9] Until 1999, the police were also under the control of the Indonesian military. A shared command and control structure allowed arms obtained through foreign aid, even if formally designated for external defense, to be used against the state's domestic opponents.

Indonesia became a parliamentary democracy upon its formal independence in 1949. Yet, less than ten years later, President Sukarno dissolved parliament and declared martial law throughout the country in response to a series of regional rebellions and coup attempts. Constitutional changes followed, culminating in a July 5, 1959, presidential decree that began Indonesia's period of "Guided Democracy." Thereafter, Sukarno ruled with the backing of the armed forces. Guided Democracy came to an end in October 1965 when a group calling itself the September 30th Movement kidnapped and executed six army generals, including the TNI's highest commander.

Although the movement claimed to be preempting a coup, it was quickly crushed. The TNI began reprisal killings and then-Major General Suharto publicly blamed the Communist Party of Indonesia for supporting the movement.[10] Hundreds of thousands throughout the country were killed by the military, militia groups, and even ordinary citizens. In 1966 Sukarno was forced to turn over emergency powers to Suharto. On March 12, 1967, Indonesia's legislative body, the People's Consultative Assembly, unanimously passed a decree declaring Sukarno incapable of fulfilling his duties, and naming Suharto as acting president. The following year, Suharto was elected to a five-year term as president of Indonesia. CIA assessments found Suharto to be a strong and resourceful, although cautious, leader, as opposed to Sukarno, who was often described as overly emotional and erratic.[11] (Sukarno died of kidney failure on June 21, 1970, while under house arrest in Jakarta.)

Under Suharto's "New Order" regime and the doctrine of dwifungsi, the TNI became a central part of the political process through mechanisms such as guaranteed parliamentary seats.[12] In practice, the military's dual roles of defending the nation and promoting national development meant that it became deeply embedded in Indonesia's political and economic life. By 1970, army officers were governors of fourteen of the country's twenty-six provinces.[13] The TNI's command structure paralleled the country's administrative bodies, making it possible for the military to dominate national, regional, and local economic opportunities.

Throughout the more than three decades of Suharto's rule, both the president and his family increasingly were targets of criticism regarding corruption and the substantial power of the TNI within the Indonesian economy. This long-standing criticism, combined with the economic shocks of the 1998 Asian financial crisis, led to the rapid erosion of popular support for Suharto. He resigned in 1998 following widespread protests; Vice President Bacharuddin Jusuf Habibie, who had been appointed by Suharto to the role in March of that year, became president. Habibie remained in power for a little over a year before Abdurrahman Wahid was elected to the presidency. In July 2001 the People's Consultative Assembly voted to remove Wahid from power after he declared a state of emergency and attempted to disband the Assembly. Megawati Sukarnoputri, Sukarno's daughter and acting vice president at the time, came to power. She served out the remainder of Wahid's term, only to face electoral defeat in 2004 by Susilo Bambang Yudhoyono, a retired army officer. Yudhoyono was subsequently reelected in 2009 with a majority of votes in the first round, marking Indonesia's full transition to a democratic political system.

U.S. Assistance to Indonesia

Truman's Point Four Program coincided with the establishment of an independent Indonesian government under Sukarno. American foreign assistance to Asia in the 1950s was intended to minimize the danger of increased communist influence in "free" countries by improving the economic strength of the region.[14] In the immediate postindependence years, the United States provided substantial amounts of food aid so that Indonesia could acquire food, cotton, and tobacco without using scarce foreign exchange.[15]

U.S. military assistance to Indonesia began as a relatively small program (equivalent to about $33 million today) authorized under Section 401 of the Mutual

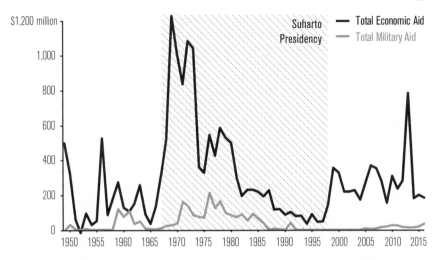

FIGURE 3.1. U.S. Bilateral Assistance to Indonesia. Note: Reported in 2016 dollars. Source: USAID, 2018.

Defense Assistance Act of 1949, and included military equipment for the police.[16] Major military assistance did not begin until 1959, as illustrated in Figure 3.1.[17] The passage of the Foreign Assistance Act in 1961 gave the president authorization "to furnish military assistance on such terms and conditions as he may determine, to any friendly country or international organization, the assisting of which the President finds will strengthen the security of the United States and promote world peace."[18] Indonesia was one such country.

The vast majority of U.S. military aid given during Sukarno's years in office took the form of MAP grants, which provided direct budgetary support to the military.[19] It was thought that this military aid would help foster increased cohesion within the armed forces and, in turn, the military would check Sukarno's power at a time when he appeared to have procommunist leanings.[20] Through IMET funds, which allowed over 4,000 Indonesian military officers to attend U.S. military academies, the United States gained valuable intelligence and created a reliably Western-oriented military. As historian Bradley Simpson notes, military assistance was a major weapon in the fight for continued Indonesian independence and the fight to increase Indonesia's receptivity to Western political and economic institutions and practices.[21] At the same time, concerns about Soviet influence in Indonesia could not be easily dismissed.[22]

The limits of military assistance as a tool of American influence were demonstrated when Sukarno began to threaten Indonesia's neighbors, pursuing a policy of *Konfrontasi* (confrontation) from 1962 to 1966 in response to the union of several former British colonies as independent Malaysia. Much of this conflict centered on the island of Borneo, where competing Dutch and British colonial interests resulted in an international border between Indonesia and Malaysia that still exists today. Peace negotiations eventually ended Indonesia's support to insurgent groups in Malaysia's half of Borneo. Indonesia then began to prepare for what seemed to many American diplomats to be territorial aggrandizement in the Dutch colony of West Irian (located on the western half of the island of New Guinea).

Throughout the early 1960s, the United States limited its economic aid due to U.S.-Indonesian diplomatic tensions over these issues.[23] The Kennedy administration tried to arrange increased aid to Indonesia, but Congress opposed it.[24] In August 1963 the House Foreign Affairs Committee adopted an amendment cutting all economic assistance to Indonesia in response to its aggression toward Malaysia. This forced the president to explicitly authorize the aid in terms of U.S. national interest, overriding Congress, in an attempt to bolster Sukarno's power vis-à-vis the Indonesian Communist Party.[25] Kennedy believed that Indonesia was in danger of being seized from within by communist forces supported by military or paramilitary efforts from both inside and outside the country.[26] The bottom line, according to Simpson, was that "Washington could not give up the game to the Soviets or the Chinese no matter how anyone felt about Sukarno."[27] As National Security Council (NSC) staff member Robert Komer wrote to President Kennedy in July 1963, "Despite all the pain, our Indo[nesia] policy is gathering speed in [the] right direction, if we can only stick it out."[28]

Given the potential volatility of U.S. foreign aid flows to Indonesia due to congressional opposition, loans extended by the Export-Import Bank were a way for Kennedy and subsequent administrations to circumvent Congress. The Export-Import Bank was created in 1934 by President Franklin D. Roosevelt to assist in financing and facilitating exports and imports and the exchange of commodities between the United States and other countries.[29] In 1945 the Export-Import Bank Act made Roosevelt's bank permanent. Over the course of Sukarno's presidency, American loans made through the Export-Import Bank totaled over $1 billion.[30] Figure 3.2 illustrates the mix of economic and military assistance provided by the United States to Indonesia.

True to his position as a leader of the nonaligned movement, Sukarno also actively sought economic and military support from the Soviet Union. In 1956 the Soviet Union extended a $100 million loan to Indonesia.[31] Other communist countries soon followed: from 1955 through 1965, Indonesia received grants and loans from Communist Bloc countries totaling approximately $1 billion.[32] Declassified Soviet Gosplan documents suggest that almost 90 percent of Soviet assistance was used for military purposes.[33] According to CIA estimates, the Soviet Union supplied about $1.1 billion in military assistance to Indonesia, including $860 million in arms

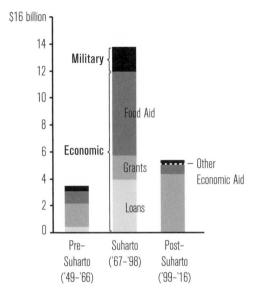

FIGURE 3.2. Types of U.S. Assistance to Indonesia. Note: Reported in 2016 dollars. Source: USAID, 2018.

shipments, prior to 1965.[34] The Joint Chiefs of Staff estimated that American military aid commitments totaled only one-fourteenth of the Soviet effort.[35] This led to concerns that the Soviet Union might be supporting a military buildup in Indonesia similar to that in Cuba, with the possible placement of submarines and long-range bomber aircraft.[36] American fears proved to be overblown, and endemic Indonesian mismanagement, continued engagement with the United States, and differences over Indonesian foreign policy moves led to a rapid drop-off in Communist Bloc assistance in the mid-1960s.

The combination of American and Soviet assistance did, however, enable Indonesia to stake a claim over the territory of West Irian (now the provinces of Papua and West Papua). The territory had formerly been part of the Dutch East Indies, but was separated in 1949 as part of the settlement for Indonesian independence. West Irian remained under Dutch control as Netherlands New Guinea. The Netherlands argued that the people of New Guinea were ethnically distinct and that the territory should undergo a decolonization process that would leave it independent from Indonesia. But Indonesia's territorial ambitions in West Irian were encouraged by the Soviet Union as part of Nikita Khrushchev's support for wars of national liberation. The Australians, for their part, firmly supported continued Dutch control. The American position was more nuanced. President Kennedy contended, "The area is a most unsuitable one for a war in which the United States would be involved. We would not wish to humiliate the Dutch, but on the other hand it would be foolish to have a contest when the Dutch really do want to get out if a dignified method can be found."[37]

The Indonesian government's emphasis on a military buildup and preoccupation with the West Irian issue and Malaysia diverted much of the country's resources to military use.[38] Indonesian military expenditures rose to an estimated 37.8 percent of the budget in 1960 and almost half of the government's budget in 1961.[39] Equipment delivered to Soviet-aided projects remained crated at ports or lay rusting at construction sites even as the Soviets officially authorized the diversion of economic aid to the military.[40]

The fungibility of aid in the Indonesian context was widely acknowledged. Scholars observed that "non-military aid increases the general amount of foreign currency available to the central government, and enables the government to spend on the armed forces more of the foreign currency obtained from non-aid sources."[41] Even U.S. food aid, exempt from any congressional restrictions, was devoted to subsidizing the military during this period. American rice was sold by the Indonesian government to the TNI for one rupiah per liter while the free-market price in the capital city of Jakarta was over sixty rupiahs per liter.[42]

The diversion of economic assistance toward military ends had a profound impact on the state's military capacity. Active duty personnel reached 330,000 by late 1962. Indonesia built a navy with at least twenty submarines, two cruisers, four destroyers, and several motor torpedo boats.[43] The country's air force included at least ninety jet fighters, alongside bombers and helicopters. Ultimately, the TNI developed the capacity to infiltrate West Irian, land 2,000 to 3,000 paratroopers, and engage in naval battles with the Dutch.[44] Military expenditures consumed over half of the government's annual budget, and the country's debt continued to mount.

The Kennedy administration eventually accepted that West Irian would come under Indonesian control one way or another, in spite of the firm stance taken by the State Department and the president himself against Indonesian use of force.[45] "We should recognize that this territory was likely eventually to go to Indonesia, even though we ourselves might deeply dislike Sukarno as an individual," argued Kennedy. "The real stake here was not West Irian but the fate of Indonesia, the most rich and populous country in the area and one which was the target of energetically pursued Soviet ambitions."[46] The CIA shared similar views. A May 1962 memo argued, "We do not wish to leave [the] impression that [the] solution of [the] West Irian problem would leave [the] door open for [a] love feast between U.S. and Indonesia. Far from that, but [a] solution would, in our opinion, open [the] door for dealing frankly with Indonesians without [the] irritant so long hindering our relations with this country."[47] Despite opposition at the UN, American and Indonesian pressure eventually led to a 1962 agreement for a phased handover of West Irian to Indonesia. President Kennedy sought to capitalize on America's role in promoting the handover to move toward a better relationship with Indonesia through expanded military aid, economic stabilization and development programs, and new diplomatic initiatives.[48]

In Indonesia, however, the situation was far from settled. A 1969 sham referendum, known legally as "the Act of Free Choice," led local elites in the newly renamed province of Papua to launch the Free Papua Movement (Organisasi Papua Merdeka). The Free Papua Movement and the TNI engaged in violent conflict from the late 1960s until the mid-1980s.[49] The movement still exists, even though its leaders are regularly assassinated. Raising the Morning Star flag of Netherlands New Guinea remains a crime punishable by prison time.[50]

Throughout these tensions, significant reductions in U.S. foreign assistance to Indonesia were never seriously considered. The CIA's Office of National Estimates concluded in January 1964 that reducing aid to Indonesia would provide a serious jolt to U.S.-Indonesian relations and invite various anti-American actions, including protest riots and demonstrations.[51] An aid reduction would undermine the limited influence the United States had with Indonesia, while a complete cutoff of aid could "provoke Sukarno to permit mob violence against U.S. nationals, expropriate U.S. property, and break diplomatic relations."[52] Aid dollars did not translate into significant influence with Sukarno, but at the same time, a cutoff in aid would potentially threaten American interests in the country and possibly throughout the region. As policymakers struggled with a solution to this dilemma, the October 1965 coup attempt and the sidelining of Sukarno in favor of Suharto provided them with the solution they had been waiting for.

Following his abrupt rise to power, Suharto came to rely heavily on foreign assistance from the United States as Soviet aid dried up. Suharto placed a great deal of emphasis on U.S. military training and made repeated requests for greater military assistance to shore up loyalty within the armed forces, a request that was hard to ignore in the wake of a coup attempt.[53] After Suharto became president in March 1967, U.S. bilateral aid to Indonesia jumped to $546 million in 1968, an almost fourfold increase. As seen in Figure 3.1, U.S. foreign aid to Indonesia reached an all-time high under Suharto in 1972, at the current equivalent of $1.22 billion.[54]

U.S. assistance to Suharto was driven by two considerations. First, the political stability of Indonesia was then, as now, tied to the central government's ability to extend its control over the entire territory. Developing Indonesia's outlying regions and tying them both institutionally and economically to the Javanese center was a major concern, and the military played an essential role in this effort. Nixon understood this and believed that it was necessary for Indonesia, with thousands of miles of coastline and an essentially military leadership, to have a substantial military capability in order to ensure its political stability.[55]

Second, requests by Suharto's government for increased U.S. military assistance were often directly framed in terms of Indonesia's economic development needs. By repeatedly stressing the importance of economic development, the leadership created a situation whereby the potential diversion of resources away from economic development and toward the military became a continual threat used to secure additional foreign assistance from the United States. In meetings, Suharto spoke of the priority given to economic development. He stressed the austerity imposed on the armed forces as a result, which left the military with barely enough for upkeep.[56] General Sumitro, head of the TNI, argued in a conversation with Henry Kissinger that "in speeding up the rebuilding of the Indonesian Armed Forces, Indonesia needed time to develop since its training facilities were limited and its management very bad. There was an additional principle: military development should not interfere with the Indonesian five-year plan. Not one penny could be expected from this plan, or it would fail."[57] As a result, both economic and military support were framed as essential to the regime's survival.

From the American perspective, Indonesia's internal security concerns—including its ability to suppress procommunist and separatist groups—were a national security priority, given the growth of communism in the region. To support Indonesia's effort to maintain internal security, the United States supplied equipment for nine infantry battalions and significant numbers of aircraft, including planes that could be converted to gunships to meet the TNI's desire for combat equipment.[58] The United States also contributed to a substantial naval buildup.[59] Requests from the Indonesian Ministry of Defense and the U.S. Defense Liaison Group in Jakarta led to an almost threefold increase in military aid in 1971.[60] President Nixon personally authorized a tripling of MAP grants to Indonesia.[61] The possibility of supplying light combat items to help Indonesia meet its internal security needs was also discussed.[62]

Beginning in 1973, FMF grants for the purchase of U.S. defense equipment and services were established to substitute for MAP grants.[63] As a result, arms sales from the United States to Indonesia quintupled between 1974 and 1975. However, this shift in U.S. foreign aid policy introduced additional tension in U.S.-Indonesian relations. Suharto believed that grant military assistance was a general indicator of U.S. support for Indonesia, and argued that MAP funding lessened the degree to which other funds needed to be diverted toward military purposes.[64] These tensions were exacerbated by the oil crises. The OPEC oil embargo in 1973 reinforced partisan opposition between Nixon and Congress, making it politically impossible to provide significant levels of assistance to Indonesia, an OPEC member.[65]

Worried that a loss of military assistance could lead elements within the TNI to demand a change in the government's orientation, the United States began providing alternative forms of assistance.[66] U.S. foreign aid began to rely heavily on PL 480 food and commodities, such as cotton, and alternative sources of financial support, including Export-Import Bank loans. Growing congressional restrictions on U.S. foreign aid made these sources of support all the more attractive. As of 1976, new legislation required annual human rights reporting to Congress by the State Department as part of a broader effort to limit military assistance to countries found to be violating human rights. In this context, the fungibility of economic aid into Indonesian military expenditure was openly acknowledged as a potential avenue for continued support to Suharto by key Ford administration figures, including Kissinger.[67]

From 1967 to 1985, the United States provided over $3 billion in favorable loans to Indonesia. This figure included a July 1973 Export-Import Bank loan of $54 million to Pertamina. In October 1982 a $292.5 million loan to Pertamina was approved by the Senate and House Banking committees.[68] At the time, Pertamina was run by Brigadier General Judo Sumbono, a close associate of Suharto's. These loans were explicitly intended to assist with Indonesia's balance of payments challenges and, by extension, to allow the country to continue financing its military. But they also supported Indonesia's military in more direct ways. For example, an $11.3 million loan was used to purchase six Sikorsky S-76 helicopters.[69] Similarly, a March 1984 Export-Import Bank loan of $104.3 million to Indonesia's state-owned shipbuilding company was used to purchase high-speed jet foils from Boeing, which were then used in Indonesian naval vessels.[70]

Despite Suharto's personal fondness for military assistance, economic assistance actually made up the overwhelming majority of U.S. foreign assistance to Indonesia (as illustrated in Figure 3.2).[71] Economic assistance was viewed as an indirect way of providing hard currency to the economically fragile state. U.S. policymakers were well aware that food aid would be sold, providing the government with a much-needed source of foreign exchange. The billions of dollars in food aid provided to Indonesia had a significant income effect, allowing the government to devote some of these funds to a policy of military expansion and hardware acquisition that was also subsidized by hundreds of millions of dollars in military assistance.

Indonesia's December 1975 invasion of East Timor abruptly changed U.S. foreign policy toward the country. While West Irian had historically been part of the same Dutch colony as Indonesia, that was not the case for East Timor, which had been a Portuguese colony for 273 years. Yet, from the Indonesian government's perspective, the incorporation of East Timor was easily rationalized. Indonesia already controlled the western half of the island of Timor. Portugal had invested little in its far-flung colony. The tiny population of about one million could be easily absorbed into Indonesia and join their ethnic compatriots, from whom they had been divided by centuries of colonialism. Such reasoning was rejected by Australia and other powers interested in limiting Indonesia's influence in the region. After East Timor was declared the twenty-seventh province of Indonesia on July 17, 1976, the United States was forced to stop providing Indonesia with foreign aid–funded military equipment because of the negative international response.

As early as January 1975, the U.S. ambassador to Indonesia, David D. Newsom, noted that unilateral Indonesian military action in East Timor could automatically involve the United States in an embarrassing problem. Newsom argued that there was a virtual inevitability that if Indonesia used military force in acquiring East Timor, U.S. military equipment obtained through MAP grants would be involved.[72] Nevertheless, members of the Ford administration, and in particular Kissinger, continued to push for greater aid to Indonesia because the strategic gains outweighed the possibility of being involved in a colonial dispute.[73]

Arguably, the surge in military aid to Indonesia in the mid-1970s occurred in anticipation of future aid restrictions by Congress. The Nixon and Ford administrations, in effect, sought to bank goodwill with Suharto. It is also possible that Suharto was aware of potential changes to U.S. foreign aid policy and acted in East Timor with that in mind. Either way, the capacity-building effect of U.S. military assistance during this period is undeniable. Indonesia acquired sixteen helicopters and sixteen OV-10 ground attack aircraft from the United States.[74] Millions of dollars were earmarked to fund helicopters and patrol craft, while millions more in military grants were given to provide modern equipment for key military units.[75]

Congress proved unpredictable. The Senate Foreign Relations Committee voted down a ban on military aid grants to Indonesia, even though its subcommittee on foreign assistance recommended the ban based on human rights concerns.[76] The Senate committee's rationale was that the United States accepted Suharto's annexation of East Timor, and therefore there was no prohibition on the use of U.S. arms there, because Indonesia was expected to use the equipment within its borders.[77] Essentially, the formal incorporation of East Timor into Indonesia made the issue a matter of internal security rather than territorial annexation. Later that year, the TNI began a violent counterinsurgency campaign in East Timor against pockets of local resistance.[78] Similar efforts were underway in Papua, where in 1977 the TNI dropped napalm on villages in response to an anti-Indonesia rebellion by 15,000 tribal group members.[79]

It is now widely accepted that roughly 90 percent of the military equipment used in the Indonesian invasion of East Timor was supplied by the United States through the foreign aid programs described here.[80] Officials in the State Department at the time knew that American equipment was being used, including the U.S. destroyers that shelled East Timor's capital city of Dili.[81] The Ford administration was aware that there would be accusations of American complicity in the murder of innocent civilians during the capture of Dili.[82] However, U.S. officials claimed to not have anticipated that 2,000 people would be killed in the first few days of the operation as 15,000 to 20,000 Indonesian troops invaded.[83] By February 1976, an estimated 60,000 Timorese had been killed.[84] Episodes of torture and sexual violence, in addition to well-known incidents of mass killings, are documented in interviews with Timorese from the cities of Balibo and Dili.[85] Human rights concerns were raised in the months following the invasion, but Ambassador Newsom defended the Suharto regime and argued that ending security assistance would not only drastically reduce U.S. influence but could cause Indonesia to turn for assistance to countries with less concern for human rights.[86] Such claims continue to be made in defense of foreign assistance to abusive governments even today. American fears about Soviet influence in Indonesia, and Southeast Asia more generally, overrode legitimate human rights concerns.

The Timor-Leste Commission for Reception, Truth, and Reconciliation found that "U.S.-supplied weaponry was crucial to Indonesia's capacity to intensify military operations from 1977 in its massive campaigns to destroy the Resistance."[87] As the occupation began to normalize, the TNI switched from a focus on civilian punishment through aerial bombardment to more targeted counterinsurgency operations in East Timor. These operations continued through the early 1980s. For example, Indonesian troops allegedly made a "clean sweep" of the area surrounding Kraras, resulting in between 300 and 500 deaths over a period of several days in September 1983.[88] Reports from the U.S. embassy in Jakarta recount episodes of indiscriminate violence.[89] In addition to counterinsurgency tactics, there was extensive use of the selective detention, interrogation, and torture of alleged members of resistance groups.[90] In Papua, at least 11,000 people fled across the border to Papua New Guinea in response to similar repressive tactics between 1984 and 1986.[91]

Throughout all of the violence experienced in East Timor, American economic and military assistance to Indonesia continued, but at reduced levels. U.S. economic aid remained significant in the 1980s and was augmented by foreign aid from Japan, which became the world's largest bilateral aid donor in 1989. Although food aid declined in importance as the country's level of development and agricultural productivity increased, U.S. foreign assistance to Indonesia declined notably only as part of a general policy of fiscal retrenchment under President Reagan.

Even as the United States began to pull back its financial support for the Suharto regime, state violence continued. On November 12, 1991, the military suppressed a funeral procession in Dili that had evolved into a proindependence demonstration. Captured on film by an Australian journalist, the approximately 2,000 demonstrators were met with active fire from the TNI, who later characterized the event as a violent riot.[92] The alleged victims of the massacre totaled 271 killed, 278 wounded, and 270 disappearances.[93] Similar demonstrations and riots in Papua were met with military abuses.[94]

Violence expanded to other areas of Indonesia as well. Civil war broke out in Aceh province as the separatist Free Aceh Movement launched attacks on the military.[95] The TNI's heavy-handed response saw more individuals killed by summary executions than in actual fighting.[96] During the first four years of the counterinsurgency operations known as *Jaring Merah,* or Red Net, scores of guerrillas and civilians were killed, tortured, and disappeared. Victims spoke of being forced to bury people shot by the military; women reported sexual assault and rape.[97] Women were also targeted for interrogation and torture for information on their husbands. The government's efforts in Aceh were supported by civilian militias. Often out of fear of being labelled guerrillas, local villagers played a notable role in the killings. As early as November 1990, mass graves were discovered. Estimates of the disappeared range from 500 to 5,000. Reports indicate that at least 3,439 individuals were tortured, and human rights groups claim that as many as 12,000 people were murdered in Aceh between 1990 and August 1998.[98]

The international attention given to the Dili massacre finally prompted Congress to restrict lethal aid to Indonesia from 1993 to 1995. In 1994 total U.S. foreign aid reached its lowest level since Suharto came to office, a paltry $36.7 million in economic assistance for a country of over 196 million people. When IMET funds were resumed in 1996, they totaled less than $1 million per year.[99] Although the changing dynamics of post–Cold War U.S. foreign policy played a role, the reduction in U.S. assistance was also due to increased international attention to human rights abuses, including the awarding of the 1996 Nobel Peace Prize to Carlos Felipe Ximenes Belo, bishop of East Timor, and José Ramos-Horta, spokesperson for the East Timor independence movement.

During the period of restricted U.S. foreign assistance, the TNI actively developed state-sponsored civilian militias.[100] The headquarters of many militia groups were located on military premises, and the militias often used military vehicles for their patrols or patrolled alongside military personnel.[101] Although some militias had rudimentary weapons such as homemade firearms and knives, others were supplied with modern firearms by military officials.[102] By August 1998, 21,600 TNI troops were stationed alongside paramilitary forces and militias in East Timor among a population of 865,000.[103] TNI Commander Wiranto acknowledged tactical control of about 1,100 militia members with 546 weapons as well as 11,950 members of "resistance organizations" opposed to East Timor's independence.[104]

Violence in East Timor rapidly escalated from November 1998 to August 1999 in the wake of Suharto's resignation. Groups favoring increased autonomy within Indonesia, as proposed by President Wahid, were pitted against proindependence groups. A peaceful UN-monitored referendum on East Timor's future status was followed by an explosion of violence and mass killings. An estimated 1,000 to 2,000 civilians were killed and approximately 500,000 more—greater than half of the population—were internally displaced. According to a subsequent human rights investigation, the violence was supported by the military, which allowed use of command headquarters.[105] Yet, only twelve individuals were tried in 2002 for orchestrating the violence. Two, including East Timor's former governor, were convicted of crimes against humanity.[106] The rest, including TNI officers and a police colonel, were acquitted.[107]

In the wake of this violence, the United States again suspended military assistance and stopped the transfer or purchase of U.S. military equipment by Indonesia. From the establishment of the UN Transitional Administration in East Timor at the end of 1999 until East Timor's official independence in 2002, the United States withheld all military assistance to Indonesia. However, in response to the Asian financial crisis and the post-Suharto political transition, U.S. economic aid more than doubled between 1998 and 1999—rising from $144 million to $356 million.[108] The curtailment of military aid was rendered meaningless by increased economic assistance.

Independence for East Timor did not change the way the Indonesian state operated. The withdrawal of TNI forces from East Timor in response to the UN mission facilitated the deployment of an additional 51,000 soldiers and police officers to Aceh province in 2003.[109] In the early 2000s Aceh was virtually cut off from independent media coverage due to the expulsion of NGOs and independent observers. Local NGOs such as Koalisi HAM Aceh (Aceh Human Rights Coalition) continued to report on human rights violations attributed to the TNI and the police.[110] In Papua, human rights abuses also continued. In one instance, TNI officers ordered subordinates to shoot those trying to escape during a crackdown on an antigovernment demonstration.[111]

A natural disaster, not any meaningful change in the government's human rights behavior, led to the full resumption of U.S. foreign assistance to Indonesia. The

December 2004 Indian Ocean tsunami killed 221,000 people across Aceh and displaced more than 500,000 others. The devastation resulted in a major increase in total U.S. economic aid, most of which came from USAID's special Tsunami Recovery and Reconstruction Fund for the region.[112] Secretary of State Condoleezza Rice waived restrictions that had made aid funds available only if the government was prosecuting, punishing, and resolving cases involving members of the TNI alleged to have committed human rights violations in East Timor and elsewhere. This allowed the United States to resume military assistance and permitted U.S. military forces to assist the TNI in the relief effort.[113] While IMET, FMF, and transfers of lethal defense articles resumed in November 2005, restrictions on U.S. engagement with Indonesia's special forces, known as Kopassus, continue. Fortunately, the tsunami also helped reinforce steps toward peace in Aceh. In return for the Free Aceh Movement's demilitarization, the Indonesian government agreed in August 2005 to withdraw all nonlocal military and police units and disarm the approximately 10,000 progovernment militia members in Aceh.[114] By the start of the new year, over 30,000 Indonesian police and army personnel had left the province.[115]

As was the case with East Timor's independence, the Aceh peace agreement allowed the TNI to redeploy 15,000 troops to Papua. Reports of extrajudicial killings, arbitrary arrests, torture, and excessive use of force surged.[116] In 2008 an army official indicted for crimes against humanity in East Timor was nominated as military commander in Jayapura, the capital of Papua province.[117] U.S. military assistance contributed to Indonesia's coercive capacity by training of thousands of TNI officers. These leaders set the tone for thousands more. In this case, there is scant evidence that exposure to American military norms had any effect in moderating their behavior.

Conclusion

American foreign policy in Indonesia played a decisive role in shaping Indonesia's direction. The most populous Muslim country in the world has, for most of its postindependence history, been firmly oriented toward the West. But the extensive U.S. foreign assistance program to Indonesia has come with significant costs. For decades, the United States provided both economic and military aid, which ensured that Indonesia could pursue military expansion while sustaining its much-needed economic development initiatives. Indonesia, in turn, became a more aggressive state, occupying territory and violently repressing internal challenges. People were silenced, imprisoned, tortured, and killed for taking part in communist organizations and supporting independence movements in Aceh, East Timor, and Papua.

Foreign aid initially played a direct and prominent role in building up the country's military strength. Through military assistance programs and subsidized military hardware purchases, foreign assistance from the United States, and to a lesser degree, the Soviet Union, enabled a military buildup under Sukarno. Sukarno used the country's new military strength to forcefully pressure the Netherlands to cede control of Papua. Under Suharto, U.S. military assistance supported the invasion and annexation of an adjacent territory, East Timor, setting the stage for decades of repression and internal conflict that exploded into mass killings in 1999.

President Suharto and members of his government effectively used the threat of diverting resources from economic development to the military to ensure continued foreign assistance from the United States. This threat was credible, given the military's deep reach into the country's economy, the country's extensive development needs, and the potential for widespread social unrest. With more money to spend, the Indonesian government could direct the excess toward the military while still providing essential public services through its many state monopolies (including on food imports, electricity, and oil).

Key U.S. government officials intended economic aid (and in particular, PL 480 food aid and commodities) to provide general budgetary support for the Indonesian government. They openly acknowledged that this aid could be diverted to fund the military. From the American perspective, the coercive effect of foreign aid served two purposes: first, to ensure that the military remained reliably Western- (as opposed to Soviet-) oriented, and second, to ensure continued support for Suharto, who proved to be a reliable partner of the United States.

Indonesia also demonstrates how improvements in military capacity brought about through foreign assistance endure beyond temporary reductions or cutoffs of aid.[118] It may be the case that it is not military assistance itself, but the lessons learned from military operations (especially in a civil war or counterinsurgency context) that create the human capital necessary for continued coercion.[119] State violence in East Timor, as well as Aceh and Papua, grew out of the coercive skills that the TNI developed during the initial occupation of East Timor from 1975 to 1976. The training of elite units such as Kopassus was funded through IMET. Although the United States did briefly cut off military assistance to Indonesia—from 1993 to 1995 and in 2001 and 2002—this sanction was not enough to lead to the punishment of most human rights abusers. By the time cuts were implemented, the TNI's role in maintaining internal security and the impunity with which its members violated human rights had been well established. It is therefore difficult to make the case that cuts to U.S. military assistance prevented any human rights abuses.

The case of Indonesia unfortunately illustrates the limits of human rights conditionality in U.S. foreign aid policy. Such conditions do not prevent human rights abuses from occurring. Rather, aid restrictions serve as a punishment for governments that have egregiously abused their own citizens and, often, have already achieved their political objectives in doing so. Continued restrictions on military assistance to Kopassus reflect the persistence of Senator Leahy, who urged Secretary of Defense James Mattis to use his January 2018 visit to Indonesia to answer the question of "whether the Indonesian government has punished the Kopassus officers who ordered and covered up these horrific crimes, and whether members of Kopassus today are accountable to the rule of law."[120] But in spite of these restrictions, the United States' policy of maintaining economic aid irrespective of Indonesia's human rights behavior was counterproductive. Even as congressional restrictions eliminated direct military-to-military ties, military professionalization, and other oversight mechanisms that result from military cooperation, U.S. economic aid continued to support a regime that regularly relied on state violence.

Foreign assistance played an important role in U.S. foreign policy by signaling support for Suharto's regime and Indonesia's status vis-à-vis its neighbors. However, the coercive effect of foreign aid played a much greater role in influencing the liberty, or lack thereof, of millions of Indonesians.

4

El Salvador

Buying Guns and Butter

THE HISTORY OF AMERICAN INVOLVEMENT in El Salvador is polarizing. On one side, critics argue that U.S. military assistance to a brutal dictatorship helped kill tens of thousands of peasants and contributed to the worst excesses of America's not-so-cold Cold War. On the other side, proponents of American aid to the Salvadoran government believed then, as now, that America could turn the tide against communism in Latin America by helping to save this little country; military dictatorships, though bad, were nothing compared to communist ones. Economic reforms and a new system of land tenure would demonstrate to the peasantry that there was a better way forward. For these defenders of U.S. involvement, the fact that El Salvador is now a robust democracy is proof that the struggle was worth the cost. The truth lies somewhere in between these two perspectives.

Following on the heels of the Vietnam War, America's interventions in its own backyard touched a nerve and led many to ask what vital national interest was at stake in Central America. But in reality, American involvement in El Salvador's civil war (which lasted from 1980 to 1992) was not like Vietnam. U.S. troops were never deployed in large numbers; fewer than 100 military advisors were in the country at any given moment. Even with hindsight, it remains difficult to pin the blame for the human cost of the civil war in El Salvador entirely on one side. Political violence has characterized much of El Salvador's history, and based on the size of the population, El Salvador's guerrillas were once the largest irregular force in the region. However, the extreme violence perpetrated by the state and state-aligned militias during the late 1970s and 1980s was not driven by local factors alone. Through the coercive effect of aid, foreign assistance from the United States crucially enabled the government of El Salvador to respond to a leftist opposition threat with widespread violence.

El Salvador, where the United States previously had little interest, became the focus of an intense project to eradicate communism in the region after leftist groups began gaining strength throughout Latin America. The United States pursued what was essentially a policy of regime stability, even as El Salvador's political leaders continued to change. U.S. military assistance was required to keep the government's war effort going. But economic assistance played an even more important role. It eased pressures for meaningful economic reform, ensured that the country staved off financial collapse and supported increased military spending. Foreign assistance from the United States disincentivized a political solution to the conflict, leaving the pursuit of a military victory as the only option.

In El Salvador, the artificial distinction between military and economic assistance was on full display. Economic aid was the dominant form of foreign assistance from the United States, and the majority of that aid was highly fungible PL 480 food aid and ESF cash transfers. With the blessing of the U.S. government, food aid was actively monetized through commercial sales to support the Salvadoran government's budget. But certain forms of military assistance were monetized as well, including millions of dollars of U.S. taxpayer-subsidized jet fuel sold to elements supporting the Nicaraguan Contras. The line between economic and military assistance was regularly blurred. Investigations by Congress found that roughly three-quarters of American assistance to El Salvador could (and should) be considered war-related. El Salvador, then, helps explain the disconnect between the perception that economic aid does no harm and empirical findings to the contrary.

Background

El Salvador's government has historically been dominated by the military. A long-standing system of collaboration between the military and the country's oligarchy has shaped state-society relations.[1] With a Spanish landed elite controlling most of the coffee-centered economy, successive governments used state repression against indigenous groups and *mestizos* (together, roughly 95 percent of the population) to avoid land reforms that would undermine the power of the country's fourteen land-owning families.[2]

In December 1931 the country's first democratically elected president, Arturo Araujo, was ousted by a military coup that eventually brought to power his vice president, General Maximiliano Martínez. Under Martínez, the country transitioned from the traditional patronage system that characterized the pre-Araujo dictatorships to a more modern military regime. Martínez also established the deadly precedent of crushing political opposition, most notably in *La Matanza* (the massacre).[3] In January 1932 at least 10,000 peasants in western El Salvador were killed following an uprising organized by a local communist leader, Agustín Farabundo Martí. The uprising also provided the impetus for Martínez to further consolidate power by expanding the government's intelligence apparatus and creating a de facto police state.[4] This helped Martínez ward off continued threats to his power, including successive coup attempts, until he was eventually forced to resign following a nationwide strike in 1944.

A similar pattern of military-dominated politics followed Martínez's resignation. Elections were overseen by the military, which approved all candidates for both local and national offices. The military responded to any perceived threats to its electoral control by brutally clamping down on reforms, rigging elections, and increasing repression.[5] Yet, the military itself remained divided. A series of coups by various military factions continued to oust the country's top leadership. In 1948 a revolt by young officers brought Major Óscar Osorio to power. Like previous reform-minded military rulers, Osorio and his successor, Lieutenant Colonel José María Lemus, instituted a number of development projects such as the creation of hydroelectric facilities and urban housing projects. But in 1960, when Lemus responded to protests against poor living standards with repressive measures, he too was ousted by a coup.

In the 1960s and 1970s El Salvador began to diversify its economy and integrate further into the global economy. Yet, continued public unrest and dissatisfaction with the economic status quo led to the formation of multiple popular front movements and guerrilla groups. The Popular Forces of Liberation Farabundo Martí (Fuerzas Populares de Liberación Farabundo Martí) was founded in 1970 and the People's Revolutionary Army (Ejército Revolucionario del Pueblo) in 1972. The government responded to these groups with ever greater repression. The nature of state violence also changed. From 1972 onwards, the National Reconciliation Party began relying on forced disappearances and mass repression in addition to electoral fraud to maintain its hold on power. Following the decree of the Law for the Defense and Guarantee of Public Order in 1977, assassinations, arrests, and forced disappearances of union members, peasant leaders, and student activists increased. A final coup in 1979, led by junior officers who ousted then-president General Carlos Humberto Romero, came shortly after the collapse of the Somoza government in neighboring Nicaragua. The communist revolutionary government established by the Sandinistas in Nicaragua stoked American fears that El Salvador, too, would soon fall to communism.

The Revolutionary Government Junta that took power in El Salvador shortly after Romero was deposed positioned itself as reformist, promising an end to violence and corruption and new national elections. It collapsed in January 1980, shortly after it formed, when the three civilian members of the junta resigned along with ten of eleven cabinet ministers, throwing the government into crisis. The Second

Revolutionary Government Junta had a civilian, José Napoleón Duarte, serving as head of state. The political turmoil unleashed a wave of violence and compelled the United States to take a more active approach to its foreign policy in El Salvador.

That same year, a paramilitary group called the Frente Farabundo Martí para la Liberación Nacional (FMLN; Farabundo Martí National Liberation Front) united five revolutionary organizations to become Latin America's most powerful guerrilla movement. Throughout the 1980s, the FMLN clashed with El Salvador's armed forces and undertook a strategy of economic sabotage, destroying key infrastructure including bridges and electrical grids. Attempts to put down the FMLN quickly deteriorated into widespread violence against civilians by the military and right-wing militias.

The country's leftist political opposition and peasantry were the main targets of state-led violence, which took the form of targeted killings and indiscriminate massacres. Rape was common and torture was used extensively. Bodies were often recovered from roadsides, fields, and the El Playon lava field near the capital city of San Salvador. During the peak of the violence, from 1980 through 1983, some 42,171 Salvadorans of a population of roughly four and a half million perished.[6] Estimates of the total number of people killed in El Salvador during the 1980s exceed 75,000.[7] A UN truth commission attributed 85 percent of the violence during this period to state-led forces and only 5 percent to the FMLN, which by late 1983 had a strength of 10,000 to 12,000 fighters (up to 30 percent of whom were women).[8]

A confluence of factors eventually pushed the civil war between the FMLN and the government toward resolution. The United States' sustained aid to the Salvadoran government, combined with the collapse of the Soviet Union and the electoral defeat of the Sandinistas in neighboring Nicaragua, undermined the FMLN both militarily and politically. Seeing an opportunity, incoming president Alfredo Cristiani called for direct negotiations between the government and the FMLN in 1989. A brutal military offensive that year underscored the necessity of a political resolution.[9] Both sides appealed to the UN for help, and a UN Observer Mission was established in May 1991. After UN-brokered negotiations and haggling over constitutional reforms and the FMLN's political future, the Chapultepec Agreement in January 1992 marked the official end to the civil war.

The war's end, and the end of the Cold War more generally, eliminated much of the United States' interest in El Salvador. While a successful democracy emerged out of the war's devastation, the peace accords failed to resolve the underlying causes of tensions in the country. The share of income held by the wealthiest 10 percent of the population fell from 41 percent in 1991 to 32 percent in 2015, but the poorest still control only 2.4 percent of wealth.[10] Over 30 percent of the population lives below the poverty line.[11] Remittances from the more than one million Salvadorans that live abroad—primarily in the United States—are the country's second largest source of revenue.[12] El Salvador also has one of the highest murder rates in the world, peaking in 2015 at 103 homicides per 100,000 persons.[13] Poverty, social inequality, and insecurity persist even as the United States channels millions of dollars in foreign aid to stem irregular migration from the country.[14]

U.S. Assistance to El Salvador

El Salvador was among the first beneficiaries of Truman's Point Four program, receiving $5 million in economic assistance in 1946.[15] To help with the country's endemic political instability, the United States offered El Salvador technical assistance to improve rural living standards.[16] Technical assistance was given in almost every imaginable area—public administration, industrial hygiene, administration of orphanages, and more.[17] Later, as part of a region-wide response to communist activities, El Salvador was declared eligible for military assistance grants under the Mutual Security Act. Nearby Nicaragua and Honduras received arms deliveries in response to the Guatemalan Revolution.[18] But it was not until the 1960s, with growing American concern over Cuban action throughout Latin America, that meaningful American support for El Salvador's security sector began.

To improve El Salvador's intelligence apparatus, the Office of Public Safety offered law enforcement training, which included the deployment of CIA operatives.[19] Counterinsurgency doctrine and technical assistance was also provided by U.S. Army Mobile Training Teams and temporary advisors.[20] However, El Salvador's five-day 1969 border war with Honduras—in which thousands died and over 130,000 Salvadoran agricultural workers were forced from Honduras—led to a rise in arms purchases by both countries. This made the United States wary of committing further military assistance for fear it might inflame tensions in the region.[21]

An attempted coup in 1972 in response to elections rigged in favor of Colonel Arturo Armando Molina added to the United States' hesitancy to pledge significant foreign assistance resources. The United States would not promise more than a modest program to demonstrate its goodwill.[22] The embassy in San Salvador felt that "on domestic political questions, there is little that the U.S. can, need or should do so long as the [government of El Salvador] does not resort to flagrant repression of the legitimate opposition during or after the scheduled legislative/municipal election process."[23] Random incidents of government repression occurred, but "the general propensity of the culture for violence, and the incapacity of the judicial system to determine facts" led the embassy to report that the Salvadoran government was not engaged in consistent, substantial, or continual violation of human rights.[24] As late as August 1975, U.S. officials could identify no vital strategic or economic interests in El Salvador that would justify an increased commitment of resources: "in global or even Latin American terms, it is a small, insignificant country."[25]

The American position changed rapidly with the Nicaraguan Revolution and the ascent of the Sandinistas. As Nicaragua was gripped by political violence, General Romero took over the Salvadoran presidency in July 1977. His brief tenure coincided with a dramatic increase in American aid: from 1975 to 1985, the United States gave the relatively tiny El Salvador roughly $2.7 billion in economic aid and $686 million in military aid. The latter included the organization and training of elite counterinsurgency units.[26] Following the Nicaraguan Revolution, U.S. officials recognized that El Salvador was stuck between a rock and a hard place: "The Salvadoran government faces the unenviable and inherently contradictory task of meeting popular aspirations for improved living conditions while maintaining the order and stability expected by vested economic interests, many of whom equate the most modest change in the status quo with socialism or communism."[27] At all costs, the United States wanted to avoid "another Nicaragua" where competing leftist groups fought for control of the Salvadoran state.

Fervently committed to the protection of human rights, the Carter administration's El Salvador policy was characterized by indecision. President Carter firmly believed that America's renewed commitment to human rights and democratization was widely understood and respected. "The military governments that once felt they could serve the U.S. interest in stability in whatever way they wanted now feel inhibited from using violence or torture to suppress political opposition or to eliminate guerrilla movements," asserted NSC staffer Robert Pastor.[28] But the administration struggled to respond to the reality of a communist takeover in Central America and the need for a coherent policy in the region—one that required engagement with historically repressive military regimes. Although foreign aid and loans were identified as a source of leverage, the administration correctly concluded that no clear strategy was driving their use.

Very quickly, the Carter administration found itself in an untenable situation. Romero appeared receptive to American suggestions for political liberalization but was also politically vulnerable if he did not respond robustly to internal opposition. As Secretary of Defense Harold Brown argued to President Carter, this placed the administration in the awkward position of needing to bolster Romero's position so he could pursue reforms, while simultaneously looking the other way if he took steps to violate citizens' rights.[29] It didn't help that the government of El Salvador was openly hostile to investigations into its internal affairs by the United States— it had formally renounced security assistance for fiscal year 1978 because of congressional hearings on its elections.[30] Tensions only grew when an October 1979 coup brought down Romero and installed the Revolutionary Government Junta, a centrist constellation of civilians and military officers that was led by Duarte from 1980 to 1982.

Early U.S. assessments saw the junta as a willing partner in the pursuit of mutually beneficial interests. Like preceding reformist regimes, the junta promised a series of social and economic reforms including higher wages, agrarian reform, and free elections. The possibility of change was evident, but the direction of that change was uncertain. "In El Salvador, there will be a lot of violence, and we should be prepared to compete with the Cubans, adopting their principal tactic of picking a group and supporting it," argued Pastor.[31] Ultimately, American officials came to recognize that the junta "was an inherently unstable compound which could contain the seeds of its own destruction."[32] Nevertheless, both economic and military assistance were rapidly rallied to help the new government succeed in putting down its leftist opposition and obtaining broad support.[33] A USAID team was dispatched to meet with Salvadoran officials to design $35 million worth of high-impact projects in rural and urban areas to generate public support for the junta.[34] This effort was assisted by a covert CIA program to serve the same basic purpose.[35]

The Carter administration tried to have it both ways—making economic and military assistance to an authoritarian regime conditional on the pursuit of political reforms and human rights investigations. But this quid pro quo strategy was largely a failure.[36] Attempts to make U.S. assistance conditional on observable improvements in human rights were repeatedly rebuffed by members of the junta. In part, this was because the junta could not meaningfully act to address past abuses. Communication between the State Department and the embassy in San Salvador details how it was impossible for the junta to reveal information about human rights abuses under the previous government without provoking a public backlash.[37] In short, ensuring punishment for human rights violators—particularly those in the military—was an impossible task for both the junta and the Carter administration.

Accepting this unfortunate reality, Carter decided that the best way forward was to continue supporting the junta as much as possible and hope that it substantiated its commitment to much-needed reforms. Military and intelligence assistance and large-scale economic assistance programs were developed even as the junta appeared to be increasingly unstable.[38] U.S. Military Training Teams, totaling thirty-six armed trainers, were offered to the Salvadoran government along with a no-cost lease of six U.S. Army UH-1H helicopters valued at $6.3 million (in 1980 dollars).[39] Tear gas, crowd control equipment, and riot gear were also sent by the U.S. government (although the proposed hand grenades and grenade launchers were held back), while the military teams assessed what materiel was most needed and could be obtained through aid-supported FMS financing.[40] David Aaron, deputy national security advisor, urged in meetings with the State Department and the NSC that El Salvador get as much aid as possible, as quickly as possible.[41] Carter's Assistant for National Security Affairs, Zbigniew Brzezinski, also tried to insulate the junta from criticism by U.S.-based human rights groups in an effort to keep it in power.[42] But internal divisions within the junta, including an alliance with Duarte and the Christian Democrats, prevented it from pursuing many of the reforms that Carter hoped for.

As news of continuing human rights abuses and atrocities in El Salvador trickled in—including at least 20 people killed and more than 120 wounded following a street demonstration in January 1980—Congress debated whether to continue military aid.[43] It ultimately decided to continue funding the junta, approving a Carter administration request for millions in "nonlethal" military assistance.[44] To its credit, the administration continued to push for a reduction in state repression, but an American proposal to implement a two-month monitoring period before delivering additional military aid fell flat with the junta. In reply, Salvadoran Colonel Bustillos essentially contended that the United States was giving them very little and demanding much in return.[45]

The election of Ronald Reagan in November 1980 upended what little direction the Carter administration had shown in its policy toward El Salvador. Internal debates raged over whether to deliver on earlier promises made to the junta. In an attempt to protect Carter's legacy, Pastor argued strongly against providing lethal military assistance prior to the presidential transition.[46] Secretary of Defense Harold Brown offered multiple justifications for the assistance while also acknowledging that the government of El Salvador fell far short of the human rights goals the administration had set.

The murder of three American nuns and a layperson in December 1980 gave Carter an excuse to stop the delivery of helicopters and suspend economic and military aid commitments. A presidential mission sent to investigate found that the Salvadoran security forces either were complicit in the crime or had helped those responsible evade investigation. However, it concluded that the killings did not have high-level government involvement.[47] These findings allowed Brzezinski and others to push for the restoration of U.S. economic and military aid to El Salvador, even as the number of Salvadorans killed by state forces that year reached almost 12,000.[48] President Carter, top-level State Department officials, and Pastor of the NSC were all aware of reports of regular mass burials at the behest of the Salvadoran National Guard. Assistant Secretary of State for Inter-American Affairs William Bowdler went so far as to acknowledge that a high percentage of the killing was being done by the security forces, but he also argued that this should not stop the United States from moving ahead with its aid package.[49]

In the face of urgent requests for military assistance, Brzezinski informed Carter that it was the almost unanimous view of members of the administration that it was in the U.S. national interest to quickly provide lethal military assistance.[50] On

January 16, 1981, just days before Reagan was to be sworn in, Carter signed off on the provision of lethal military assistance to El Salvador.[51] In rationalizing the decision, Brzezinski contended, "It would be extremely dangerous not only to our national interest but to the historical record of this Administration to leave office unwilling to take the hard decision to provide lethal assistance to an essentially middle of the road government."[52]

Ronald Reagan began his first term as president with a keen focus on El Salvador. In contrast to the indecisive Carter, Reagan was crystal clear: "We can't afford a defeat. El Salvador is the place for a victory."[53] No longer an insignificant country, El Salvador was now at the heart of the Cold War. Reagan's foreign policy team immediately drafted a replacement plan for the U.S. ambassador to El Salvador. The Reagan administration actively ensured that arms and aid were delivered to the country, arguing that emergency military assistance was necessary to save El Salvador from a "probable victory" by communist insurgents.[54] From the new administration's perspective, the attempts by Carter's team to pressure the Salvadoran military to stop or even to decrease the violence and repression had failed, and Reagan's own human rights agenda focused on victory over communism.

Between 1979 and 1980, economic aid from the United States to El Salvador increased by 700 percent, as shown in Figure 4.1. Under the first Reagan administration,

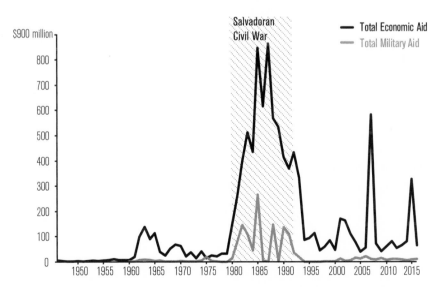

FIGURE 4.1. U.S. Bilateral Assistance to El Salvador. Note: Reported in 2016 dollars. Source: USAID, 2018.

U.S. foreign assistance continued its upward trajectory. American funds accounted for 85 percent of all the economic aid received by El Salvador. Once Reagan assumed the presidency, the United States ratcheted up military aid as well. Between fiscal years 1980 and 1984, U.S. funds to the Salvadoran government, central bank, and armed forces increased nearly tenfold.

Arguing in support of increased foreign assistance to El Salvador's military government, Secretary of State Alexander Haig testified before Congress that "American arms are a crucial factor, even more in political and psychological terms than in actual material terms."[55] According to this logic, support from the United States would turn the tide in El Salvador and make the opposition realize they were outgunned, both figuratively and literally. Military spending had been slowly creeping upward since 1975, but in 1980 it increased by more than 60 percent. The country's armed forces rapidly expanded from 8,000 personnel in 1977 to 23,000 in 1981, and eventually reached 48,000 troops in 1985—a sixfold increase in less than a decade.[56] Of these new military personnel, 29,000 were trained by U.S. advisers.[57] (Less than 3 percent of their training time dealt with human rights or related issues, even peripherally.)[58] The government also had unofficial state-aligned militias at its disposal. These militias served as a force multiplier while also distancing the military from some of the war's most egregious violence.

With control of Congress split between the two parties, the Reagan administration's wholehearted support for El Salvador led to heated battles. Congress adopted a bill introduced by Representative Stephen J. Solarz (D-NY) that required the president to certify to the House Speaker and the Senate Foreign Relations Committee that El Salvador's government (1) was not consistently violating internationally recognized human rights; (2) had substantial control over its armed forces; (3) was making progress in implementing essential economic and political reforms; (4) was committed to holding free elections; and (5) had demonstrated its willingness to negotiate a political resolution of the conflict.[59] The president had to vouch for the government of El Salvador in all five areas in order for Congress to authorize military and economic assistance. The bill also prohibited the president from making this certification before he *also* certified that El Salvador had made good faith efforts to investigate the murders of U.S. citizens in El Salvador and bring those responsible to justice. In effect, the bill shifted all responsibility for the United States' involvement in El Salvador directly onto the president—absolving Congress just as the Reagan administration began giving weapons to the Salvadoran army to counter Cuba and Nicaragua's support for the FMLN.[60]

In 1982 Reagan told Congress that the government of El Salvador's human rights record entitled it to receive U.S. foreign aid, even though reports indicated that all parties—leftist guerrillas, right-wing militias, and members of the government's military and security forces—continued to seriously and frequently violate basic human rights.[61] No independent human rights organization agreed with Reagan's assessment.[62] The certification came despite overwhelming evidence of a December 1981 massacre in the town of Mozote by the U.S.-trained Atlacatl Battalion—one of six rapid-reaction battalions (of 850 to 1,000 soldiers) created through American assistance at the onset of the war. IMET funded the training of at least 490 Salvadoran officers at the School of the Americas at Fort Benning, Georgia, and an additional 1,000 infantry troops underwent basic training at Fort Bragg, North Carolina.[63] (In later years, many more were trained in Honduras by U.S. Special Forces Green Berets.)[64] In Mozote, Atlacatl was accused of killing between 733 and 926 villagers.[65] The accounts were chilling. "'They said they wanted our weapons. But we said we didn't have any. That made them angry, and they started killing us.' Many of the peasants were shot while in their homes, but the soldiers dragged others from their houses and the church and put them in lines, women in one, men in another," detailed reports.[66]

Reagan had to again certify in July 1982 that El Salvador was making progress on human rights. The report submitted by the administration went further than the first in attributing some blame to government forces, but argued that deaths due to political violence were on a downward trend.[67]

Reagan's repeated human rights certifications revealed the weakness of congressionally imposed restrictions on U.S. foreign aid. Human rights groups later claimed that Salvadoran state forces killed between 11,727 and 16,266 individuals in the year before Reagan's human rights certifications.[68] Abuses by the Salvadoran military were widely covered in the American media, with the *New York Times* sharing details of "the charred skulls and bones of dozens of bodies buried under burned-out roofs, beams and shattered tiles."[69] Lurid details were made public: "There were more [bodies] along the trail leading through the hills into the village, and at the edge of a nearby cornfield were the remains of 14 young men, women and children."[70]

As the Salvadoran civil war continued, the military's tactics expanded from targeted disappearances and executions to indiscriminate violence against civilians in areas where the FMLN enjoyed support.[71] Aerial bombardments killed thousands.[72] The Salvadoran truth commission estimates that 5,962 civilians died at the hands of government forces in 1982, as military and economic assistance from the United States surged.[73] While all armed branches of the state were implicated in the violence, including the National Guard, the Treasury Police, and the National Police, small military-backed civilian death squads conducted joint operations with and received logistical support from branches of the military.[74] However, the violence was not enough to save the junta, which was dissolved following the March 1982 legislative elections. Álvaro Alfredo Magaña assumed the presidency while Duarte worked to consolidate his control over the Christian Democratic Party in advance of the 1984 presidential elections.

In the midst of these political changes, the Reagan administration launched a foreign aid offensive in El Salvador. In a March 1983 speech, Reagan took aim at Congress for undercutting his military assistance requests for El Salvador and urged the reallocation of appropriated funds to make up the difference. Reagan also called for $50 million in supplemental military assistance to "train Salvadorans so that they can defend themselves" and for expanded economic assistance to the region.[75] Arguing that "human rights means working at problems, not walking away from them," Reagan's total request for supplemental aid to El Salvador reached $110 million (in 1983 dollars). In the end, total U.S. foreign assistance to El Salvador for 1983 equalled the current equivalent of $619 million.[76] Reagan's address to a joint session of Congress justifying these aid requests invoked Carter's decision to send lethal military assistance as an indication of America's will to aid the government of El Salvador. Highlighting the preponderance of economic assistance, Reagan argued: "We do not view security assistance as an end in itself, but as a shield for democratization, economic development, and diplomacy."[77] American assistance ensured that neither the economy nor the Salvadoran armed forces collapsed, but it was clear that without an end to the conflict, America's investments in reform—both economic and political—could not bear fruit.

The Reagan administration increasingly adopted rhetoric similar to the Carter administration in justifying its support for El Salvador's military government: by allowing elections and other social and economic reforms, the military government was bringing the country closer to democracy. During a December 1983 trip to El Salvador, Vice President George H. W. Bush attempted to draw a line between the government and right-wing militias, stating, "These cowardly death-squad terrorists are just as repugnant to me, to President Reagan, to the U.S. Congress and to the American people as the terrorists of the left."[78] Indeed, U.S. foreign assistance funded judicial reform projects that included a program to protect witnesses, jurors, and judges involved in the prosecution of death-squad members.[79] A massive increase in military assistance, including additional aircraft, was also promised as a reward for improved human rights conditions.[80] The pressure exerted by Congress on the administration helped back up Bush's admonition that abuses must decline, and in the following months, death-squad violence did decline considerably—although roughly 300 civilians continued to be killed each month.[81]

The results of El Salvador's 1984 election saw Duarte return to the presidency. This, combined with the findings of the National Bipartisan Commission on Central America led by Kissinger, reinforced the upward trend in U.S. foreign aid.[82] While the commission as a whole recognized the importance of human rights conditionality in determining U.S. foreign assistance policy toward El Salvador, Kissinger himself dissented and argued that conditionality should be weighed by Congress against the probability of a Marxist-Leninist victory. Ultimately, it was Duarte's reelection that prompted Congress to approve the Reagan administration's request to resupply the Salvadoran military, which the administration claimed was running out of bullets.[83]

Congress went on to approve the administration's military assistance requests for fiscal years 1985, 1986, and 1987.[84] Congress's about-face on military aid to El Salvador was achieved in part through Duarte's in-person assurances during a visit to Washington, D.C., that he planned to remove from office Treasury Police Chief Nicolas Carranza, who was accused of links to right-wing death squads and whose removal had been a key component of Carter's human rights demands.[85] (Carranza had, in fact, been paid as a CIA informant and later sought refuge in the United States.)[86] Evidence also suggests that the Reagan administration was regularly providing false or incomplete information to Congress by omitting or classifying relevant details and providing overly optimistic assessments of the impact of U.S. foreign assistance in the country.[87]

In contrast to the way the deaths of Salvadorans were often characterized, the murder of six Americans and seven others at a San Salvador café in June 1985 was declared an act of indiscriminate terrorism and barbarism—one that justified expedited delivery of U.S. assistance to the government.[88] Reagan downplayed human rights abuses in El Salvador even as substantial civilian fatalities continued to mount.[89] "If the communists can start a war against the people of El Salvador, then El Salvador and its friends are surely justified in defending themselves," Reagan argued. "If the Soviet Union can aid and abet subversion of our hemisphere, then the United States has a legal right and a moral duty to help resist it. . . . It would be profoundly immoral to let peace-loving friends depending on our help be overwhelmed by brute force if we have any capacity to prevent it."[90]

American bilateral military assistance to El Salvador reached its zenith in 1985 at $265 million.[91] That year, El Salvador's military expenditure reached $252 million. It peaked at $794 million two years later.[92] While U.S. military aid officially amounted to one-quarter of El Salvador's military expenditure in 1987, U.S. economic aid equaled the country's military expenditure.[93] The import of these official figures was contested at the time. Representatives Jim Leach (R-IA) and George Miller (D-CA) and Senator Mark Hatfield (R-OR) argued in a 1985 report, "By developing more precise and more realistic categories of aid, based on its *use* rather than what U.S. *agency* administers it, we find instead that direct war-related aid is double the amount of our aid for reform and development; and that the largest single category of aid is indirect war-related economic maintenance, which merely neutralizes the effects of the civil war."[94] The bipartisan Congressional Arms Control and Foreign Policy Caucus report found that three-quarters of U.S. foreign assistance to El Salvador was being used to further the war effort. Specifically, there was credible evidence that local military commanders forced people to join civil-defense patrols by withholding U.S. economic aid (including food aid) from villages until the patrols were formed.[95] Cash transfers to the government from USAID constituted 76 percent of what the report deemed indirect war-related aid. The fungible nature of this assistance was explicitly noted:

> In fact, the local currencies raised by the Cash Transfer have been made "fungible" (i.e. can be used anywhere in the budget) through a special waiver. This waiver is the only one of its kind [US]AID has granted anywhere in Central America. The fungible nature of the Cash Transfer means that these funds, while not being directly traceable, are indeed "indirectly war-related." . . . Without the Cash Transfer, the Salvadoran government could never have tripled its spending on the Armed Forces.[96]

As the civil war raged, Congress was aware that U.S. foreign aid was financing the war effort while simultaneously ensuring that the Salvadoran government remained in power long enough to successfully prosecute the war.

Other investigations followed. A report by the U.S. General Accounting Office (GAO), though more optimistic than the caucus report, found that the United States relied heavily on El Salvador's government for oversight; Department of Defense officials in El Salvador did not closely monitor how the Salvadoran armed forces used and controlled U.S. military assistance.[97] The fungibility of aid was at the forefront of oversight concerns. Between June 1987 and September 1989 El Salvador monetized $1.1 million in grants through unauthorized sales of U.S. aid-funded fuel to the Nicaraguan Contras. The GAO expressed concern that "countries are able to generate cash from the FMS program and are not subject to controls over its use. . . . We found no provision in the [Arms Export Control Act] authorizing cash transfers as a means of assistance."[98] Yet, the government of El Salvador obtained cash by reselling more than 60,000 gallons of jet fuel not only to the Contras, but also directly to the U.S. military. In this scheme, U.S. taxpayers subsidized jet fuel for the Salvadoran military, which then turned around and sold the fuel back to the Department of Defense for cash. This meant that a very specific form of military assistance, jet fuel, was in fact highly fungible and could be used to fund a range of activities beyond what the aid was initially authorized for (in this case, support for the air war against the FMLN).

Evidence of the fungibility of aid was not limited to U.S. military assistance. Key to the coercive effect of foreign aid were USAID's highly fungible cash transfers and food aid in El Salvador. From 1980 to 1989 cash transfers and PL 480 food aid totaled $1.6 billion, or 62 percent of U.S. economic assistance.[99] In addition to the $40 million worth of U.S. food aid that was sold by the Salvadoran government in 1989, the United States deposited $157 million in cash into Salvadoran government accounts at four U.S. commercial banks as part of the ESF program.[100] Local currency raised from ESF cash grants and PL 480 food aid sales amounted to almost one-quarter of Salvadoran government expenditures that fiscal year.[101] Food aid wasn't feeding El Salvador's citizens—it was being sold. U.S. economic assistance was subsidizing government spending by supplying the Salvadoran government with cold, hard cash.

Even as the oversight of U.S. foreign assistance to El Salvador continued to expand, exceptional acts of violence were occurring as part of the war. The 1989 murders of six Jesuit priests and two women by the Atlacatl Battalion were widely reported in the American press.[102] The *New York Times* reported: "Most of the priests were dragged from their beds in cubicles in a dormitory at the Jose Simeon Canas University of Central America on the outskirts of the capital and shot in the head with high-powered rifles, apparently of the same type issued by the army. The Jesuits' cook and her 15-year-old daughter were also shot to death."[103] The Spanish priests' murders galvanized international opposition to the Salvadoran government and remain a political flash point in the country even now.[104]

In spite of growing media attention and international pressure on the Salvadoran government, it wasn't until 1992, after more than a decade of war, that the government and the FMLN laid down their arms. By then, U.S. assistance to the Salvadoran government had had the strategic effect that Reagan hoped for. The FMLN's fighting forces had declined to between 5,000 and 7,000 guerrillas by the late 1980s—a drop of up to 50 percent.[105] The peace process led to a series of political reforms, including the creation of a State Council for Human Rights and the removal of standing Supreme Court justices who had been criticized for being tools of the president. But the reforms also allowed members of the Salvadoran military to transition into civilian police forces and ultimately undermined attempts to hold them accountable for human rights violations. Following the peace deal, U.S. military assistance declined dramatically—by more than 50 percent from 1992 to 1993. By 1994 it totaled less than $1 million. U.S. economic aid to El Salvador declined as well. In times of peace, El Salvador returned to its former status as a small, insignificant country.

Conclusion

A common narrative about U.S. assistance to El Salvador is that "only massive U.S. assistance allowed the Armed Forces of El Salvador to turn the tide and achieve a stalemate against the FMLN."[106] Indeed, this was the explicit plan laid out by

Kissinger's commission. But historian Hal Brands argues that U.S. military assistance to El Salvador was in fact counterproductive, rather than the game changer
that the Reagan administration claimed: "In the hands of a repressive army, U.S.
weapons enabled the very practices that had alienated the population. The military
used U.S.-supplied helicopters and planes in attacks that caused large numbers of
civilian casualties and gruesome cases of 'peasants' skin being burned off by white
phosphorous bombs.'"[107] But the role that foreign aid played in El Salvador's civil
war is more complicated than either of these perspectives suggests. It was not just
military assistance that was crucial in El Salvador—extensive economic support
from the United States was also vital.

The majority of U.S. economic assistance provided to El Salvador supported the
war effort. The budgetary support received from the United States allowed military
expenditures to steadily increase. Food aid and ESF kept the government financially
afloat. Successive military governments presented themselves as reformist. They
undertook efforts at land reform and the reconstruction of infrastructure damaged
by the FMLN, but in the absence of the local currency and balance-of-payments
support from the United States, the economy might have rapidly collapsed. The
military government would likely have followed.

To be fair, the United States did try to use foreign aid as a form of leverage to
improve human rights conditions in El Salvador. The Carter administration sent
multiple lists of human rights demands to the junta and pushed for legitimate investigations into the killings of Americans. The Reagan administration successfully
used Vice President Bush's visit to bring about a temporary reduction in death-squad
killings in response to the promise of increased aid. And USAID withheld ESF in
an attempt to pressure the Salvadoran government to adhere to agreements for reform.[108] But by allowing political concerns to dominate and continuing to provide
foreign aid regardless of the military's conduct, the U.S. government ultimately
squandered its leverage over the Salvadoran government.

Other important lessons can be gleaned from this case. First, El Salvador highlights both the pros and cons of relying on cross-country statistical analysis to
understand the complex relationship between foreign assistance and state violence.
The situation in El Salvador exemplifies the association identified in Chapter 2
between economic assistance from the United States and subsequent increased
levels of state violence. However, while military assistance was associated with
improvements in human rights in the statistical analysis, there is little evidence to
support this in the case of El Salvador. Instead, U.S. military assistance was key in
training and arming counterinsurgency units that went on to commit egregious
acts of violence. Second, El Salvador highlights the difficulty of disentangling civil
war violence from government repression and other human rights violations. Much

of the violence perpetrated by the state was justified by the government by the broader context of a communist insurgency. Conditions on the ground, including a limited in-country U.S. military presence, made it difficult to determine the full extent of civilian casualties. The UN-sponsored truth commission and human rights NGOs vary significantly in their estimates of violence and disappearances.

Foreign aid to El Salvador and the role that it played in defeating the FMLN came at a cost to the United States' standing in the world. Presciently, the 1985 caucus report argued, "Tragically, if U.S. aid is composed in the future as it is at present, the next five years will be as violent and unproductive for El Salvador as the past five years. Under current U.S. aid strategy, there is no light at the end of this tunnel."[109] The eventual resolution of the civil war in December 1992 in the government's favor did not force a much-needed reckoning with the costs and consequences of U.S. foreign assistance policy in El Salvador, or indeed anywhere else.

5

South Korea
Constraining Coercion

SOUTH KOREA'S ECONOMIC MIRACLE—which turned a decimated, agrarian country into a technology hub and the envy of its neighbors—is the oft-touted success story of U.S. foreign assistance. In 1960, shattered by two successive wars, South Korea had a per person GDP that was only 5.5 percent of the United States', and less than Ghana's.[1] In the five decades since, spurred by foreign aid and shrewd economic planning, the country's per capita gross national income has increased by 330 percent. In a single generation, life expectancy rose by twenty-seven years. South Korea's infant mortality rate dropped to almost *half* that of the United States. Literacy jumped from 21 percent in 1945 to 88 percent by 1970. Now, South Korea is among the fastest-growing developed economies in the world.

It is undeniable that foreign assistance played an essential role in the transformation of South Korea. But there is another aspect of this story that often goes untold. South Korea's economic transformation occurred in a climate of widespread fear and repression, far from the liberal democracy its citizens currently enjoy. For decades, U.S. foreign assistance supported successive authoritarian governments that relied on an extensive coercive apparatus for support. Leaders suppressed political opposition by intellectuals, students, and even clergy in order to maintain their hold on power. And yet, despite extensive government repression and other conditions conducive to state-led violence, the use of outright force against civilians was relatively rare in South Korea.

Several factors help explain why state violence was constrained in this case. First, the United States' long-standing military involvement in the country includes direct operational control of the South Korean armed forces in the event of a major armed conflict. Second, the ongoing military threat from North Korea led to a strong focus on external defense. The Korean War demonstrated the need for a large standing army to defend against future invasions. This led to universal conscription and the cultivation of the military as a professional class interested in the country's stability. Although the military intervened in domestic politics through multiple coups, the armed forces never became an extension of the surveillance state that dominated political life. Third, the democratic nature of the political opposition and the lip service that South Korea's leaders paid to democracy and political competition made it difficult to use the struggle against communism as a pretext for state violence, as was common elsewhere during the Cold War. Communist organizations were officially banned and intense purges of suspected communists took place during the Korean War, rendering this threat largely symbolic.

From the perspective of the United States, its strong interest in South Korea's political stability and its reliance on South Korean bases for forward positioning in Asia meant that it had significant incentives to ensure that the military was not a destabilizing factor. Thus, it was the civilian police and the intelligence services that were the primary agents of government repression. And whenever repression escalated into outright violence, the United States quickly applied its considerable leverage to bring South Korea's leadership back in line. This balancing act persisted until a rapid reduction in U.S. foreign assistance coincided with a period of intense political instability in South Korea. Declining American influence failed to check increased political restrictions in the aftermath of yet another military coup. However, these additional restrictions on political life galvanized popular opposition, which eventually forced the authoritarian regime to accept greater political liberalization in the interest of stability. At the end of the 1990s, South Korea emerged as both democratic and independent of foreign aid.

Background

The Korean peninsula has seen its fair share of conflict. In eight centuries of dynastic rule, Korea endured three major wars with the Mongols, Japanese, and Manchus. Following the collapse of the Chosŏn dynasty and the Russo-Japanese War, President Theodore Roosevelt brokered a deal in 1905 that saw Korea become first a protectorate and then a colony of Japan, until its liberation at the end of the Second World War. At first, Koreans strongly resisted Japanese annexation; more than 69,000 took up arms against the Japanese in 1908. But by 1910, fewer than 2,000 active guerrillas remained, by Japanese estimates.[2] Imperial Japan ruled Korea through a military governor-generalship and deprived Koreans of freedom of assembly, association, and the press. Those who defied the Japanese regime were thrown into prison. Political prisoners numbered as many as 50,000 in 1912 and 140,000 by 1918.[3]

Inspired by President Woodrow Wilson's commitment to self-determination and the death of the former emperor, Kojong, an estimated two million Koreans took to the streets in peaceful anti-Japanese demonstrations in March 1919.[4] In Seoul, protestors read aloud the Korean Declaration of Independence. The Japanese responded with characteristic brutality—killing some 7,500 Koreans and wounding 16,000 more.[5] Roughly 47,000 protestors were arrested. Seeing little opportunity for immediate change from within, a group of Koreans formed a provisional government in exile in Shanghai. For the next two decades, Syngman Rhee—a former student of Wilson's at Princeton who had spent six years in prison for anti-Japanese activities—served as president of the Provisional Government of Korea. During World War II, Rhee stepped down and moved to Washington, D.C., to rally American and Allied support for Korea's independence.

During World War II, hundreds of thousands of Koreans were forced to labor in support of the Japanese war effort—in factories, on military bases, and as "comfort women."[6] Imperial Japan industrialized parts of Korea through the development of steel mills, hydroelectric facilities, and petrochemical plants.[7] This economic shift led to widespread dislocation as peasants were uprooted and land was expropriated. Japanese colonization was generally characterized by cultural and political repression, but many members of the Korean elite collaborated with the Japanese to maintain power and influence. However, rapid industrialization in a colonial context also meant that an indigenous managerial class never developed, which impeded the country's economic growth once Japan withdrew.

World War II fundamentally shaped American engagement in the region. The terms of Japanese surrender saw forces north of the thirty-eighth parallel capitulate to the Soviets, while those south of the thirty-eighth parallel surrendered to the Americans. From 1945 to 1948 the United States formally occupied the southern part of Korea. It implemented a military government with the Representative Democratic Council headed by Rhee serving as an advisory body. Later, it established a partially elected legislative assembly. But the December 1945 UN trusteeship agreement that determined Korea's postwar fate called for no more than five years of great power involvement in the peninsula. In November 1947 the UN General Assembly adopted a resolution calling for general elections. Although the Soviet Union barred UN observers from entering the north, delaying elections until August 25, elections proceeded in the south on May 10, 1948. Rhee was elected president and, following the adoption of a constitution, the Republic of Korea was formed in the south on August 15. This marked the transition from U.S. military government to a formally independent South Korea. The following month, the Democratic People's Republic of Korea was proclaimed in the north, marking the official political separation of the two Koreas. Shortly thereafter, the United States and the Soviet Union withdrew their occupying forces.

When North Korea invaded South Korea on June 25, 1950, the United States responded by immediately offering military assistance. Days later, the United States committed its own ground troops. During the Korean War, approximately 35,000 American troops were killed and more than 100,000 wounded. At least 2.2 million Koreans perished. Following the war's end in 1953, the United States and South Korea signed the Mutual Defense Treaty, which serves as the foundation of the present-day United States–Republic of Korea alliance. The 28,500 U.S. troops stationed in South Korea today and the extension of the U.S. nuclear umbrella are both part of the United States' ongoing commitment to South Korea's defense.

In the immediate aftermath of the Korean War, U.S. foreign assistance played a pivotal role in allowing South Korea to continue functioning as a state. American aid accounted for 50 percent of the government's budget. Until 1960, foreign aid grants financed most of the country's imports, as well as three-quarters of South Korean investment.[8] Economic recovery was slow. Many economists felt that South Korea was doomed to economic stagnation. Production had increased, but the country's trade deficit continued to rise. Both domestic Korean policy and protectionist American policy favored import-substitution growth strategies that saw only limited results. But suddenly, everything changed.

Park Chung Hee, a military officer who had served in the Japanese army during World War II and the Republic of Korea army during the Korean War, led a military coup in May 1961 that toppled the parliamentary system created after Rhee resigned as president in 1960. Under Park, South Korea embarked on a revolutionary path of export-oriented industrialization. Whereas exports accounted for less than 5 percent of GDP in the late 1950s, they made up more than 35 percent of a much larger GDP by 1980. South Korea's economy advanced in almost every measurable area. USAID closed its country office. But Park's rule was also characterized by political restrictions, periods of martial law, and the ever-expanding reach of the Korean Central Intelligence Agency (KCIA). Eventually, the dragon that he created took Park down: he was assassinated by the director of the KCIA on October 26, 1979.

General Chun Doo Hwan rose to power in December 1979 to lead a regime that was described by CIA analysts as more authoritarian and more imperial than Park's. A graduate of the Korean Military Academy, Chun trained in the United States at the Army's Special Warfare and Infantry Schools. From 1970 to 1971, Chun fought in the Vietnam War and was awarded the Bronze Star from the United States for his service.[9] Once in power, he banned politicians of the Park era, disbanded political parties, and promoted the creation of new ones. Dissent from South Korea's intellectuals, students, labor groups, and Christians persisted. Almost a decade later, South Korea finally began a transition to democratic rule under General Roh Tae-woo. Mass protests in June 1987 were followed by free parliamentary elections in 1988. Presidential elections followed in 1993, with Kim Young Sam, a former regime opponent, succeeding Roh. During this period of uncertainty, South Korea succeeded in reducing its reliance on foreign aid. In 1998 former opposition leader Kim Dae Jung became president. To improve relations with North Korea, Kim launched the Sunshine Policy, which used unconditional economic and humanitarian assistance to engage North Korea. South Korea joined the OECD's Development Assistance Committee in 2010, marking its official transition from aid recipient to aid donor.

U.S. Assistance to South Korea

American perceptions of the Cold War that pitted the democratic West against the communist East—the Soviet Union, Communist China, and their allies—defined the initial relationship between the United States and South Korea. South Korea was to be a bulwark against the expansion of communism throughout Asia; it needed to be clearly allied with the United States to achieve this. Against this backdrop, USAID and its predecessor agency provided more than $18 billion to South Korea. The forms that U.S. assistance took in the decades following the Second World War varied widely. Economic assistance for reconstruction and food aid were quickly overtaken by military assistance. Both forms of foreign assistance began a rapid decline in the mid-1970s before being abruptly curtailed in the early 1980s.

The political consequences of these shifts in U.S. foreign assistance have received far less attention than the changes in the military relationship between the two countries. Yet, U.S. foreign assistance was consequential in shaping state-society relations in South Korea. The fact that the transition to democracy took place when U.S. foreign assistance to South Korea was at its lowest point reflects the highly stabilizing role that this assistance played.

The United States was an occupying force when it first began providing foreign assistance to South Korea. From 1945 to 1952, the United States disbursed more than $500 million through U.S. Army Military Government in Korea programs and an additional $200 million through the Economic Cooperation Administration, which was established in 1948 to administer the Marshall Plan. Much of this assistance took the form of emergency relief, including food aid and agricultural supplies. However, the American occupation—like the other occupations that preceded it—faced stiff resistance. The U.S. military resorted to suppressing local governments known as People's Committees throughout the southern provinces. As historian Bruce Cummings notes, "This provoked a massive rebellion that spread over four provinces in the fall of 1946; after it was suppressed, radical activists developed a significant guerrilla movement in 1948 and 1949."[10]

The proclamation of the Republic of Korea in 1948 finally gave Rhee his own government. He almost immediately used the threat of communism to justify restrictions on political freedoms, targeting the Left through harassment and imprisonment. In October of that year, Rhee purged the military of suspected communist sympathizers. The National Security Law of 1948 and other executive orders were used to conduct an anticommunist drive that included the arrests of opposition leaders and bans on political parties.[11] The law defined sedition so broadly that it could be used as a political tool to suppress virtually any kind of opposition. By the spring of 1950, more than 30,000 people had been imprisoned by their new government.[12] American perceptions of Rhee as "venerable but wily and irascible" led the United States to impose strict controls on its foreign assistance in an attempt to ensure that the South Korean government actually pursued economic stabilization and other long-term objectives.

At the same time, the United States was working to develop the South Korean constabulary around a small group of officers who had been trained by the Japanese or involved in guerrilla-type operations against them.[13] The constabulary expanded from a core of 5,000 men in early 1946 to a sizable force of more than 50,000 by 1950. The June 25, 1950, invasion by some 75,000 North Korean soldiers drew into sharp relief the need for a standing army. By the war's end, the American military had trained, equipped, and maintained over 600,000 South Korean troops.[14]

The outbreak of war also brought additional emergency assistance. The UN established the Civilian Relief to Korea program and the Korea Reconstruction Agency to assist with recovery. In the early 1950s U.S. assistance included contributions to both agencies, but especially to the UN Korean Reconstruction Agency (amounting to 65 percent of its total funds).[15] War damages were estimated to be $1 billion (in 1953 dollars) and income per capita declined by one-third.[16] Close to half of all homes and industrial facilities were damaged. Assistant Secretary of State for Far Eastern Affairs John Moore Allison observed shortly after the end of the war: "When the destruction and disorganization of war were superimposed on previously existing difficulties [such as inflation and administrative backwardness], the tasks of creating adequate standards of living, supporting defense forces, commencing reconstruction, and preserving fiscal stability called for superhuman efforts."[17]

Foreign aid accounted for roughly 74 percent of South Korean government revenue in the decade after the July 1953 armistice between the two Koreas. Military aid initially made up only a small percentage of U.S. foreign assistance. American efforts were devoted largely to reconstructing infrastructure that had been destroyed and ensuring that South Korea had adequate food stocks. Food aid, raw materials, and other products made up about three-quarters of official foreign assistance. The UN's Civilian Relief program is credited with relieving widespread starvation.[18] But food aid did more than that. PL 480 wheat flour given by the United States was also used to pay government workers mobilized for public works programs. However, the large quantity of food aid provided by the United States eventually distorted local food prices.[19]

Beyond ensuring the country's immediate survival, U.S. foreign assistance policy in South Korea lacked clear objectives. President Dwight Eisenhower wanted to strengthen the economy in light of U.S. security interests. He appointed Henry J. Tasca (a career foreign service officer) to undertake a study of the country's economic prospects. Tasca recommended that the United States pump $1 billion (1953) dollars into South Korea over the course of three years to support the armed forces, ensure adequate living standards for the population, and develop the country into a self-defending and self-supporting nation as soon as possible.[20] The idea underlying Tasca's recommendations was that the need for U.S. military assistance would decline considerably if South Korea could be made more economically productive. More than 90 percent of the assistance Tasca called for was economic in nature. He projected that over the same three-year period, the United States could draw down its military assistance by 60 percent. Many of these recommendations were included in a July 1953 NSC report on how to strengthen the South Korean economy.[21] Despite the emphasis placed on increased economic aid, it was U.S. military assistance to South Korea that grew rapidly following Eisenhower's reelection. This assistance enabled a military buildup to deter the provocative actions of North Korea and was intended to ensure South Korea's success in any future armed conflict between the two states.

Expanding U.S. military assistance did little to solve South Korea's economic woes or its internal political divisions. Rhee clung to power while the new country stagnated. The March 1960 presidential elections were rigged in favor of Rhee, who received 88.7 percent of the vote at the advanced age of eighty-five. Rhee's independently elected running mate, Lee Ki-poong, defeated his more popular opponent by a margin that the public was simply unwilling to accept. On March 15, students demonstrated in the city of Masan against the fraudulent election results. When one of the protestors was found dead a month later, further protests erupted. Participants declared they "were so mad, angry and frustrated by the election riggings and police brutalities we wanted to demonstrate to the people and to the government that we [students] were not a 'living corpse.'"[22] Days later, the protests spread to the capital, Seoul. On April 18, students protesting at Korea University were attacked by counterprotestors mobilized by the government. The following day, police fired on 30,000 students as they marched on the Blue House, the president's official residence, demanding new elections and Rhee's resignation.[23]

In what became known as the April Revolution, approximately 130 student demonstrators were killed and many more wounded.[24] The government declared a state of emergency and troops moved into Seoul to enforce a curfew. Rhee attempted to ease the unrest by offering some political concessions, including firing his cabinet, but the protests and marches continued. A CIA assessment written in the days following the protests noted that Rhee's "authoritarian tendencies have been exacerbated by near senility and are no longer subject to the check of a strong sense of the living political situation." The assessment concluded that "as graciously, and even compassionately, as possible, we should ease him out of power along with his party lieutenants."[25]

The crisis came to a head when the general in charge of quelling the demonstrations refused to take further military action against the protestors. In the face of mounting American pressure, Rhee resigned as president on April 26 and went into exile in Hawai'i, where he died five years later. Lee Ki-poong was found dead along with his wife and children on the grounds of the Blue House—killed by his son as a part of a suicide pact—hours after assuming the presidency. The minister of foreign affairs, Huh Chung, finally assumed power as acting president. One of his first public statements condemned alleged waste and mismanagement in the United States' aid program to the country, which had been identified by the CIA as a factor contributing to popular opposition to Rhee.

Months of political turmoil and constitutional changes followed the chaos surrounding Rhee's resignation. A feckless prime minister was overthrown in a bloodless military coup led by General Park on May 16, 1961. The Supreme Council for National Reconstruction, essentially a military junta, was established with Park as chairman. In this capacity, he met with President Kennedy at the White House in November 1961—a move that legitimized his continued rule. The Supreme Council was succeeded by the Third Republic upon Park's election as president in 1963. As president, Park established a system of governance that combined formally representative institutions with an authoritarian rule grounded in a coercive state.[26] Constitutional changes that followed only served to strengthen the presidency. The 1972 Yushin Constitution effectively made Park president for life.

Park's style of governance strongly reflected the CIA's vision for South Korea, which advocated deliberately sponsoring a quasi-military regime in order to keep the country's only reasonably nonpartisan force in control and ensure that U.S. foreign assistance was used for the sound buildup of the economy.[27] The objective of U.S. foreign assistance shifted from postwar reconstruction to sustained economic growth.

In the early years of Park's rule, South Korea received levels of American financial support similar to what it had under Rhee. U.S. foreign aid accounted for more than 50 percent of the government's budget and more than 70 percent of military expenditures. Signs of political stability appeared: in 1963 thousands of political prisoners were released and political activity was resumed in advance of elections. When Park attempted to extend military rule beyond 1963, American pressure— including the threat to withhold millions in economic aid—ensured that elections took place.[28] Park won the elections with a plurality of the vote and a promise that American aid would continue.

During Park's first decade in office, U.S. bilateral foreign aid averaged the current equivalent of $2.8 billion a year, as illustrated in Figure 5.1. Export-Import Bank loans to South Korea increased throughout the 1960s as economic aid declined.[29] It was during this time that the South Korean economy entered an impressive phase of growth under export-oriented industrialization. Aid-financed imports dropped from 68 percent of imports in 1960 to 10 percent in 1968.[30] But Park's reelection in 1969 began a new wave of militarization that culminated in his declaration of martial law three years later.

Park's military buildup was motivated by what was initially called the Guam Doctrine and later referred to as the Nixon Doctrine—the idea promulgated by President Nixon that both internal subversion and external aggression should increasingly be dealt with by Asian nations themselves rather than by the United States.[31] As one of the enduring legacies of the Korean War, South Korea was (and remains) host to a large number of U.S. troops and bases. In keeping with his new

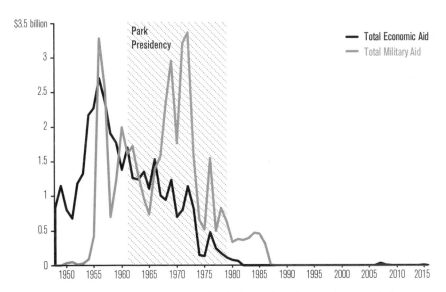

FIGURE 5.1. U.S. Bilateral Assistance to South Korea. Note: Reported in 2016 dollars. Source: USAID, 2018.

doctrine, Nixon announced that 20,000 of those troops would be withdrawn. In response, the Park government established the Five-Year Plan to Reinforce Military Equipment and solicited U.S. military assistance as compensation. If Nixon wanted South Korea to be solely responsible for its own security, then it would need even more aid to get there.[32] U.S. military assistance was increased yet again, to almost $3.2 billion in 1971, amounting to 80 percent of total U.S. bilateral aid to the country. In contrast to Rhee's presidency, which was characterized by postwar reconstruction, Park's regime relied heavily on U.S. military assistance. Indeed, South Korea is one of only a handful of countries where military assistance exceeded economic assistance from the United States for a sustained period.

With the dominance of military aid and the provision of cheap American military equipment to South Korea, the capacity-building mechanism of foreign aid was hard at work. U.S. military assistance ensured that South Korean military spending did not detract from the country's economic development. But the South Korean military also began to take on internal security functions. For example, the military was called on when the police failed to effectively suppress student demonstrations about on-campus military training, labor rights, and political freedoms, among other issues. In 1971, a 50,000 person–strong riot erupted in the city of Gwangju in anticipation of the next presidential election.[33] When Park was reelected yet again, protests intensified and the government proclaimed a Garrison Decree (October 15 to November 19, 1971) that empowered the military to maintain public order in Seoul.[34] These authoritarian practices culminated in Park's December 6, 1971, Declaration of the State of National Emergency.[35]

Park repeatedly used martial law as a way of mobilizing the army for internal security purposes. He was aware of the negative impact this would have on U.S.–South Korean relations, but bilateral relations were deteriorating anyway. The CIA concluded that Park "calculated that U.S. forces will soon be withdrawn from the South in any case and U.S. military assistance sharply reduced if not terminated."[36] U.S. military assistance dropped precipitously between 1972 and 1974, from $3.14 billion to $616 million.

Despite the size and strength of the state's coercive apparatus—the military, police, and intelligence services—South Korea did not experience the levels of overt violence seen in comparable military dictatorships. Park's regime cracked down on political opposition and banned numerous political parties and organizations, but the use of violence by the state was fairly restrained, even under martial law. Soldiers were deployed to Seoul's universities and more than 1,800 protestors were arrested in 1971. Student leaders were accused of being communist agents, but relatively few were imprisoned. During the first thirteen years of Park's rule, despite numerous and large-scale antigovernment protests, no demonstrators were shot.[37] However, the discovery in April 1974 of a student group—the National Federation of Democratic Youth and Students—committed to attaining democratic reforms through organized demonstrations led to an emergency decree that dictated the death penalty for anyone involved in the group. More than 300 people were arrested for violating this decree, including religious leaders, student organizers, lawyers, writers, and intellectuals.[38] But no executions took place.

On August 8, 1974, Nixon resigned. A week later, on August 15, an assassination attempt on Park took the life of his wife, Yuk Young Soo.

Park's increasing authoritarianism and overt suppression of democratic activists alarmed some members of Congress. During the Ford administration, committee hearings in the House of Representatives referred to human rights abuses in South Korea as a "challenge for U.S. foreign policy."[39] Testimony at these hearings noted that mass arrests, prolonged detentions without trial, surveillance by the KCIA, and other repressive features were rife in the country. In February 1975 Park announced the release of 203 noncommunist political prisoners in an attempt to ease criticism.[40] But the following month, he issued Emergency Measure No. 9, which outlawed public criticism of the 1972 Yushin Constitution, banned student participation in political activities, and prohibited the spreading of "false rumors." News agencies were prevented from reporting on any criticism or protests against the constitution or the decree.[41] In spite of clear evidence of government repression, Congress voted down further reductions in U.S. military assistance to South Korea in May 1975.[42] The Park regime responded to these mixed signals by accelerating the sentencing of individuals so that it could lift its emergency measures, rather than canceling the trials. By December 1977 more than 500 people had been charged with violating the emergency measure, and approximately 150 were imprisoned.[43]

President Carter's human rights agenda clearly conflicted with the support the United States was providing to South Korea. Carter believed that "in distributing the scarce resources of our foreign assistance programs, we will demonstrate that our deepest affinities are with nations which commit themselves to a democratic path to development."[44] But his attempts to reduce foreign aid to South Korea were complicated by influence peddling on Capitol Hill. The *New York Times* reported that "J. Edgar Hoover personally sent warnings to John N. Mitchell and Henry A. Kissinger that South Korean agents were on Congressional staffs, had paid off representatives and had contributed large sums to the Democratic party."[45] What became known as the Koreagate investigation uncovered that South Korean agents used nearly $1 million in cash generated from the sale of taxpayer-supported U.S. rice to influence Congress.[46] A $10,000 cash payment to one of Nixon's aides was personally returned by the U.S. ambassador to South Korea, Philip Habib.[47] The initial objectives of these extraordinary measures to influence American policy and opinion were congressional approval of a $1.5 billion military aid package and an end to future U.S. troop withdrawals. After the 1972 constitutional changes,

South Korean attempts to influence Congress broadened to include selling Park's newly expanded powers. Despite the media attention on influence peddling, the House voted down an amendment that would have cut $56 million in PL 480 funds for South Korea, even after criminal charges were brought against a South Korean businessman implicated in the scandal.[48]

The assassination of Park on October 26, 1979, by KCIA director Kim Jae Kyu followed on the heels of another Garrison Decree in reaction to protests in Pusan, Masan, and Ch'angwon. General Chun of the KCIA became the de facto leader of South Korea, although a civilian, Choi Kyu Hah, was the official head of state. Choi repealed Emergency Measure No. 9, but maintained martial law. Although some modest political reforms occurred and select batches of political prisoners were released under Chun, he continued to rely on the military and competing branches of the intelligence services for influence.[49] In the process of consolidating his control, Chun added purged politicians, media figures, and bureaucrats to the existing mix of dissidents. He also expanded the overall size of the state's coercive apparatus to deal with the continued threat of popular protest.

The government's increasing reliance on coercion was obvious in its response to the May 1980 demonstrations by students at Gwangju's Chonnam University. Labeled by the government as an insurrection by communist sympathizers and rioters, the protests against Chun's military government have since been referred to as the May 18th Democratic Uprising. The local police and, later, paratroopers attempted to suppress student protests that had quickly swelled to tens of thousands of demonstrators. Some of the demonstrators armed themselves with guns stolen from barracks, Molotov cocktails, and other improvised weapons.[50] Many had been trained as part of the country's mandatory military service. The protestors succeeded in forcing the military out of Gwangju for several days. With the United States' blessing, 20,000 South Korean troops fought to regain control of the city, including by firing into crowds gathered at the Provincial Hall. There were anywhere from 200 to 600 civilian fatalities and roughly 2,710 injuries as a result of the military's actions.[51] Decades later, a government investigation confirmed that South Korean troops committed rapes, sexual assaults, and sexual torture (including against teenagers and a pregnant woman) during the ten days of protest in Gwangju.[52] Once the protests were suppressed, all existing political parties were dissolved and hundreds of individuals were banned from participating in political activities.

The exorbitant violence seen in Gwangju appeared to mark an inflection point in U.S.–South Korean relations. Observers at the time noted, "It is inconceivable that South Korea can endure a nearly total freeze on freedom and strained relations with the U.S. indefinitely."[53] Yet, only months later, Chun was welcomed in Washington, D.C., as one of President Reagan's first official visitors. Reminiscent of

Kennedy's controversial endorsement of Park's rule, Reagan's meeting with Chun took place even as 1,500 South Koreans arrested in the wake of the Gwangju protests remained in prison. The only notable human rights concession in advance of the meeting with Reagan was the release of opposition leader Kim Dae Jung, who had been sentenced to death for sedition and conspiracy after the Gwangju protests. (As president, Kim would later pardon Chun when he was sentenced to death for his involvement in the 1980 coup and the violence in Gwangju.)

During his meetings with Reagan and other U.S. government officials, Chun sought guarantees that the remaining American troops in South Korea would continue to be stationed there. He also requested expanded U.S. military assistance in the form of FMS credits. The Reagan administration admitted that military assistance was an area where the United States could do better; only $160 million of the $275 million the administration estimated South Korea needed had been authorized by Congress.[54] However, the most important point of consensus to emerge from the meeting was that past American statements on human rights in South Korea had been deeply problematic for U.S.–South Korean relations. Reagan's position on this issue was clear: the question of human rights needed to be considered in the proper manner. The United States had ignored the greatest violators of human rights, most of whom were behind the bamboo and iron curtains, and needed to focus attention on them rather than key allies such as South Korea.[55]

U.S. military assistance to South Korea continued through 1986 as Chun consolidated control. U.S economic aid, however, continued its rapid decline. At the outset of political reforms in 1987, up to 2,000 political prisoners were still held by Chun. But by then, the United States had abandoned foreign aid as a means of influencing events in South Korea.

Conclusion

Few countries have succeeded in reducing their dependence on foreign aid, much less witnessed the rapid economic growth seen in South Korea. Foreign aid must be recognized for its role in supporting the country's economic development. But it should also be acknowledged that U.S. foreign assistance helped establish the country's military and its internal security agencies, ranging from the police to the KCIA. These agencies were responsible for the repression and arrest of thousands of South Koreans who opposed authoritarian rule. On occasions when government repression failed to end criticism and protests, the military itself was called on to respond. Yet those who suffered oppression under successive authoritarian regimes would ultimately shape the country's democratic future.

In comparison with the cases of Indonesia and El Salvador, the limited violence seen in South Korea better fits the general finding identified in Chapter 2 that

U.S. military aid differs from economic aid in its impact on human rights. U.S. foreign aid undoubtedly supported the military capacity of the South Korean state; indeed, that was the explicit goal of the vast majority of U.S. assistance to South Korea. However, U.S. military assistance to South Korea peaked during a period of relative political liberalization as Park tried to build domestic and external support for his rule. The security relationship between the United States and South Korea always took precedence, but the strength and nature of that relationship may have helped restrain the use of state violence under Rhee and Park. For instance, the extensive presence of U.S. troops in the country combined with U.S. command and control to ensure that the South Korean military maintained a high degree of professionalism. The importance of this was demonstrated in 1960 when the military leadership refused to follow Rhee's orders to forcefully put down protests against his reelection.

The ever-present threat posed by North Korea also helped to ensure the outward, conventional orientation of the South Korean military. In low-threat environments, military resources can (and often are) directed toward internal security. This was not the case in South Korea, where there was a clear and present external danger and where internal and external security institutions were sharply divided. External constraints on the use of the military as a tool of coercion were strengthened by universal conscription, which raised the social cost of internal violence. Conscripts were reluctant to use violence against friends, family, and neighbors.[56]

The punctuated nature of state violence in South Korea also illustrates the complex character of government repression. Electoral cycles had a strong influence on the timing of protests. State violence occurred largely in response to these protests and the failure of widespread government repression to prevent them. This pattern differs from Indonesia and El Salvador, where armed opposition groups and their presumed supporters were the targets of state violence. And unlike in the other two countries, there were no meaningful attempts to leverage foreign aid as a tool for improving human rights in South Korea. This was partly because the rationale for military assistance was unassailable. Maintaining South Korea's independence was always the primary goal. South Korea's importance as an anticommunist state in East Asia meant that cutting off foreign aid could not credibly be used as a bargaining chip—even though this was proposed in 1963.

The United States undermined any human rights leverage it may have had in South Korea by announcing its phased military withdrawal from the country and significantly reducing economic aid levels. The prospect of decreased financial support meant that the United States was in a weaker position to censure Park and also had fewer tools with which to do so. Once Chun came to power with the backing of the intelligence services, the United States' ability to influence his behavior was almost nonexistent. Reagan's meeting with Chun served only to legitimate the last and most brutal dictator in modern South Korean history.

6

Aiding and Abetting in the Twenty-First Century

DURING THE COLD WAR, U.S. foreign aid was often used for explicitly political purposes: to contain the spread of communism and to counter perceived communist threats throughout the so-called Third World.[1] Foreign aid was provided to
oppressive but anticommunist regimes such as those of Suharto and Park. Covert
assistance was also given to violent nonstate actors such as the Afghan mujahedeen,
some of whom eventually came to lead a highly repressive regime in Afghanistan as
the Taliban. Most of the history discussed thus far took place in this context—a
struggle between East and West, communism and the free world. But what happened after the Cold War ended?

The political interests of the United States during the Cold War helped define the
acceptable limits of state-led violence in the developing world. The repression of communist groups was fine; the overt suppression of prodemocracy protestors was not.
The ideological struggle against communism also determined who was an acceptable
partner of the United States, which in turn determined who was eligible for U.S.
foreign assistance. Although communist regimes were certainly deadly—roughly 94
million people were killed or starved to death by communist governments since the
end of World War I[2]—the policies adopted by the United States helped to legitimize
dictators and despots. Billions of dollars were spent to keep communism out of countries that were far from free. Then, communism suddenly imploded in Eastern
Europe (though it marched on elsewhere) and an end to the Cold War was declared.

The end of the Cold War made some countries on the front line of anticommunist efforts less strategically valuable. On the whole, however, U.S. foreign aid policy

did not change dramatically immediately after the Soviet Union's collapse.[3] Both during and after the Cold War, dictators were among the top recipients of U.S. foreign aid.[4] Although foreign aid's negative effect on democratization was more pronounced during the Cold War, even in the post–Cold War period, strategically important nondemocratic aid recipients can still use aid to thwart political change, according to Sarah Blodgett Bermeo.[5] One exception to business as usual was the creation of aid programs for Eastern Europe and the successor states of the Soviet Union. This was part of a general post–Cold War trend of redirecting aid toward relatively developed countries that were undergoing political transitions, and away from politically and economically stagnant ones. This strategy was both a bid to gain political influence in a part of the world that had previously been closed to U.S. influence and a return to using foreign aid to promote American principles of democracy and free markets in countries where these ideals had a reasonable chance of succeeding.

As priorities abroad shifted, a debate raged at home over what America's responsibilities in the world should be. During the second televised debate of the 1992 presidential campaign, President George H. W. Bush responded to a question about the United States' role as a superpower in the new world order with his characteristic eloquence:

> You know, it's so easy now to say "Hey, cut out foreign aid, we got a problem at home." I think the United States has to still have the Statue of Liberty as a symbol of caring for others. We're—right this very minute we're sending supplies in to help these little starving kids in Somalia. We're trying to get—we're—it's the United States that's taken the lead in, in humanitarian aid into Bosnia. We're doing this all around the world.[6]

Democratic presidential candidate Bill Clinton's response to the same debate question did not mention U.S. foreign assistance. Nor did Clinton's 1993 or 1997 inaugural addresses. As president, Clinton, who ran on a domestically focused economic platform, presided over the deepest cuts to U.S. foreign aid ever seen.

But after the 9/11 terrorist attacks and the ensuing invasions of Afghanistan and Iraq, the United States under the George W. Bush administration returned to the original model established by Truman of foreign aid for postconflict reconstruction and state-building. Massive amounts of foreign assistance were devoted to reconstruction and security-sector reform in Afghanistan and Iraq. Neighboring countries received greater assistance for their cooperation in multilateral military operations.[7] Since the wars began, Afghanistan and Iraq have dominated U.S. foreign assistance flows, alongside long-standing aid recipients such as Egypt and Israel. Whether these changes affected the relationship between U.S. foreign assistance and state violence is the focus of this chapter.

The End of the Cold War and the Beginning of the War on Terror

The evolution of U.S. foreign assistance policy since the end of Cold War has been analyzed primarily in terms of whether security objectives have declined in importance relative to economic or ideological goals.[8] On the whole, U.S. foreign aid policy has actually remained fairly consistently driven by security considerations, despite rhetorical shifts among policymakers. Prior to 9/11—the first foreign attacks on American soil since the bombing of Pearl Harbor—the U.S. foreign aid budget had been in decline generally since the mid-1980s as part of a push to reduce the deficit. In 1997 total U.S. bilateral foreign aid hit its lowest point ever, as shown in Figure 6.1. The United States rolled back both military and economic aid (particularly to Asian countries) due to human rights abuses, weapons proliferation, and terrorism concerns.[9] But after 9/11, U.S. foreign aid skyrocketed. For an unprecedented five-year period (fiscal years 2008–2012), the United States' foreign aid budget exceeded $50 billion annually.[10]

The surge in aid to Iraq and increases to some neighboring countries contributed to an overwhelming prioritization of the Middle East in U.S. foreign aid policy in the 2000s. Although a similar dynamic occurred in Southeast Asia during the Vietnam War, albeit on a much smaller scale, the war in Iraq heightened an already existing imbalance in the distribution of U.S. military aid toward the Middle East,

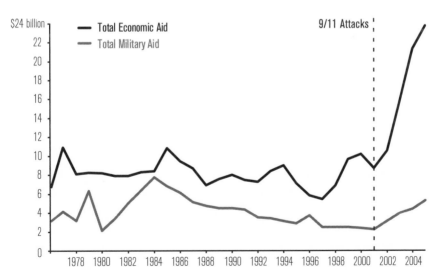

FIGURE 6.1.   U.S. Military and Economic Assistance. Note: Reported in 2016 dollars. Source: USAID, 2018.

home to other major aid recipients such as Egypt, Jordan, and Israel. The sheer scale of foreign assistance to Afghanistan and Iraq (shown in Figures 2.1 and 2.2) is hard to fathom. Reconstruction programs in these two countries alone totaled more than the combined budgets of all other U.S. foreign aid programs in fiscal year 2004; more American aid went to Afghanistan and Iraq than to all the rest of the world.

Snapshots of the top U.S. foreign aid recipients in the decades after the Cold War demonstrate evolving U.S. strategic interests as well as the dramatic recovery in the size of the foreign aid budget. Other than Egypt and Israel, no country was consistently in the top fifteen aid recipients in the years 1995, 2005, and 2015. Over time, sub-Saharan African countries began receiving larger shares of foreign aid funding, thanks largely to initiatives to address HIV/AIDS and other public health crises such as Ebola outbreaks. In 1995 aid to Africa comprised 11 percent of the U.S. foreign assistance budget, but rose to 32 percent by 2015. South and Central Asia's share of the foreign aid budget increased fivefold over the same period (from 5 percent in 1995 to 25 percent in 2015), due to increased aid to Pakistan for counterterrorism cooperation and the neighborhood effects of the war in Afghanistan for some Central Asian countries.[11] Aid to Southeast and East Asia was also reoriented to focus on key partners in the War on Terror, including Indonesia and the Philippines.[12]

The George W. Bush administration sought to codify its approach to foreign aid policy by focusing on what it called "transformational development." Enhancing U.S. national security abroad and promoting democracy became central tenets of U.S. foreign aid policy. For its part, the Obama administration aimed to integrate development more fully into its foreign policy approach by elevating it to a position of equality with defense and diplomacy, if only rhetorically. But on the whole, the Obama administration continued many of the foreign aid programs and policies established under Bush, even as foreign assistance programming expanded into new areas such as climate change adaptation and global food security.

To assess whether the relationship between U.S. foreign assistance and human rights abuses differed systematically during and after the Cold War, I analyze the data in two parts: 1976 to 1990 and 1991 to 2016.[13] This specification treats the end of the Cold War as a structural break that may have fundamentally altered the human rights impact of U.S. foreign aid policy. An alternative specification with a control variable for Cold War years (1976–1990) yields similar results (not reported).

U.S. Military Assistance

When looking solely at the Cold War period, U.S. military aid is associated with a decreased likelihood of state killings (defined as twenty-five or more civilian fatalities intentionally caused by state agents) and government repression. This differs

TABLE 6.1. *U.S. Foreign Aid and State Violence during and after the Cold War.*

VARIABLE	COLD WAR (1976–1990)				POST–COLD WAR (1991–2016)			
	MASS KILLINGS	STATE KILLINGS	REPRESSION	TORTURE 1981–1990	MASS KILLINGS	STATE KILLINGS	REPRESSION	TORTURE 1991–2011
Military aid$_{t-1}$	1.002	0.913***	0.977*	0.981	0.932***	0.967***	1.001	0.971***
	(0.030)	(0.020)	(0.012)	(0.019)	(0.016)	(0.009)	(0.008)	(0.009)
Economic aid$_{t-1}$	1.082**	1.081***	1.080***	1.049*	1.189*	1.016	1.019	0.924***
	(0.045)	(0.026)	(0.014)	(0.027)	(0.117)	(0.015)	(0.012)	(0.020)
Controls	Yes	Yes	Yes	Yes	Yes	Yes	Yes	Yes
Observations	1102	792	914	797	2962	2313	2492	2246
Pseudo R^2	0.3539	0.2597	0.1455	0.2114	0.2101	0.2265	0.1306	0.0361
Wald Chi^2	184.31	152.14	343.30	531.29	202.54	498.21	739.14	76.80
Log pseudo-likelihood	–183.692	–306.804	–1051.728	–280.843	–363.648	–980.511	–3122.901	–1136.915

NOTE: Odds ratios with bootstrapped standard errors. Cut points and other explanatory variables not reported for brevity. ***p<0.01, ** p<0.05, *p<0.10.

SOURCES: Cingranelli, Richards, and Clay, 2014; Eck and Hultman, 2007; Gibney et al., 2017; Marshall, 2017; Marshall, Gurr, and Harff, 2017; Marshall, Gurr, and Jaggers, 2017; Schrodt and Ulfelder, 2016; USAID, 2018; World Bank, 2018.

somewhat from the results presented in Chapter 2, which found a negative association between U.S. military aid and all forms of state violence—except government
repression—for the period 1976 to 2016. The relationship between U.S. military
assistance and state violence is much clearer for the post–Cold War period. On
average, the United States has actually provided more military assistance in the
decades after the Cold War. The results show that U.S. military aid is negatively
associated with all forms of state violence in the post–Cold War period.

Several possible explanations can help account for the seemingly counterintui-
tive finding that U.S. military assistance may improve human rights conditions.
First, it is possible that this finding is actually a mirage of sorts, that it is more about
the countries to which the United States does and does not give aid rather than a
reflection of what aid achieves in the recipient countries. The passage in the late 1990s
of the Leahy Laws means that military assistance is now less likely to go to abusive
militaries. Beginning with restrictions on counternarcotics assistance and eventually expanding to all foreign operations assistance, Congress prohibits the use of
funds for foreign security forces where there is credible evidence that a foreign military or police unit committed gross violations of human rights. Although the human
rights restrictions of the Foreign Assistance Act had little impact during the Cold
War, in large part because the president could easily circumvent them, human rights
conditionality may now have more bite. If so, this suggests that at least part of the
observed effect results from a shift away from providing foreign aid to abusive armed
forces rather than improvements in the behavior of those forces. Simply put, the
United States may now be less likely to give military aid to human rights abusers in
the first place. This, however, does not explain the association between U.S. military assistance and improvements in human rights conditions prior to the enact-
ment of the Leahy Laws.

Alternatively, increased oversight and a reduction in the strategic use of military
assistance as an instrument of anticommunism may mean that military assistance
is now a more effective tool for military professionalization. If so, this would mean
that countries receiving U.S. military assistance, and especially training, would see
actual improvements in human rights conditions as militaries increasingly abide by
international human rights norms. With the loss of the Soviet Union as an alternative supplier of military assistance, it is also possible that U.S. military assistance is
now so valuable that governments are less likely to risk its loss through poor human
rights behavior. Although such an explanation is unlikely to apply to major allies
such as Pakistan or Egypt, it could help explain why military assistance is associated
with improvements in various human rights behaviors, on average. Adjudicating
between these and other possible explanations for the moderating effect of U.S.
military assistance is an important issue for future research.

Because the global distribution of military assistance has been significantly affected by the wars in Afghanistan and Iraq, I excluded these cases and repeated the analysis (results not reported). U.S. military assistance remains associated with a decreased likelihood of all forms of state violence in the post–Cold War period. All other findings remain the same.

U.S. Economic Assistance

Both during and after the Cold War, U.S. economic aid is associated with increased levels of multiple forms of state violence in countries receiving aid. The most notable difference is that although U.S. economic assistance was associated with the use of torture during the Cold War, it is associated with *decreased* levels of torture in the post–Cold War period. But what is perhaps most surprising is that U.S. economic aid continues to be associated with increased mass killings and government repression over the past twenty-five years. Because many forms of U.S. economic aid are generally not subject to the same oversight or human rights conditionality as U.S. military aid, economic aid continues to be both easier to divert and more likely to be put to coercive use by governments that seek to maintain their hold on power. Sometimes the links between economic aid and state violence are clear, as when economic aid is used to procure crowd-control equipment or to support the construction of state infrastructure linked to torture, such as prisons. As policing has become increasingly militarized around the globe, American support for civilian security sector institutions abroad may have unexpected consequences for human rights. But at other times, the linkages are indirect, as is the case when food aid is monetized and the resulting government income is directed toward the state's coercive capacity.

Aid and State Violence in the Twenty-First Century

The events of 9/11 dramatically affected the amount of foreign aid given by the United States, as well as which countries received U.S. foreign aid windfalls. Besides Afghanistan and Iraq, the countries that received the most foreign aid were those aligned with the United States in the War on Terror, including Indonesia and lesser-known examples such as Poland and Uzbekistan. At the same time, a concern about weak states emerged in U.S. national security policy: "The events of September 11, 2001, taught us that weak states, like Afghanistan, can pose as great a danger to our national interests as strong states. Poverty does not make poor people into terrorists and murderers. Yet poverty, weak institutions, and corruption can make weak states vulnerable to terrorist networks and drug cartels within their borders."[14] Foreign aid became a tool for preventing supposedly weak states such as Pakistan, Kenya, and Sudan from failing, collapsing into anarchy, and requiring foreign intervention to put them back together again.

The American response to 9/11 may have also influenced the use of state-led violence in other countries. The invasion of Afghanistan allowed many countries to reframe their own internal conflicts as part of the Global War on Terror, which was interpreted as targeting radical Islamist movements.[15] Some authoritarian regimes began a systematic crackdown on Islamist opposition groups and/or Muslim minorities. The ongoing persecution of China's Muslim Uighur minority, including their forced participation in government reeducation camps in Xinjiang province, is one of the most appalling examples of this phenomenon.[16] In addition, many have argued that U.S. policies during the Iraq War, such as extraordinary rendition and extended detentions at Guantanamo Bay, contributed to an international climate where the use of torture and repression by governments could be justified as an extension of state sovereignty.[17]

To assess whether these changes may have affected the relationship between U.S. foreign assistance and state violence after 9/11, I limit the scope of the analysis to 2002 to 2016.[18] The results, reported in Table 6.2, suggest some important differences from the general post–Cold War period. U.S. military assistance continues to be associated with reductions in state killings and mass killings. However, U.S. military assistance does not have a statistically significant relationship with government repression or torture in the years after 9/11. Even so, the negative association between U.S. foreign aid and mass killings and state killings in the post-9/11 years is notable.

When looking at the post-9/11 period, the findings for U.S. economic aid also change somewhat. The magnitude of the observed relationship between economic aid and mass killings increases. And contrary to prior results, torture is positively correlated with U.S. economic aid during the years 2002 to 2011. The results are the same even when Afghanistan and Iraq are excluded from the analysis, which means that the relationship between U.S. economic aid and state violence seen in the post-9/11 period is not driven by those countries. The inconsistent results for torture may stem from changes in its use as part of the Global War on Terror. In particular, countries hosting black sites used by the CIA to detain, interrogate, and torture suspects may have received increased U.S. foreign assistance as either an incentive or a reward. Either way, the results clearly show that the relationship between U.S. economic assistance and state violence persists.

To understand how the coercive effect of foreign aid operates in the twenty-first century, it is useful to look at South Sudan—the world's newest country and a product of extensive American political and financial support. South Sudan allows us to examine how high levels of economic aid are undermining human freedoms *at this very moment*. This case also demonstrates the difficulty of upending U.S. foreign aid policy in the absence of economic growth or significant political changes in the country receiving aid.

TABLE 6.2. *U.S. Foreign Aid and State Violence post-9/11.*

VARIABLE	MASS KILLINGS 2002–2016	STATE KILLINGS 2002–2016	REPRESSION 2002–2016	TORTURE 2002–2016
Military aid$_{t-1}$	0.897***	0.964**	1.008	0.995
	(0.027)	(0.017)	(0.035)	(0.009)
Economic aid$_{t-1}$	2.090***	1.028	1.072***	1.079***
	(0.376)	(0.060)	(0.028)	(0.024)
Controls	Yes	Yes	Yes	Yes
Observations	1758	1136	2922	1412
Pseudo R^2	0.2672	0.2849	0.2185	0.1611
Wald Chi^2	70.67	265.31	1846.01	585.95
Log pseudo-likelihood	–148.043	–397.237	–3286.18	–1692.777

NOTE: Odds ratios with bootstrapped standard errors. Cut points and other explanatory variables not reported for brevity. ***p<0.01, ** p<0.05, *p<0.10.

SOURCES: Cingranelli, Richards, and Clay, 2014; Eck and Hultman, 2007; Gibney et al., 2017; Marshall, 2017; Marshall, Gurr, and Harff, 2017; Marshall, Gurr, and Jaggers, 2017; Schrodt and Ulfelder, 2016; USAID, 2018; World Bank, 2018.

South Sudan: Aiding and Abetting the World's Newest Country

South Sudan joined the international community as one of its poorest members. For almost four decades, the country had been wracked by civil war with the central government of Sudan, based in Khartoum, but also among armed groups operating in the south. In the Western press, this conflict was often characterized as racial and religious in nature, with an Arab-Muslim government in the north of Sudan oppressing African Christians in the south. Only a country of their own would safeguard the rights of this persecuted minority, according to the prevailing logic. Although the south gained autonomy in 2005 and then independence in 2011, decades of civil war and massive amounts of foreign aid continue to deeply affect the governance of South Sudan.

During the course of the Sudanese civil war, international support for the Sudan People's Liberation Movement/Army (SPLM/A), which would ultimately form the government and military of an independent South Sudan, often took the form of humanitarian assistance. Unfortunately, humanitarian aid provided the SPLA with a seemingly unlimited resource to plunder with impunity. As Alex de Waal notes, "Looting food aid was elevated to military strategy in the 1990s, when the contending factions of the SPLA staged hunger camps to attract humanitarian relief, which was then stolen."[19] The practice was so extensive that aid officials speculated that the SPLA's leader, John Garang, "must have been told by U.S. officials that indirect support of him (at that time) would come in the form of plentiful food assistance, which is easily diverted and bartered."[20] Foreign aid, along with other local lootable resources such as gold and timber, financed the SPLA's war with Khartoum.

Once South Sudan's autonomy was guaranteed, the focus of the SPLA's leadership was redirected from financing warfare to buying the support of competing armed factions. Rival groups in the south were folded into the SPLA, and the Southern Sudan Legislative Assembly repeatedly voted to raise soldiers' pay to more than twice that of the north's Sudan Armed Forces.[21] In the years between autonomy and independence, more than 80 percent of defense spending was on wages and allowances for the SPLA. A significant portion of these funds was pocketed by commanders of "ghost soldiers"—fighters who appeared on the payroll but did not actually exist.[22] By the time independence rolled around, the SPLA had a force of about 240,000 soldiers that could be supplemented by roughly 90,000 police and other armed guards, for a population of ten million South Sudanese. The newly minted president, Salva Kiir, also maintained his own personal security force.

Months after independence, defense spending amounted to 35 percent of the new government's expenditures. Oil revenues initially underwrote much of what was the region's highest levels of public spending per capita. Patronage networks rapidly spread through the government and armed forces. This was disrupted by the decision in January 2012 to shut down oil production. Halting production for what eventually amounted to more than a year led South Sudan's government to rapidly draw down its reserves and borrow against future oil production. In December 2013 renewed fighting sparked a massive humanitarian crisis.

Throughout South Sudan's infancy, the United States assumed a significant financial responsibility for its independence—totaling $3.76 billion in bilateral foreign assistance alone. This amount dramatically underestimates the full extent of the United States' contributions to the country. The United States has effectively bankrolled the UN Mission in South Sudan (UNMISS), which has operated in the country since July 2011.[23] UNMISS currently has a staff of roughly 19,000, 7,900 of whom are uniformed troops and police officers, and a budget of more than $1 billion.[24] In fiscal year 2017 alone, the United States contributed $267 million to UNMISS.[25] In total, the United States has devoted more than $11 billion to South Sudan, including humanitarian assistance to the 180,000 civilians living in camps operated by the UN in South Sudan. One million more

South Sudanese have fled to refugee camps in neighboring countries since independence. One of the world's largest refugee camps now sits just across the border in Uganda.

From its creation, South Sudan has featured all of the characteristics that facilitate the coercive effect of foreign aid: a history of civil war, a military-backed government, weak state institutions, and a leader who has proven unaccountable to both his people and the international community. South Sudan is a clear example of how the pernicious effects of foreign aid continue to operate today. Although foreign aid is not a root cause of the violence seen in South Sudan, it has undoubtedly helped insulate Kiir's government from political pressure as foreign donors and NGOs have taken on most of the obligations of the state. These same international actors pay extremely high registration and work permit fees for the dubious pleasure of doing what the government of South Sudan is unwilling to do—provide services to its people.[26] The end result of foreign intervention in South Sudan is an aid-dependent government that regularly resorts to violence because it lacks any real legitimacy.

South Sudan is also yet another example of the limits of congressional attempts to regulate U.S. foreign assistance. More than 19,000 child soldiers are estimated to be fighting in South Sudan, according to UNICEF.[27] In spite of legislation prohibiting funds to parties that actively recruit or use child soldiers, the Obama administration issued a waiver of the 2008 Child Soldiers Prevention Act for South Sudan in 2016. The waiver—another example of the president's ability to overcome congressional restrictions—allowed the U.S. government to provide South Sudan with military training through IMET and to support ceasefire monitoring in a country actively at war with itself.[28] This decision made the United States a target for South Sudan's political opposition. The spokesperson for the ousted former first vice president, Riek Machar, claimed that Kiir's government did not direct funds for the country's security sector budget to actual security sector reforms, but instead used the funds to purchase weapons in order to maintain his dictatorial rule.[29] If that is true, then Kiir understands the fungibility of foreign assistance as well as Suharto did.

Worst of all, South Sudan illustrates what happens when the coercive effect of foreign aid is brought full circle. In July 2016 uniformed South Sudanese troops invaded a secure compound housing international aid workers. Over the course of more than four hours, they singled out Americans for abuse and beatings, executed an ethnic Nuer reporter employed by a foreign NGO while his colleagues watched, carried out mock executions, and gang-raped several humanitarian aid workers.[30] UN peacekeepers and the U.S. embassy did not respond to repeated pleas from those trapped inside, even though UN troops were only minutes away.[31] A South Sudanese army spokesperson refused to confirm the military's involvement, noting that

"everyone is armed, and everyone has access to uniforms."[32] South Sudan was subsequently named the world's most dangerous country for aid workers.[33] It was not
until late 2018 that ten South Sudanese soldiers were sentenced for charges related
to the attack, including murder, rape, sexual harassment, armed robbery, and theft.[34]

The UN Commission on Human Rights in South Sudan released a jarring report in 2018 detailing the extent of war crimes and crimes against humanity perpetrated by the South Sudanese armed forces against civilians over the preceding two
years.[35] Government forces were accused of destroying humanitarian compounds,
schools, a church, and a hospital in the town of Pagak, as well as many other crimes.
In the area around Malakal, soldiers purportedly shot civilians as they fled from a
ground offensive. Those too infirm to leave were burned to death inside their homes.
On June 24, 2016, the military intervened following an outbreak of fighting between
armed groups in Wau, an ethnically mixed town. Between 39 and 69 bodies were
collected and recorded by the police, including those of at least 15 women and 10
children. The UN believes the actual death toll to be much higher, based on the
testimony of witnesses who recounted that government soldiers intentionally shot
and killed civilians as they fled their homes for the protection of a UN base.

Despite repeated calls at the UN Security Council and other venues to hold
the government of South Sudan accountable, there appears to be little change on the
horizon following the initial promise of a September 2018 peace deal. By April 2019,
a USAID Disaster Assistance Response Team had been in South Sudan for almost
five and a half years. Six and a half million South Sudanese were in need of food
assistance and U.S. humanitarian funding for fiscal year 2018 reached $625 million
for the country.[36] As U.S. Ambassador to the UN Nikki Haley remarked, "South
Sudan, in particular, is a tragic case of shattered dreams and unrealized potential.
It is the youngest country in the world but the promise of its hard-fought independence is slipping away. . . . The government is primarily responsible for ethnically
based killings and for blocking the delivery of humanitarian assistance to suffering
people. The realities of the South Sudan crisis are difficult to truly comprehend."[37]
What is even more difficult to comprehend is how the United States and other international donors can possibly extract themselves from a crisis that their foreign
assistance is actively fueling.

Conclusion

The coercive effect of foreign aid is not some long-gone Cold War phenomenon. It
persists even today. Decades after the Cold War's end, U.S. economic aid remains
associated with acts of violence and repression by states all over the world. Contrary
to what many might expect, the linkage between economic aid and state violence
does not depend on the massive influx of U.S. foreign aid to Afghanistan and Iraq

and the continuing violence in those countries. Instead, the robust evidence in support of the coercive effect of foreign aid is rooted in decades of U.S. foreign assistance policy. It is a structural feature of bilateral foreign assistance, and it demands remedy.

The lost promise of South Sudan, a country built on U.S. foreign assistance, should serve as a caution to those who attribute internal violence during the Cold War to high levels of military assistance and assume that a retrenchment in U.S. military aid (to most countries) has solved the problem. Although military aid undoubtedly played an important role in developing the coercive capacity of many states, on the whole, military aid is associated with lower levels of state violence both during and after the Cold War. In this context, it is important to note that the United States gives much more economic aid than it does military assistance. The persistent finding that U.S. economic aid is associated with worse human rights practices in countries receiving aid is chilling.

Conclusion
Can "Do No Harm" Be Done?

"WE SHOULD NOTE THE WORDS that the Hippocratic oath addresses to would-be interveners, 'First do no harm.'"[1] These words graced a memo to Reagan's first secretary of state on the reinvigoration of U.S. human rights policy. "First, do no harm." This commonly invoked maxim urges us to consider the possible injury or damage that any intervention might do. It calls to mind harms that are obvious, and pushes us to consider those that we cannot foresee. It reminds us of the power that interveners have over the subjects of their intervention, and that outcomes, not intentions, determine the justice of an action. But despite the lip service paid to Hippocratic principles, U.S. foreign assistance policy has never seriously weighed the benefits and costs of intervening in the politics, economies, and societies of others. Good intentions have helped diminish the responsibility of state actors who try to use foreign aid to manipulate the course of history in their favor. The imperative to do something has not been balanced by an obligation *not* to do something that makes the problem worse.

It is true that weighing the potential positive and negative effects of foreign assistance is a challenging task. This is particularly apparent when considering security sector assistance. Yet, even when "nonlethal" forms of security assistance—such as radios or GPS equipment that can be used for logistical purposes—are provided during a conflict, they are intended to support violent actors.[2] As demonstrated by cases ranging from Carter's nonlethal aid to the Salvadoran government to the hundreds of millions of dollars the Obama administration funneled to the opposition to Bashar al-Assad in Syria, the fundamental ability of aid recipients on either side of a conflict to weaponize foreign assistance serves to extend the length and costs of war.[3]

The negative effects of foreign aid—aid dependence, market distortions, constraints on civil liberties, and others—continue to be uncovered by rigorous research. This book has focused on the type of aid that constitutes the vast majority of foreign assistance provided by the United States: bilateral foreign aid that is given by the people of the United States through the U.S. government to the governments (and ostensibly, the people) of developing countries. In 2017 this amounted to roughly $38 billion; a similar amount is planned for fiscal year 2019.[4] The evidence shows how U.S. foreign assistance plays an important role in supporting state actors that abuse human rights—an obvious harm, with no clear policy benefits. This is especially true of economic aid, which is highly fungible and can easily be directed toward alternate uses. The pernicious relationship between U.S. foreign assistance and state violence detailed here is not limited to the Cold War era and the United States' support for dictators such as Suharto in Indonesia and Park Chung Hee in South Korea. Even decades after the Cold War's end, South Sudan is witness to how the negative effects of foreign aid continue to affect the lives of millions of individuals.

Aiding Violence and Abetting Harm: What We've Learned

The coercive effect of foreign aid helps explain why foreign assistance can actually undermine human freedoms. Foreign aid can build up a state's coercive capacity—its military and security services—which can then, under certain conditions, be used to repress, torture, and even kill its citizens. Contrary to popular belief, the evidence powerfully demonstrates that economic aid supports state violence and government repression abroad through an income effect. In constrained political environments or during periods of civil war, foreign economic aid is unlikely to be spent on public goods such as health or education. Instead, it frees up resources that a government can then devote to its own security. Foreign aid enables recipient governments to divert precious resources toward security sector spending or other means of maintaining power, such as patronage networks. Both the income effect and the capacity-building effect of foreign aid, where aid directly increases the coercive capacity of a state, play an important role in channeling additional resources to insecure governments.

Although foreign aid was seen as a powerful tool for confronting the perils of communism during the Cold War, continuing U.S. foreign assistance to repressive countries—even strategically important ones—may have been more damaging in the long run for both recipient countries and U.S. national security than cutting off American aid to abusive regimes. This is because the coercion that foreign aid facilitates can become institutionalized. Governments that resort to force are more likely to rely on force in the future. State institutions adapt and evolve so that militaries designed to defend against external threats become focused on internal ones, and police forces set up to protect civilians instead target them. The human capital dimension of the coercive effect of foreign aid means that the damaging effects of aid can persist even after aid dollars cease to flow, because state-society relations are profoundly changed by shifts in the state's coercive capacity.

In Indonesia, for example, American (and to a lesser degree, Soviet) military assistance directly supported increases in the country's military capacity through the acquisition of military hardware. U.S.-funded military buildups included naval vessels and aircraft that played an essential role in Indonesia's confrontation with the Netherlands over the Dutch colony of Papua. Indonesia's increased military capacity also enabled it to invade and occupy East Timor, a Portuguese colony. Indonesia succeeded in claiming both of these territories as its own, which set the stage for decades of government repression of ethnic minorities. But American military assistance also increased human capital by training the TNI. Thousands of Indonesian soldiers received counterinsurgency training through IMET, which aimed to increase their effectiveness and, by extension, their lethality. The TNI's experience pacifying resistance groups in East Timor further increased their specialized knowledge of coercion. This expertise was brought to bear throughout the Indonesian archipelago as soldiers who served in East Timor were redeployed to Aceh and Papua, where they worked to crush separatist movements.

Similarly, the United States openly and actively supported the Salvadoran military government in its prosecution of a brutal and bloody war against a leftist insurgency during the 1980s. More than 75,000 people were killed or went missing over a period of twelve years. The United States was temporarily successful in using the threat of aid reductions to pressure the Salvadoran government to reign in the most egregiously violent state-led groups, the militias known as death squads. But high levels of U.S. economic aid also fueled the war effort through an income effect. The goal of U.S. foreign assistance—to ensure that a noncommunist government remained in place—was achieved, and the United States withdrew most of its assistance after the Salvadoran government and the rebel group, the FMLN, signed a peace treaty. However, the lingering legacy of state violence in El Salvador suggests that the long-term harmful effects of foreign aid endure there.[5]

The full implications of U.S. military assistance to El Salvador remain in dispute. Some argue that specialized military training funded through U.S. military assistance helped professionalize the Salvadoran military. Improved behavior by both the military and the government then helped turn the tide of local public opinion against the rebels.[6] An alternative position argues that U.S. military assistance contributed to both the brutality and length of the war by increasing the human capital (through counterinsurgency training) and coercive capacity (through arms sales and transfers) of the Salvadoran military. This may have forestalled negotiations between the government and the FMLN by allowing the government to continue fighting longer than it otherwise could have. The evidence presented here supports the latter interpretation but also suggests that economic aid, not military assistance, was decisive in the Salvadoran civil war.

Military assistance had a different outcome in South Korea, where it quickly outpaced economic aid from the United States. The United States had tens of thousands of troops stationed in the country and maintained operational control of the South Korean armed forces as a legacy of the Korean War. This radically increased U.S. oversight of South Korea's military and how it used American military assistance. In El Salvador, the U.S. troop presence was restricted by Congress to a few dozen military advisors, and the Department of Defense routinely failed to monitor its operations there. These differences suggest that public scrutiny does not necessarily compensate for actual government oversight of foreign assistance programs.

South Korea presents a stronger case for the argument that U.S. military assistance helps create professional, human rights–respecting militaries. Government repression was widespread in South Korea and driven by an extensive intelligence apparatus modeled on the CIA. However, most episodes of state violence were instigated by the police in response to prodemocracy protests. Troops were called in only when the police failed in disrupting mass protests, though the military played a much greater role in maintaining order during periods of martial law. State violence in South Korea was constrained by the military's preoccupation with a conventional war with North Korea and its reliance on universal conscription. The latter meant that the protestors, too, were well trained, as seen in Gwangju in 1980. But universal conscription also meant that troops were drawn from the general population and often posted in their local communities. This differed from the Indonesian approach, which relied heavily on nonlocal forces to maintain order in troublesome regions. In addition to these factors, because of the South Korean opposition's prodemocracy and Christian character, U.S. policymakers could not easily dismiss it as a communist threat. This meant that when state violence was used against South Korean protestors, it had serious international repercussions.

Recognizing the link between U.S. military assistance and repressive behavior by foreign governments, Congress decided to make military assistance conditional on a military's human rights behavior. Specific units that violate human rights can be excluded from future foreign assistance, but other parts of that same military may continue to receive support. This has proven to be an imperfect solution to a difficult problem. Although there are many reasons why the collective punishment of a military for one unit's abuses is not a practical way to resolve human rights concerns, the effectiveness of any restrictions on military assistance is limited by the ability of aid recipients to divert other forms of aid toward military spending. As a result, human rights conditionality has not created the expected incentives for improved human rights behavior. Nor has the actual cutoff of aid been an effective tool for punishing repressive regimes. Time and again, congressionally mandated foreign aid cuts or restrictions are either circumvented by the executive branch through presidential waivers or undermined by the continued provision of other forms of foreign aid, such as economic assistance. Other reasons for continuing foreign assistance—be they U.S. national security interests or supposed economic need—take precedence over human rights.

The historical record shows that for decades, American policymakers have been well aware that economic aid can be harnessed for military purposes. In fact, they often anticipated this use of aid. In some instances, the connections between U.S. economic aid and military robustness were clear. In one example, Kissinger wrote to President Ford that congressional revisions to military aid grants to Indonesia meant that "we will need to rely more heavily on economic aid ties."[7] American rice provided as PL 480 food aid was used by the Indonesian government to feed its soldiers. Purchased by the military at one-sixtieth the market price, American rice subsidized the Indonesian armed forces and allowed the government to direct its savings toward increasing arms imports.

At other times, the connections are more oblique, as when PL 480 cotton was sold by the Indonesian government to raise foreign exchange funds. U.S. economic aid was intended to increase the overall financial resources available to Indonesia, which in turn allowed for greater military spending than would otherwise have been possible. Congress's own assessments of U.S. foreign assistance to El Salvador held that three-quarters of all U.S. foreign aid funds were supporting the Salvadoran government's war effort, even though the majority of U.S. assistance was economic aid. Aid in the form of highly fungible cash transfers and food aid meant that the Salvadoran government could invest all of its resources into winning the war and leave other priorities to the Americans to fund.

The coercive effect of foreign aid is driven by economic assistance in part because food aid is cheap to provide, both politically and financially. It is supported by the American public and backed by an important constituency: American farmers. The fungibility of food aid makes it a vital asset to the governments that receive it. Even now, U.S. food aid is being sold abroad for cold, hard cash. The practice of monetization, or the selling of donated food aid into overseas markets, continues to be widespread and is even required under U.S. law. Approximately 60 percent of non-emergency food aid is monetized each year.[8] Generating cash from food aid is grossly inefficient, with typical returns of only fifty to seventy cents on the dollar.

The control of food aid also has significant political consequences that are rarely acknowledged. Food aid can support repressive governments by providing resources that can be distributed to regime supporters; this was tragically the case with humanitarian assistance to Mengistu's dictatorship in Ethiopia and the Assad regime in Syria.[9] In Uganda the diversion of food aid has been linked to widespread government fraud.[10] And in Sudan, Omar al-Bashir's control of food aid meant that decades of assistance did little to change overall human conditions.[11] Together, this evidence suggests that what is perhaps the most easily justified form of foreign assistance—food to alleviate hunger—may also be the most harmful.

Containing the Harmful Effects of Aid

One proposed way to get around the problems associated with governments' manipulation of foreign aid is to cut out the middleman; that is, to stop providing governments with aid at all and instead focus on NGOs and other voluntary associations that can provide services directly to people. Indeed, some donors are more likely to deliver aid through nonstate actors in countries that are poorly governed.[12] But it is unreasonable to expect that such organizations can or should have the capacity or accountability of a state, and in many contexts, the extensive presence of NGOs can actually undermine state institutions. The presence of international development NGOs has no meaningful effect on the bureaucratic capacity of nondemocracies over the short or long terms. Supporting NGOs in authoritarian contexts does not necessarily help build more capable or responsive states that would lay the foundations for more accountable governments.[13] As Afghanistan, Haiti, and South Sudan aptly demonstrate, replacing the state with NGOs is not a real solution to development challenges.[14] There is nothing to prevent individuals or countries from becoming reliant on NGOs, be they local or foreign, to provide basic services. And NGOs, unlike states, have only a limited ability to tax local populations and become self-sustaining. Ultimately, they, too, are dependent on foreign aid. As a result, foreign-funded NGOs tend to be more accountable to donors than beneficiaries and are more focused on service delivery than social change.[15]

In practice, diverting foreign aid away from governments and toward NGOs has had its own unintended consequence of incentivizing governments to restrict civil society. Higher levels of foreign aid increase the probability that a country will adopt restrictive NGO laws, particularly when governments feel vulnerable to domestic challenges.[16] And foreign-backed NGOs often pose a legitimate concern for governments; increased international NGO activity is associated with higher levels of both violent and nonviolent protest.[17] As of 2016, 39 of the world's 153 low- and middle-income countries had adopted laws restricting the delivery of foreign aid to NGOs operating within their borders, and more are poised to do so.[18] That international support for civil society is actually undermining the freedom of local civil society actors is yet another pernicious effect of foreign aid.

Many governments in the developing world are clearly unwilling to give up the core functions of the state and become republics of NGOs. What we are left with, then, is a status quo where states remain the dominant actors and where foreign assistance feeds the ability of insecure governments to remain in power by any means necessary. Given this, it is reasonable to ask why the U.S. government does not do more to ensure that its aid is spent in ways that support its objectives. One possibility would be for the U.S. government to impose maintenance-of-effort requirements abroad, as it does with federal grants to states at home. Unlike cost-sharing or matching requirements, which force aid recipients to fund a portion of a program's cost, maintenance-of-effort requirements commit governments to funding a program at the same level as they did prior to receiving aid. This is intended to ensure that the assistance given actually results in increased service provision rather than the replacement of local government funding by aid. For example, countries receiving public health funds for vaccinations would have to demonstrate that they are actually vaccinating more people as a result of foreign assistance, rather than vaccinating similar numbers and redirecting the additional funds elsewhere. Such requirements are one way to limit the income effect of foreign aid. Under such a system, donor oversight and monitoring would be crucial to enforcement, and therein lies the rub. Given the perpetual willingness of donors to look the other way and the real challenges of on-the-ground oversight, this or similar fixes may not be enough to constrain the coercive effect of foreign aid.

Another way to avoid the coercive effect of foreign aid is simply to do away with (most) foreign assistance. Public opinion polling in the United States has consistently demonstrated limited public support for foreign aid. A 2016 YouGov survey reported that 68 percent of Republicans and 42 percent of Democrats agreed with the statement that the United States spends too much on foreign aid.[19] In a survey one year later, 57 percent of respondents said that the $42.4 billion in U.S. economic and military assistance slated for 2017 was excessive.[20] In January 2018 a majority of survey respondents believed that the billions of dollars spent on weapons and military aid to foreign countries was counterproductive to the goal of protecting American interests.[21] A survey of likely voters that same month found that most agreed with President Trump that U.S. foreign aid "isn't a good deal for America."[22]

The American public largely does not know or care that foreign aid constitutes only about 1 percent of the federal budget (though when citizens learn this, they are less likely to support cuts to foreign assistance).[23] Many Americans understandably want to know why their government does not invest these billions of dollars in its own health-care or education systems rather than spending them abroad. And to date, no policymaker has come up with an adequate answer.

Cuts to foreign aid are prominent in the Trump administration's budget proposals. Trump's agenda is in many ways the mirror image of Truman's. Trump has questioned Truman's core beliefs, including the value of the NATO alliance and the premise that trade is mutually beneficial. Trump has also taken sharp aim at the principles behind Truman's Four Points speech. The America First Budget for 2018 proposed a $10.1 billion (28 percent) reduction in base funding for the State Department and USAID.[24] A merger of USAID with the State Department, which would undo one of Kennedy's great achievements and the foundation for modern U.S. foreign aid policy, was also floated.

Congress rejected many of the proposed cuts through the appropriations process. But again, the Trump administration proposed a foreign aid budget for fiscal year 2019 that was 28.6 percent lower than what Congress had funded the previous year. Similar requests are expected throughout Trump's time in office. Although critics argue that the Trump administration is overseeing the gutting of the U.S. foreign policy establishment, a more charitable interpretation would be that the foreign assistance budget is being rightsized after years of postwar reconstruction and a major expansion of global public health funding.

There are, however, some compelling arguments for continuing to use foreign assistance as a foreign policy tool. Just as during the Cold War, when the United States and the Soviet Union competed for geopolitical influence, it remains the case that you can't compete if you don't spend. Reagan was clear in his position on this matter: "We must change the attitude of our diplomatic corps so that we don't bring down governments in the name of human rights. . . . We don't throw out our friends just because they can't pass the 'saliva test' on human rights."[25] For most of U.S. foreign aid's history, Reagan's position has ruled the day. Increases in human rights abuses only rarely result in cuts to U.S. foreign aid, and such cuts are often implemented well after egregious harm has occurred.

But the geopolitical balance of power is changing in ways that affect the strategic calculus behind U.S. foreign aid policy.[26] Over the course of the last decade, China has emerged as a major foreign aid donor. In 2013 experts ranked China as the sixth-largest aid donor country.[27] According to AidData, Chinese official finance totaled $354.3 billion from 2000 to 2014. During the same period, U.S. official finance was $394.6 billion.[28] Although it is difficult to draw a hard line between China's aid and investment activities, the country's footprint in developing countries continues to grow.

Those who argue that the United States should use its foreign assistance to help contain China's growing influence point to evidence that countries receiving aid from democracies are more likely to experience democratization.[29] The inverse is also true. Aid from authoritarian countries is associated with a movement away from democracy—a finding that bodes ill for many countries. U.S. foreign aid policy is highly transparent, whereas China's is not. We know how much money the United States gives a country and how it wants that aid to be applied. China published its first white paper on foreign aid only in 2011, despite having provided foreign aid in some capacity since the 1950s. We have no way of knowing the human rights impacts of Chinese foreign aid, given the lack of political transparency and oversight both in China and in many of the countries receiving Chinese aid. (The top recipient of Chinese official development assistance is Cuba.) And as other countries with questionable human rights practices such as Turkey and Saudi Arabia increase their own foreign aid giving programs (estimated to be roughly $6.2 billion and $2.8 billion, respectively, in 2016), the idea of promoting human rights through foreign aid may become obsolete.[30]

Today in my mother's homeland of the Philippines, an autocrat has used the police to wage a deadly and extrajudicial war on drugs that has killed thousands of civilians—including children. In addition to the human cost of this violence, millions of dollars in aid from the MCC has been forfeited by the Philippines due to growing and justified concerns about the contraction of civil liberties and weakening rule of law. President Duterte also rejected $280 million in aid from the European Union because of the proposed human rights conditions.[31] As ties between the Philippines and the West atrophy, China is stepping in, providing arms and ammunition to the Philippine military in its confrontation with Islamic State–inspired militants in the southern province of Mindanao.[32] This tragic result—growing presidential abuses of power and closer ties to an authoritarian state—is a profound demonstration of the limitations of foreign aid as a tool for promoting human rights. Neither the United States' decades-long attempt to buy influence in the Philippines through foreign aid nor the more recent contraction of that aid have brought about meaningful improvements in Filipinos' personal freedoms or their safety from the excesses of their own government. If freedom is a measure of American influence in the world, then the efforts of the United States are falling short.

This is true not only in the Philippines but also in the many other countries where U.S. policy has assumed that political liberalization will engender advances in human rights and rewarded tiny steps taken in that direction.[33] The massive humanitarian crisis that resulted from the persecution of Rohingyas in Myanmar reveals how foreign assistance policy can be dead wrong when rewarding apparent movement toward democracy. Despite a government led by a human rights heroine, democracy activist Aung San Suu Kyi, the military continues to act with impunity in Myanmar. The international community's response—providing aid to Bangladesh to ease tensions over its refugee host country status—fails to address the underlying causes of the violence that precipitated the crisis. In Indonesia, human rights abuses continue to be perpetrated by Kopassus, and senior military officers remain impervious to justice even as the country has successfully transitioned to a vibrant democracy. South Sudan continues to receive hundreds of millions of dollars in U.S. foreign assistance even as its military exploits thousands of child soldiers in a civil war that has killed at least 380,000 people and made the country one of the deadliest places on earth for humanitarian aid workers.[34]

One major implication of this evidence is that reducing a government's reliance on foreign aid may be a better way to usher in a political transition. The period of political instability following the assassination of South Korea's dictator in 1979 ultimately led to a transition to democracy, which occurred largely in the absence of U.S. foreign assistance. The rapid drawdown of U.S. foreign assistance following the peace deal between the government and the FMLN did not doom democracy in El Salvador. Instead, the end of foreign aid may have facilitated democratization by forcing the government to be more accountable to its citizens. The conditions most conducive to a democratic transition may ultimately involve the reduction of U.S. assistance to dictatorial regimes.

Putting Freedom First

President Carter once declared that no force on earth could separate the United States from its commitment to enhancing human rights throughout the world:

> Our human rights policy is not a decoration. It is not something we've adopted to polish up our image abroad or to put a fresh coat of moral paint on the discredited policies of the past. Our pursuit of human rights is part of a broad effort to use our great power and our tremendous influence in the service of creating a better world, a world in which human beings can live in peace, in freedom, and with their basic needs adequately met.[35]

Foreign aid has so far proven to be a flawed instrument for advancing freedom. The strategic use of foreign assistance, the propping up of military dictatorships, costly internal wars—all of these supposed features of the Cold War persist today. The coercive effect of foreign aid is not a thing of the past, it is part of our current moment.

What has changed is that aid donors can no longer claim that they are unaware of the negative consequences of foreign aid. The question is, how will they reconcile this knowledge with the imperative to do no harm? Achieving a positive vision for the future of foreign aid involves a radical rethinking of its purposes and a renewed focus on its true beneficiaries. The pursuit of American interests abroad should be measured not only in terms of the dollars spent but also with regard to the myriad costs imposed on countries where the national interest compels the United States to intervene. The costs and benefits of the strategic use of foreign assistance must be openly weighed. Policymakers need to do the extremely difficult work of revisiting long-standing quid pro quos with countries such as Egypt, Jordan, Pakistan, and Ethiopia that fail to live up to American standards of human rights and democracy even after decades of U.S. support. Food aid and democracy promotion programs need to be judged by both their successes and their failures. Human rights abuses should be a focal point, not a talking point, in U.S. foreign assistance policy. For because we are free, we can never be indifferent to the fate of freedom elsewhere.[36]

Acknowledgments

Without President Ferdinand Marcos's fateful declaration of martial law in September 1972, I wouldn't be here and this book would not have been written. So, there's that.

This book benefited from the support of many institutions and individuals. Scholarships from the Social Sciences and Humanities Research Council of Canada and the Canadian Department of Defense's Security and Defense Forum provided much-needed support during my time at McGill University. The Program on Order, Conflict, and Violence at Yale University's MacMillan Center offered a group of engaged scholars and a rigorous environment in which to lay the foundation for this book. I am also grateful to the Yale Jackson Institute for Global Affairs for a teaching fellowship that enabled me to spend even more time surrounded by very smart people. The political science department at Western University, where I held my first faculty position, enthusiastically funded additional research, including a trip to Timor-Leste. The Bridging the Gap project at American University, funded by the Carnegie Corporation of New York, allowed me to improve on early drafts. The American Enterprise Institute's Jeane Kirkpatrick Fellowship both challenged me and gave me the intellectual freedom to complete this book.

Without the patience and guidance of Stephen Saideman, Juliet Johnson, and T. V. Paul, this project would not have evolved as it did. I am grateful for their continued support. Erica Chenoweth provided valuable insights on an early draft, which helped clarify what this book is and is not about. Thanks are also due to Stathis Kalyvas, Jason Lyall, and Nuno Monteiro for their guidance during my time at Yale, as well as to the network of OCV scholars for their insights. Nils Weidmann, in particular, should be commended for putting up with my incessant questions. Boaz Atzili, Joe Young, and the Political Violence Research Cluster at American University's School of International Service also provided feedback on portions of the manuscript. I had the pleasure of presenting my research at academic conferences and on college campuses in Canada, Singapore, South Korea, and the United States. I thank everyone who attended these talks and shared their thoughts.

Bringing this project across the finish line was a team effort. Olivier Ballou and Allison Torban brought their keen design sensibilities to the book's graphics. Heeseo Kim, Kevin Reagan, and Danni Wang contributed indispensable research assistance. Evan Abramsky went above and beyond in helping prepare the manuscript for production and memorizing the entire *Chicago Manual of Style* along the way.

I was able to write the book that I wanted to write thanks to the encouragement of Suzy Hansen, who is not only a brilliant writer but also an extremely perceptive reader. Suzy helped me find my voice. Leah Pennywark of Stanford University Press thoughtfully commented on the entire manuscript and secured excellent and constructive anonymous reviewers. Gabe Aaronson's willingness to read the manuscript at the last minute was a serious mitzvah. All of their comments made the book much stronger. I also thank Alan Harvey of Stanford University Press for his openness to projects like this.

Throughout the many years this book took to complete, I benefitted from the emotional support of my friends and colleagues. I especially appreciate the uplift I received from Stefanie von Hlatky, Reo Matsuzaki, Jonah Schulhofer-Wohl, and Joshua Shifrinson, who read chapters, tossed around ideas, and motivated me to get the book into the hands of readers. Stephen Saideman and Jim Goldgeier have been indispensable mentors and policy-relevant scholars of remarkable depth. Thank you all.

My family and their journey are my inspiration. My grandparents taught me that survival comes from inner strength. That knowledge carried me through this project. My parents never once asked about the status of this book, and for that I am incredibly grateful. My sister has always patiently listened to me complain, and this was no exception. Mishka, my glorious Pomeranian, exemplified companionship and dedication in sitting on my desk for countless hours over the past thirteen years. Most importantly, my two amazing and hilarious boys have taught me that there is so much more to life than meeting other people's deadlines. My hope is that they will grow up in a world full of freedoms. Finally, I am incredibly grateful to my husband, Keith, who believes in me more than I believe in myself. His confidence in me shaped this book in more ways than I can describe. He brought both understanding and humor while traveling with me on this journey—all the way from Dili to Washington, D.C.

REFERENCE MATTER

Appendix
Empirical Model and Data

Using a dataset of foreign aid allocations from the United States to 142 developing countries for the period of 1976 to 2016, I estimate an ordered logit model:

$$y = 0 \text{ if } y^* \leq \mu_1, \, y = 1 \text{ if } \mu_1 < y^* \leq \mu_2, \, y = 2 \text{ if } \mu_2 < y^* \leq \mu_3, \, \ldots, y = N \text{ if } \mu_N < y^* \qquad (1)$$

The odds ratio forms the parameter of interest and is reported in the tables in Chapters 2 and 6. The odds ratio is the ratio, given a one-unit increase in the covariate, of the odds of being in a higher rather than a lower category. The odds ratio is calculated as:

$$\Theta_j = \text{prob}(\text{category} \leq j) \, / \, (1 - \text{prob}((\text{category} \leq j)) \qquad (2)$$

The ordered logit model is therefore estimated as:

$$\text{Ln}(\Theta_j) = \beta_0 + \beta_1 x_1 + \beta_2 x_2 + \cdots + \beta_k x_k \qquad (3)$$

In the standard estimation of my models, all independent variables are lagged by one year to avoid reverse causality. I use the natural logarithm of all continuous variables. I also estimate the models with multiple lag structures in consideration of differing potential lagged effects and report these as appropriate.

VARIABLE	DESCRIPTION	CODING
Mass killings	Binary variable indicating 300 or more state-caused fatalities in a given country-year. *Sources*: Eck and Hultman (2007); Marshall, Gurr and Harff (2017); Schrodt and Ulfelder (2016).	0–1
State killings	Binary variable indicating 25 or more state-caused fatalities in a given country-year. *Sources*: Cingranelli, Richards, and Clay (2014); Eck and Hultman (2007); Schrodt and Ulfelder (2016).	0–1
Repression	Ordinal variable indicating the extent of human rights violations in a given country-year. *Source*: Gibney et al. (2017).	1–5
Torture	Binary variable indicating allegations of torture in a given country-year. *Source*: Cingranelli, Richards, and Clay (2014).	0–1
Military aid	Continuous variable indicating the logarithm of U.S. bilateral military aid in millions of constant (2016) dollars. *Source*: USAID (2018).	0–23.13
Economic aid	Continuous variable indicating the logarithm of U.S. bilateral economic aid in millions of constant (2016) dollars. *Source*: USAID (2018).	0–22.97
Anocracy	Binary variable indicating semiauthoritarian or anocratic regime types. *Source*: Marshall, Gurr, and Jaggers (2017).	0–1
Dictatorship	Binary variable indicating a dictatorship. *Source*: Marshall, Gurr, and Jaggers (2017).	0–1
Armed forces size	Continuous variable indicating the natural logarithm of number of military personnel. *Source*: World Bank (2018).	3.91–15.37

VARIABLE	DESCRIPTION	CODING
Govt spending	Continuous variable indicating the natural logarithm of government consumption expenditure as a percentage of GDP. *Source*: World Bank (2018).	0.4–163.58
Resource wealth	Binary variable indicating states where natural resource rents exceed 10 percent of GDP. *Source*: World Bank (2018).	0–1
Interstate war	Binary variable indicating the country's involvement in an interstate war. *Source*: Marshall (2017).	0–1
Civil war	Binary variable indicating the country's involvement in a civil war. *Source*: Marshall (2017).	0–1
GDP	Continuous variable indicating the natural logarithm of the country's GDP. *Source*: World Bank (2018).	18.92–29.88
Population	Continuous variable indicating the natural logarithm of the country's population. *Source*: World Bank (2018).	12.49–21.04

Notes

PREFACE

1. Isaiah Berlin, "A Message to the Twenty-First Century," (speech, University of Toronto, Toronto, ON, Canada, November 25, 1994).

INTRODUCTION

1. See, for instance, Christopher J. Coyne, *Doing Bad by Doing Good: Why Humanitarian Action Fails* (Stanford, CA: Stanford University Press, 2013) or Rajan Menon, *The Conceit of Humanitarian Intervention* (Oxford: Oxford University Press, 2016) for exceptions to this trend.

2. The terms *U.S. foreign assistance* and *U.S. foreign aid* are used interchangeably in this study to refer to U.S. government resources provided to foreign countries, as defined by the Foreign Assistance Act. This includes both economic and military assistance. See Foreign Assistance Act of 1961, 22 U.S.C., § 2151 et seq. (1961).

3. Harry S. Truman, "Inaugural Address" (speech), January 20, 1949.

4. Truman, "Inaugural Address."

5. Amanda McVety, *Enlightened Aid: U.S. Development as Foreign Policy in Ethiopia* (Oxford: Oxford University Press, 2012), 95.

6. McVety, *Enlightened Aid*, 94.

7. David Ekbladh, "Harry S. Truman, Development Aid, and American Foreign Policy," in *Foreign Aid and the Legacy of Harry S. Truman*, ed. Raymond H. Gezelbracht (Kirksville, MO: Truman State University Press, 2015), 65.

8. McVety, *Enlightened Aid*, 169.

9. Mark Moyar, *Aid for Elites: Building Partner Nations and Ending Poverty Through Human Capital* (Cambridge: Cambridge University Press, 2016), 110.

10. Erin C. Lentz, Stephanie Mercier, and Christopher B. Barrett, *Food Aid and Assistance Programs and the Next Farm Bill* (Washington, DC: American Enterprise Institute, 2017), 3.

11. John F. Kennedy, "Inaugural Address," January 20, 1961.

12. Foreign Assistance Act of 1961, 22 U.S.C. § 2151 et seq. (1961).

13. The OECD defines official development assistance (ODA) as "government aid designed to promote the economic development and welfare of developing countries. Aid may be provided bilaterally, from donor to recipient, or channeled through a multilateral development agency such as the United Nations or the World Bank. Aid includes grants, soft loans (where the grant element is at least 25 percent of the total) and the provision of technical assistance."

Notably, loans and credits for military purposes are excluded. See Organisation for Economic Co-operation and Development, "Net ODA," accessed January 3, 2018, https://data.oecd .org/oda/net-oda.htm.

14. John F. Kennedy, "Special Message to the Congress on Foreign Aid" (speech), March 22, 1961.

15. Carol Lancaster, *Foreign Aid: Diplomacy, Development, Domestic Politics* (Chicago: University of Chicago Press, 2007), 71.

16. Hans Morgenthau, "A Political Theory of Foreign Aid," *American Political Science Review* 56, no. 2 (1962): 301–9.

17. Anne D. Boschini and Anders Olofsgård, "Foreign Aid: An Instrument for Fighting Communism?" *Journal of Development Studies* 43, no. 4 (2007): 622–48; James Meernik and Steven C. Poe, "US Foreign Aid in the Domestic and International Environments," *International Interactions* 22, no. 1 (1996): 21–40; James Meernik, Eric L. Krueger, and Steven C. Poe, "Testing Models of U.S. Foreign Policy: Foreign Aid During and After the Cold War," *Journal of Politics* 60, no. 1 (1998): 63–85.

18. John F. Kennedy, "Remarks upon Signing the Foreign Assistance Act" (speech), August 1, 1962.

19. McVety, *Enlightened Aid*, 181.

20. Lancaster, *Foreign Aid*, 25.

21. The Harkin amendment establishing Section 116 of the Foreign Assistance Act has itself been amended numerous times to expand and clarify applicable human rights violations and establish the executive branch's reporting requirements.

22. U.S. Congress, Committee on International Relations and Committee on Foreign Relations, *Legislation on Foreign Relations Through 2002*, vol. I-A, 108th Cong., 1st sess., July 2003 (Washington, DC: Government Printing Office, 2003).

23. Nancy Qian and David Yanagizawa-Drott, "Government Distortion in Independently Owned Media: Evidence from U.S. News Coverage of Human Rights," *Journal of the European Economic Association* 15, no. 2 (2017): 463–99.

24. Nancy Qian and David Yanagizawa-Drott, "The Strategic Determinants of US Human Rights Reporting: Evidence from the Cold War," *Journal of the European Economic Association* 7, no. 2/3 (2009): 446–57.

25. Department of State to Delegation Secretary, Telegram 233405, September 21, 1976, D760355-0833, Central Foreign Policy Files, 1973-79/D-Reel Microfilm, Records Group 59: General Records of the Department of State, U.S. National Archives.

26. Nina M. Serafino, June S. Beittel, Lauren Ploch Blanchard, and Liana Rosen, "'Leahy Law' Human Rights Provisions and Security Assistance: Issue Overview," CRS Report No. 7-5700 (Washington, DC: Congressional Research Service, 2014).

27. Amnesty International, "Indonesia: Kopassus Conviction Small Step Towards Ending Impunity," September 5, 2013, https://www.amnesty.org/en/latest/news/2013/09/indonesia -kopassus-conviction-small-step-towards-ending-impunity/.

28. Declan Walsh and Helen Pidd, "US to Cut Aid to Pakistan Military Units over Human Rights Abuses," *Guardian*, October 22, 2010, https://www.theguardian.com/world /2010/oct/22/us-cut-pakistan-military-aid.

29. Elizabeth Malkin and Azam Ahmed, "U.S. Withholds $5 Million in Antidrug Aid to Mexico as Human Rights Rebuke," *New York Times*, October 19, 2015, https://www .nytimes.com/2015/10/20/world/americas/us-withholds-5-million-in-antidrug-aid-to -mexico-over-human-rights.html.

30. Andrew M. Leonard, "Getting the Leahy Law Right: How to Improve U.S. Funding of Foreign Forces," *Foreign Affairs*, June 29, 2017, https://www.foreignaffairs.com/articles /2017-06-29/getting-leahy-law-right.

31. Charles "Ken" Comer, "Leahy in Indonesia: Damned if You Do (and Even if You Don't)," *Asian Affairs: An American Review* 37, no. 2 (2010): 53–70.

32. U.S. Government Accountability Office, "Human Rights: Additional Guidance, Monitoring, and Training Could Improve Implementation of the Leahy Laws," GAO-13-866 (Washington, DC: Government Accountability Office, 2013).

33. U.S. Department of State, Office of Inspector General, "Inspection of the Bureau of African Affairs' Foreign Assistance Program Management," ISP-I-18-02 (Washington, DC: Department of State, 2017).

34. Mark S. Martins, "The Commander's Emergency Response Program," *Joint Force Quarterly*, no. 37 (2005): 46–52.

35. George W. Bush, "George W. Bush: PEPFAR Saves Millions of Lives in Africa. Keep It Fully Funded," *Washington Post*, April 7, 2017, https://www.washingtonpost.com/opinions /george-w-bush-pepfar-saves-millions-of-lives-in-africa-keep-it-fully-funded/2017/04/07 /2089fa46-1ba7-11e7-9887-1a5314b56a08_story.html.

36. President's Emergency Plan for AIDS Relief, "PEPFAR Funding," July 2016, https:// www.pepfar.gov/documents/organization/252516.pdf.

37. U.S. Department of State, *Department of State & USAID Joint Strategy on Countering Violent Extremism* (Washington, DC: Department of State, May 2016); Jessica Trisko Darden, "Compounding Violent Extremism? When Efforts to Prevent Violence Backfire," *War on the Rocks*, June 6, 2018, https://warontherocks.com/2018/06/compounding-violent -extremism-when-efforts-to-prevent-violence-backfire/.

38. Barack Obama, *National Security Strategy* (Washington, DC: White House, May 2010), 11.

39. U.S. Department of State, *Leading Through Civilian Power: The First Quadrennial Diplomacy and Development Review* (Washington, DC: Department of State, 2010), ix.

40. Curt Tarnoff and Marian Leonardo Lawson, "Foreign Aid: An Introduction to US Programs and Policy," CRS Report R40213 (Washington, DC: Congressional Research Service, 2018), 14.

41. Takashi Yamano, Harold Alderman, and Luc Christiaensen, "Child Growth, Shocks, and Food Aid in Rural Ethiopia," *American Journal of Agricultural Economics* 87, no. 2 (2005): 273–88.

42. Nathan Nunn and Nancy Qian, "U.S. Food Aid and Civil Conflict," *American Economic Review* 104, no. 6 (2014): 1630–66; David Tschirley, Cynthia Donovan, Michael T. Weber, "Food Aid and Food Markets: Lessons from Mozambique," *Food Policy* 21, no. 2 (1996): 189–209.

43. Richard Nixon, "Special Message to the Congress on Foreign Aid" (speech), May 28, 1969.

44. Foreign Aid Transparency and Accountability Act of 2016, H.R. 3766, 114th Cong. (2016).

45. Amanda Shendruk, "Many UN Agencies Are in a Precarious Position if the US Decides to Cut Foreign Aid," *Quartz*, September 29, 2018, https://qz.com/1405965/many-un -agencies-are-in-a-precarious-position-if-the-us-decides-to-cut-foreign-aid/; Felicia Schwartz and Jessica Donati, "U.S. Cuts Millions in Funding to U.N. Palestinian Agency," *Wall Street Journal*, August 31, 2018, https://www.wsj.com/articles/u-s-will-cut-millions-in-funding-to-u

-n-palestinian-agency-1535739845; Associated Press, "UN Operating Budget Cut by $285M; US Claims Credit for It," December 26, 2017, https://www.apnews.com/6558eea166404e76 9df6a93ccdb10240.

46. See James H. Lebovic and Erik Voeten, "The Politics of Shame: The Condemnation of Country Human Rights Practices in the UNHCR," *International Studies Quarterly* 50, no. 4 (2006): 861–88; H. Richard Friman, ed., *The Politics of Leverage in International Relations: Name, Shame, and Sanction* (New York: Palgrave Macmillan, 2015); Jacob Ausderan, "How Naming and Shaming Affects Human Rights Perceptions in the Shamed Country," *Journal of Peace Research* 51, no. 1 (2014): 81–95.

47. See Oona A. Hathaway, "Why Do Countries Commit to Human Rights Treaties?" *Journal of Conflict Resolution* 51, no. 4 (2007): 588–621; and James Raymond Vreeland, "Political Institutions and Human Rights: Why Dictatorships Enter into the United Nations Convention Against Torture," *International Organization* 62, no. 1 (2008): 65–101.

48. For example, Thania Sanchez, "After Ratification: The Domestic Politics of Treaty Implementation and Compliance" (PhD diss., Columbia University, 2009); Emilie M. Hafner-Burton, "Sticks and Stones: Naming and Shaming the Human Rights Enforcement Problem," *International Organization* 62, no. 4 (2008): 689–716; Eric Neumayer, "Do International Human Rights Treaties Improve Respect for Human Rights?" *Journal of Conflict Resolution* 49, no. 6 (2005): 925–53; Oona A. Hathaway, "Do Human Rights Treaties Make a Difference?" *Yale Law Journal* 111, no. 8 (2002): 1935–2042.

49. Amanda Murdie and Dursun Peksen, "Women's Rights INGO Shaming and the Government Respect for Women's Rights," *Review of International Organizations* 10, no. 1 (2015): 1–22.

50. Justin Esarey and Jacqueline H. R. DeMeritt, "Political Context and the Consequences of Naming and Shaming for Human Rights Abuse," *International Interactions* 43, no. 4 (2017): 589–618; James H. Lebovic and Erik Voeten, "The Cost of Shame: International Organizations and Foreign Aid in the Punishing of Human Rights Violators," *Journal of Peace Research* 46, no. 1 (2009): 79–97; James C. Franklin, "Shame on You: The Impact of Human Rights Criticism on Political Repression in Latin America," *International Studies Quarterly* 52, no. 1 (2008): 187–211.

51. See Michael J. Gilligan and Nathaniel H. Nesbitt, "Do Norms Reduce Torture?" *Journal of Legal Studies* 38, no. 2 (2009): 445–70; Emilie M. Hafner-Burton and Kiyoteru Tsutsui, "Human Rights in a Globalizing World: The Paradox of Empty Promises," *American Journal of Sociology* 110, no. 5 (2005): 1373–411.

52. "UN Human Rights Chief Points to 'Textbook Example of Ethnic Cleansing' in Myanmar," *United Nations News*, September 11, 2017, http://www.un.org/apps/news/story .asp?NewsID=57490#.Wcla6oyZOYY.

53. "Sergei Lavrov: Russia Rejects Use of Force in Syria," BBC News, June 9, 2012, http:// www.bbc.co.uk/news/world-middle-east-18384519.

54. Karen DeYoung, "How the U.S. Came to Abstain on a U.N. Resolution Condemning Israeli Settlements," *Washington Post*, December 28, 2016, https://www.washingtonpost.com /world/national-security/how-the-us-came-to-abstain-on-a-un-resolution-condemning -israeli-settlements/2016/12/28/fed102ee-cd38-11e6-b8a2-8c2a61b0436f_story.html; "UN Committees Adopt 10 Resolutions Against Israel in a Single Day," *Times of Israel*, November 9, 2016, https://www.timesofisrael.com/un-committees-begin-voting-on-10-resolutions-against -israel-in-a-single-day/.

55. Sonia Cardenas, "Norm Collision: Explaining the Effects of International Human Rights Pressure on State Behavior," *International Studies Review* 6, no. 2 (2004): 213–31.

56. David L. Richards, Ronald D. Gelleny, and David H. Sacko, "Money with a Mean Streak? Foreign Economic Penetration and Government Respect for Human Rights in Developing Countries," *International Studies Quarterly* 45, no. 2 (2001): 219–39; Seymour Martin Lipset, "Some Social Requisites of Democracy: Economic Development and Political Legitimacy," *American Political Science Review* 53, no. 1 (1959): 69–105.

57. Eric Neumayer, "Self-Interest, Foreign Need, and Good Governance: Are Bilateral Investment Treaty Programs Similar to Aid Allocation?" *Foreign Policy Analysis* 2, no. 3 (2006): 245–67; Eric Neumayer and Laura Spess, "Do Bilateral Investment Treaties Increase Foreign Direct Investment to Developing Countries?" *World Development* 33, no. 10 (2005): 1567–85.

58. See Emilie M. Hafner-Burton, "Right or Robust? The Sensitive Nature of Repression to Globalization," *Journal of Peace Research* 42, no. 6 (2005): 679–98.

59. William H. Meyer, "Human Rights and MNCs: Theory Versus Quantitative Analysis," *Human Rights Quarterly* 18, no. 2 (1996): 368–97; Richards, Gelleny, and Sacko, "Money with a Mean Streak?," 219–39.

60. Emilie M. Hafner-Burton, "Trading Human Rights: How Preferential Trade Agreements Influence Government Repression," *International Organization* 59, no. 3 (2005): 593–629.

61. M. Rodwan Abouharb and David L. Cingranelli, "The Human Rights Effects of World Bank Structural Adjustment, 1981–2000," *International Studies Quarterly* 50, no. 2 (2006): 233–62; L. M. McLaren, "The Effect of IMF Austerity Programs on Human Rights Violations: An Exploratory Analysis of Peru, Argentina, and Brazil" (paper, 56th Annual Meeting of the Midwest Political Science Association, Chicago, IL, April 1998); James C. Franklin, "IMF Conditionality, Threat Perception, and Political Repression: A Cross-National Analysis," *Comparative Political Studies* 30, no. 5 (1997): 576–606.

62. William H. Meyer, *Human Rights and International Political Economy in Third World Nations: Multinational Corporations, Foreign Aid, and Repression* (Westport, CT: Praeger, 1998).

63. Daniel W. Drezner, "The Hidden Hand of Economic Coercion," *International Organization* 57, no. 3 (2003): 643–59; Daniel W. Drezner, *The Sanctions Paradox: Economic Statecraft and International Relations* (Cambridge: Cambridge University Press, 1999); Dursun Peksen and A. Cooper Drury, "Economic Sanctions and Political Repression: Assessing the Impact of Coercive Diplomacy on Political Freedoms," *Human Rights Review* 10, no. 3 (2009): 393–411.

64. Dursun Peksen, "Better or Worse? The Effect of Economic Sanctions on Human Rights," *Journal of Peace Research* 46, no. 1 (2009): 59–77; Peksen and Drury, "Economic Sanctions and Political Repression," 393–411; Reed M. Wood, "'A Hand upon the Throat of the Nation': Economic Sanctions and State Repression, 1976–2001," *International Studies Quarterly* 52, no. 3 (2008): 489–513; Dursun Peksen and A. Cooper Drury, "Coercive or Corrosive: The Negative Impact of Economic Sanctions on Democracy," *International Interactions* 36, no. 3 (2010): 240–64.

65. David Cortright and George A. Lopez, eds. *Smart Sanctions: Targeting Economic Statecraft* (New York: Rowman and Littlefield, 2002); Daniel P. Ahn and Rodney D. Ludema, "Measuring Smartness: Understanding the Economic Impact of Targeted Sanctions" (U.S. Department of State, Office of the Chief Economist Working Paper 2017–01, Washington, DC, 2016); Daniel W. Drezner, "Sanctions Sometimes Smart: Targeted Sanctions in Theory and Practice," *International Studies Review* 13, no. 1 (2011): 96–108.

66. *Testimony Before the House Foreign Affairs Committee*, 115th Cong. (2018) (statement by Robert S. Ford, Ambassador of the United States (Ret)). https://docs.house.gov/meetings

/FA/FA13/20180206/106832/HHRG-115-FA13-Wstate-FordR-20180206.pdf; Nick Hopkins and Emma Beals, "How Assad Regime Controls UN Aid Intended for Syria's Children," *Guardian*, August 29, 2016, https://www.theguardian.com/world/2016/aug/29/how-assad-regime-controls-un-aid-intended-for-syrias-children; Reinoud Leenders and Kholoud Mansour, "Humanitarianism, State Sovereignty, and Authoritarian Regime Maintenance in the Syrian War," *Political Science Quarterly* 133, no. 2 (2018): 225–57.

67. Sarah Sunn Bush, *The Taming of Democracy Assistance: Why Democracy Promotion Does Not Confront Dictators* (Cambridge: Cambridge University Press, 2015), 6.

68. Woodrow Wilson, "Address Delivered at Joint Session of the Two Houses of Congress" (speech), April 2, 1917, U.S. 65th Congress, 1st Session, Senate Document 5.

69. Ronald Reagan, "Remarks at a White House Briefing for the Citizens Network for Foreign Affairs" (speech), October 21, 1987.

70. William J. Clinton, "Inaugural Address" (speech), January 20, 1993.

71. U.S. Department of State, "Memorandum from the Deputy Secretary of State (Clark) and the Under Secretary of State for Management (Kennedy) to Secretary of State Haig," in *Foreign Relations of the United States* (hereafter *FRUS*), *1981–1988*, vol. XLI, *Global Issues II*, ed. Alexander O. Poster (Washington, DC: Government Publishing Office, 2017), Document 54.

72. On the provision of foreign aid, see Marina Ottaway and Thomas Carothers, eds., *Funding Virtue: Civil Society Aid and Democracy Promotion* (Washington, DC: Carnegie Endowment for International Peace, 2000); Stephen Knack, "Does Foreign Aid Promote Democracy?" *International Studies Quarterly* 48, no. 1 (2004): 251–66; Jakob Svensson, "Aid, Growth and Democracy," *Economics and Politics* 11, no. 3 (1999): 275–97; Joseph Wright, "How Foreign Aid Can Foster Democratization in Authoritarian Regimes," *American Journal of Political Science* 53, no. 3 (2009): 552–71.

73. Inter alia, Bruce Bueno de Mesquita, James D. Morrow, Randolph M. Siverson, and Alastair Smith, "An Institutional Explanation of the Democratic Peace," *American Political Science Review* 93, no. 4 (1999): 791–807; Zeev Maoz and Bruce Russett, "Normative and Structural Causes of Democratic Peace, 1946–1986," *American Political Science Review* 87, no. 3 (1993): 624–38.

74. Michael McFaul, "Democracy Promotion as a World Value," *Washington Quarterly* 28, no. 1 (2004): 147–63.

75. Jack L. Snyder, *From Voting to Violence: Democratization and Nationalist Conflict* (New York: Norton, 2000); Emilie M. Hafner-Burton and James Ron, "Seeing Double: Human Rights Impact Through Qualitative and Quantitative Eyes," *World Politics* 61, no. 2 (2009): 360–401.

76. Human Rights Watch, "India: Events of 2016," December 19, 2016, https://www.hrw.org/world-report/2017/country-chapters/india.

77. Nita Bhalla, "India Uses Foreign Funding Law to Harass Charities: Rights Groups," Reuters, November 8, 2016, http://www.reuters.com/article/us-india-ngos-crackdown-idUSKBN134056; Amnesty International, "Hungary: Plan to Brand NGOs Has Somber Echoes of Russia's 'Foreign Agents' Law,'" April 7, 2017, https://www.amnesty.org/en/latest/news/2017/04/hungary-plan-to-brand-ngos-has-sombre-echoes-of-russias-foreign-agents-law/; Amnesty International, "Russia: Four Years of Putin's 'Foreign Agents' Law to Shackle and Silence NGOs," November 18, 2016, https://www.amnesty.org/en/latest/news/2016/11/russia-four-years-of-putins-foreign-agents-law-to-shackle-and-silence-ngos/; Ahmed Aboulenein, "Egypt Issues NGO Law, Cracking Down on Dissent," Reuters, May 29, 2017, http://www.reuters.com/article/us-egypt-rights-idUSKBN18P1OL.

78. Amanda Murdie and Tavishi Bhasin, "Aiding and Abetting: Human Rights INGOs and Domestic Protest," *Journal of Conflict Resolution* 55, no. 2 (2011): 163–91.

79. Bush, *Taming of Democracy Assistance*.

80. Christopher J. Coyne, *After War: The Political Economy of Exporting Democracy* (Stanford, CA: Stanford University Press, 2007).

81. Eric Schmitt, "Warnings of a 'Powder Keg' in Libya as ISIS Regroups," *New York Times*, March 12, 2017, https://www.nytimes.com/2017/03/21/world/africa/libya-isis.html.

82. Andrew J. Enterline and J. Michael Greig, "Perfect Storms? Political Instability in Imposed Polities and the Futures of Iraq and Afghanistan," *Journal of Conflict Resolution* 52, no. 6 (2008): 880–915.

83. Amanda Murdie and Dursun Peksen, "The Impact of Human Rights INGO Shaming on Humanitarian Intervention," *Journal of Politics* 76, no. 1 (2014): 215–28.

84. Scholars typically examine the responsiveness of foreign aid flows to human rights abuses abroad (i.e., whether human rights are a determinant of foreign aid), rather than the human rights impact of foreign aid. For example, Bethany Barratt, *Human Rights and Foreign Aid: For Love or Money?* (New York: Routledge, 2008); Clair Apodaca and Michael Stohl, "United States Human Rights Policy and Foreign Assistance," *International Studies Quarterly* 43, no. 1 (1999): 185–98; David L. Cingranelli and Thomas E. Pasquarello, "Human Rights Practices and the Distribution of US Foreign Aid to Latin American Countries," *American Journal of Political Science* 29, no. 3 (1985): 539–63.

85. Doug Johnson and Tristan Zajonc, "Can Foreign Aid Create an Incentive for Good Governance? Evidence from the Millennium Challenge Corporation" (CID Working Paper No. 11, Center for International Development, Harvard Kennedy School of Government, Harvard University, Cambridge, MA, 2006); Craig Burnside and David Dollar, "Aid, Policies, and Growth," *American Economic Review* 90, no. 4 (2000): 847–68; Thomas Carothers, *Aiding Democracy Abroad: The Learning Curve* (Washington, DC: Carnegie Endowment for International Peace, 1999); Paul Collier, *The Bottom Billion: Why the Poorest Countries Are Failing and What Can Be Done About It* (Oxford: Oxford University Press, 2007); Steven Radelet, *The Great Surge: The Ascent of the Developing World* (New York: Simon and Schuster, 2015); Jeffrey D. Sachs, *The End of Poverty: Economic Possibilities for Our Time* (New York: Penguin, 2005).

86. For example, Simeon Djankov and Marta Reynal-Querol, "Poverty and Civil War: Revisiting the Evidence," *Review of Economics and Statistics* 92, no. 4 (2010): 1035–41; William Easterly, *The White Man's Burden: Why the West's Efforts to Aid the Rest Have Done So Much Ill and So Little Good* (New York: Penguin, 2006); Sarah Kenyon Lischer, "Collateral Damage: Humanitarian Assistance as a Cause of Conflict," *International Security* 28, no. 1 (2003): 79–109; Paul Collier and Anke Hoeffler, "Aid, Policy and Peace: Reducing the Risks of Civil Conflict," *Defence and Peace Economics* 13, no. 1 (2002): 435–50; Stephen Knack, "Aid Dependence and the Quality of Governance: Cross-Country Empirical Tests," *Southern Economic Journal* 68, no. 2 (2001): 310–29; Mary B. Anderson, *Do No Harm: How Aid Can Support Peace—or War* (Boulder, CO: Lynne Rienner, 1999).

87. Christian Davenport, "State Repression and Political Order," *Annual Review of Political Science* 10, no. 1 (2007): 1–23.

88. On the former, see Amanda Murdie and Simone Dietrich, "Human Rights Shaming Through INGOs and Foreign Aid Delivery," *Review of International Organizations* 12, no. 1 (2017): 95–120; Lebovic and Voeten, "Cost of Shame"; Rhonda L. Callaway and Elizabeth G. Matthews, *Strategic US Foreign Assistance: The Battle Between Human Rights and National Security* (Burlington, VT: Ashgate, 2008); James H. Lebovic, "National Interests and US

Foreign Aid: The Carter and Reagan Years," *Journal of Peace Research* 25, no. 2 (1988): 115–35; Michael Stohl, David Carleton, and Steven E. Johnson, "Human Rights and US Foreign Assistance from Nixon to Carter," *Journal of Peace Research* 21, no. 3 (1984): 215–26. Early research on the human rights effects of foreign aid found little evidence of an impact. Patrick M. Regan, "US Economic Aid and Political Repression: An Empirical Evaluation of US Foreign Policy," *Political Research Quarterly* 48, no. 3 (1995): 613–28.

CHAPTER I

1. H. H. Gerth and C. Wright Mills, eds. and trans., *From Max Weber: Essays in Sociology* (New York: Oxford University Press, 1946).

2. Stathis N. Kalyvas, *The Logic of Violence in Civil War* (Cambridge: Cambridge University Press, 2006).

3. Similar perspectives define repression as government regulatory action directed at those challenging existing power relationships between the state and citizens. See Christian Davenport, "Assessing the Military's Influence on Political Repression," *Journal of Political and Military Sociology* 23, no. 1 (1995): 119–44; Christian Davenport, "Multi-Dimensional Threat Perception and State Repression: An Inquiry into Why States Apply Negative Sanctions," *American Journal of Political Science* 39, no. 3 (1995): 683–713.

4. United Nations, General Assembly, *Universal Declaration of Human Rights*, A/RES/217 (New York: United Nations, 1948).

5. For example, Nicholas Sambanis and Annalisa Zinn, "From Protest to Violence: An Analysis of Conflict Escalation with an Application to Self-Determination Movements" (paper, Annual Meeting of the American Political Science Association, Washington, DC, September 2005); Christopher J. Anderson, Patrick M. Regan, and Robert L. Ostergard, "Political Repression and Public Perceptions of Human Rights," *Political Research Quarterly* 55, no. 2 (2002): 439–56; Paul Rich and Richard Stubbs, *The Counter-Insurgent State: Guerrilla Warfare and State-Building in the Twentieth Century* (New York: St. Martin's Press, 1997); Scott Sigmund Gartner and Patrick M. Regan, "Threat and Repression: The Non-Linear Relationship Between Government and Opposition Violence," *Journal of Peace Research* 33, no. 3 (1996): 273–87; Davenport, "Multi-Dimensional Threat Perception"; T. David Mason and D. Krane, "The Political Economy of Death Squads: Toward a Theory of the Impact of State-Sanctioned Terror," *International Studies Quarterly* 33, no. 2 (1989): 175–98.

6. Charles Tilly, *From Mobilization to Revolution* (New York: Addison-Wesley, 1978); Sabine C. Carey, "The Use of Repression as Response to Domestic Dissent," *Political Studies* 58, no. 1 (2010): 167–86.

7. Jan Henryk Pierskalla, "Protest, Deterrence, and Escalation: The Strategic Calculus of Government Repression," *Journal of Conflict Resolution* 54, no. 1 (2010): 117–45; Sam R. Bell and Amanda Murdie, "The Apparatus for Violence: Repression, Violent Protest, and Civil War in a Cross-National Framework," *Conflict Management and Peace Science* 35, no. 4 (2016): 336–54.

8. Ted Robert Gurr, *Why Men Rebel* (Princeton, NJ: Princeton University Press, 1970).

9. See Todd Landman and Marco Larizza, "Inequality and Human Rights: Who Controls What, When, and How," *International Studies Quarterly* 53, no. 3 (2009): 715–36; Christopher Cramer, "Does Inequality Cause Conflict?" *Journal of International Development* 15, no. 4 (2003): 397–412; Mark Irving Lichbach, "An Evaluation of 'Does Economic Inequality Breed Political Conflict?' Studies," *World Politics* 41, no. 4 (1989): 431–70; Manus I.

Midlarsky, "Rulers and the Ruled: Patterned Inequality and the Onset of Mass Political Violence," *American Political Science Review* 82, no. 2 (1988): 491–509; Edward N. Muller and Mitchell A. Seligson, "Inequality and Insurgency," *American Political Science Review* 81, no. 2 (1987): 425–52; Lee Sigelman and Miles Simpson, "A Cross-National Test of the Linkage Between Economic Inequality and Political Violence," *Journal of Conflict Resolution* 2, no. 1 (1977): 105–28.

10. For example, Paul Collier and Nicholas Sambanis, eds., *Understanding Civil War: Evidence and Analysis* (Washington, DC: World Bank, 2005); Collier and Hoeffler, "Aid, Policy and Peace"; Ibrahim A. Elbadawi and Nicholas Sambanis, "How Much War Will We See? Explaining the Prevalence of Civil War," *Journal of Conflict Resolution* 46, no. 3 (2002): 307–34.

11. Michael L. Ross, "Resources and Rebellion in Aceh, Indonesia," in *Understanding Civil War: Evidence and Analysis*, ed. Paul Collier and Nicholas Sambanis (Washington, DC: World Bank, 2005), 35–58.

12. Collier and Hoeffler, "Aid, Policy and Peace."

13. Hannah Arendt, *The Origins of Totalitarianism* (New York: Schocken Books, 1951).

14. Juan J. Linz, *Totalitarianism and Authoritarian Regimes* (Boulder, CO: Lynne Rienner, 2000).

15. Larson and colleagues provide contemporary evidence of this in South Sudan. See Greg Larson, Peter Biar Ajak, and Lant Pritchett, "South Sudan's Capability Trap: Building a State with Disruptive Innovation" (CID Working Paper No. 268, Center for International Development, Harvard University Kennedy School of Government, Harvard University, Cambridge, MA, 2013).

16. For example, Tarhan Feyzioglu, Vinaya Swaroop, and Min Zhu, "A Panel Data Analysis of the Fungibility of Foreign Aid," *World Bank Economic Review* 12, no. 1 (1998): 29–58; Howard Pack and Janet Rothenberg Pack, "Foreign Aid and the Question of Fungibility," *Review of Economics and Statistics* 75, no. 2 (1993): 258–65; Rick Travis and Nikolaos Zaharadis, "Aid for Arms: The Impact of Superpower Economic Assistance on Military Spending in Sub-Saharan Africa," *International Interactions* 17, no. 3 (1992): 233–43.

17. Nasir M. Khilji and Ernest M. Zampelli, "The Fungibility of US Military and Non-Military Assistance and the Impacts on Expenditures of Major Aid Recipients," *Journal of Development Economics* 43, no. 2 (1994): 345–62; Mark McGillivray and Oliver Morrissey, "Aid Fungibility in *Assessing Aid*: Red Herring or True Concern?" *Journal of International Development* 12, no. 3 (2000): 413–28; David Dollar and Lant Pritchett, *Assessing Aid: What Works, What Doesn't, and Why* (New York: Oxford University Press, 1998); Phillippe Le Billon, "Buying Peace or Fuelling War: The Role of Corruption in Armed Conflicts," *Journal of International Development* 15, no. 4 (2003): 413–26.

18. University of Washington, Institute for Health Metrics and Evaluation, *Financing Global Health 2010: Development Assistance and Country Spending in Economic Uncertainty* (Seattle, WA: Institute for Health Metrics and Evaluation, 2010).

19. Bruce Bueno de Mesquita and Alastair Smith, "Foreign Aid and Policy Concessions," *Journal of Conflict Resolution* 51, no. 2 (2007): 254.

20. Cited in McVety, *Enlightened Aid*, 152.

21. Syed Mansoob Murshed and Somnath Sen, "Aid Conditionality and Military Expenditure Reduction in Developing Countries: Models of Asymmetric Information," *Economic Journal* 105, no. 429 (1995): 498–509.

22. Khilji and Zampelli, "Fungibility of US Military and Non-Military Assistance."

23. Daniel Yuichi Kono and Gabriella R. Montinola, "The Uses and Abuses of Foreign Aid: Development Aid and Military Spending," *Political Research Quarterly* 66, no. 3 (2012): 615–29.

24. Jan Pettersson, "Foreign Sectoral Aid Fungibility, Growth and Poverty Reduction," *Journal of International Development* 19, no. 8 (2007): 1074–98.

25. McGillivray and Morrissey, "Aid Fungibility"; Feyzioglu, Swaroop, and Zhu, "A Panel Data Analysis."

26. "What Fuels, Bread and Water Reveal About How Egypt Is Mismanaged," *Economist*, February 10, 2018, https://www.economist.com/news/middle-east-and-africa/21736552 -egyptians-are-addicted-subsidies-make-them-poorer-what-fuel-bread-and.

27. Ruth Michaelson, "'We Want Bread': Subsidy Cut Sparks Protests Across Egypt," *Guardian*, March 8, 2017, https://www.theguardian.com/world/2017/mar/08/egypt-protests -we-want-bread-subsidy-cut.

28. For example, Jean-Paul Azam, "How to Pay for the Peace? A Theoretical Framework with References to African Countries," *Public Choice* 83, no. 1/2 (1995): 173–84; Heng-Fu Zou, "A Dynamic Model of Capital and Arms Accumulation," *Journal of Economic Dynamics and Control* 19, no. 1/2 (1995): 371–93; Saadet Deger and Somnath Sen, "Military Expenditure, Aid, and Economic Development," in *Proceedings of the Annual Conference on Development Economics 1991*, ed. Lawrence H. Summers and Shekhar Shah (Washington, DC: World Bank, 1992), 159–86.

29. Palda's model includes a third option of corruption wherein rulers pocket some portion of aid funds. Filip Palda, "Can Repressive Regimes Be Moderated Through Foreign Aid?" *Public Choice* 77, no. 3 (1993): 535–50.

30. Saadet Deger and Somnath Sen, "Military Expenditure and Developing Countries," in *Handbook of Defense Economics*, vol. 1, ed. Keith Hartley and Todd Sandler (Amsterdam: Elsevier Science BV, 1995), 267–307.

31. Deger and Sen, "Military Expenditure, Aid, and Economic Development," 298.

32. Martin C. McGuire, "US Assistance, Israeli Allocation, and the Arms Race in the Middle East: An Analysis of Three Interdependent Resource Allocation Processes," *Journal of Conflict Resolution* 26, no. 2 (1982): 199–235; Kono and Montinola, "Uses and Abuses of Foreign Aid," 624.

33. Paul Collier and Anke Hoeffler, "Unintended Consequences: Does Aid Promote Arms Races?" *Oxford Bulletin of Economics and Statistics* 69, no. 1 (2007): 1–27.

34. Nikolaos Zahariadis, Rick Travis, and Paul F. Diehl, "Military Substitution Effects from Foreign Economic Aid: Buying Guns with Foreign Butter?" *Social Science Quarterly* 71, no. 4 (1990): 774–85.

35. Peter Gill, *Famine and Foreigners: Ethiopia Since Live Aid* (Oxford: Oxford University Press, 2010); Central Intelligence Agency, Directorate of Intelligence, Office of African and Latin American Analysis, "Ethiopia: Political and Security Impact of the Drought," ALA 85-10039, April 3, 1985, https://www.cia.gov/library/readingroom/docs/CIA-RDP86T00589 R000200160004-5.pdf.

36. McVety, *Enlightened Aid*, 196.

37. Haley Swedlund, *The Development Dance: How Donors and Recipients Negotiate the Delivery of Foreign Aid* (Ithaca, NY: Cornell University Press, 2017).

38. Christian Davenport, "State Repression and the Tyrannical Peace," *Journal of Peace Research* 44, no. 4 (2007): 485–504; Christian Davenport and David A. Armstrong, "Democracy and the Violation of Human Rights: A Statistical Analysis from 1976 to 1996," *American Journal of Political Science* 48, no. 3 (2004): 538–54; Håvard Hegre, Tania Ellingsen, Scott

Gates, and Nils Petter Gleditsch, "Towards a Democratic Civil Peace? Democracy, Political Change, and Civil War, 1816–1992," *American Political Science Review* 95, no. 1 (2001): 33–48.

39. Christian Davenport, *State Repression and the Domestic Democratic Peace* (Cambridge: Cambridge University Press, 2007).

40. James C. Scott, *Weapons of the Weak: Everyday Forms of Peasant Resistance* (New Haven, CT: Yale University Press, 1985).

41. Edward N. Muller, "Income Inequality, Regime Repressiveness, and Political Violence," *American Sociological Review* 50, no. 1 (1985): 47–61; Muller and Seligson, "Inequality and Insurgency."

42. Gartner and Regan, "Threat and Repression"; Helen Fein, "More Murder in the Middle: Life-Integrity Violations and Democracy in the World, 1987," *Human Rights Quarterly* 17, no. 1 (1995): 170–91; Hegre et al., "Towards a Democratic Civil Peace"; Patrick M. Regan and Errol A. Henderson, "Democracy, Threats and Political Repression in Developing Countries: Are Democracies Internally Less Violent?" *Third World Quarterly* 23, no. 1 (2002): 119–36.

43. For example, Lars-Erik Cederman, Simon Hug, and Lutz F. Krebs, "Democratization and Civil War: Empirical Evidence," *Journal of Peace Research* 47, no. 4 (2010): 377–94; Patrick M. Regan and Sam R. Bell, "Changing Lanes or Stuck in the Middle: Why Are Anocracies More Prone to Civil Wars?" *Political Research Quarterly* 63, no. 4 (2010): 747–59; James Raymond Vreeland, "The Effect of Political Regime on Civil War: Unpacking Anocracy," *Journal of Conflict Resolution* 52, no. 3 (2008): 401–25; James D. Fearon and David D. Laitin, "Ethnicity, Insurgency, and Civil War," *American Political Science Review* 97, no. 1 (2003): 75–90; Edward Mansfield and Jack Snyder, "Democratic Transitions, Institutional Strength, and War," *International Organization* 56, no. 2 (2002): 297–337.

44. Robert I. Rotberg, *State Failure and State Weakness in a Time of Terror* (Washington, DC: Brookings Institution Press, 2003).

45. Mason and Krane, "Political Economy of Death Squads."

46. Aaron Zelin, "The Islamic State of Iraq and Syria Has a Consumer Protection Office," *Atlantic*, June 13, 2014, https://www.theatlantic.com/international/archive/2014/06/the-isis-guide-to-building-an-islamic-state/372769/.

47. James A. Piazza, "Incubators of Terror: Do Failed and Failing States Promote Transnational Terrorism?" *International Studies Quarterly* 52, no. 3 (2008): 469–88.

48. Faisal Z. Ahmed and Eric D. Werker, "Aid and the Rise and Fall of Conflict in the Muslim World," *Quarterly Journal of Political Science* 10, no. 2 (2015): 155–86.

49. Travis and Zahariadis, "Aid for Arms"; Collier and Hoeffler, "Unintended Consequences."

50. Eliana Balla and Gina Yannitell Reinhardt, "Giving and Receiving Foreign Aid: Does Conflict Count?" *World Development* 36, no. 12 (2008): 2566–85; Collier and Hoeffler, "Unintended Consequences."

51. Michael E. Flynn, "Before the Dominos Fall: Regional Conflict, Donor Interests and US Foreign Aid," *Conflict Management and Peace Science,* June 16, 2017. 1–19.

52. Böhnke and Zürcher find that postconflict foreign assistance neither increases perceived security nor fosters more positive attitudes toward international actors. Jan Rasmus Böhnke and Christoph Zürcher, "Aid, Minds and Hearts: The Impact of Aid in Conflict Zones," *Conflict Management and Peace Science* 30, no. 5 (2013): 411–32.

53. Nunn and Qian, "U.S. Food Aid": Neil Narang, "Assisting Uncertainty: How Humanitarian Aid Can Inadvertently Prolong Civil War," *International Studies Quarterly,* 59,

no. 1 (2015): 184–95. De Ree and Nillesen, by contrast, find that foreign assistance has decreased civil war duration in sub-Saharan Africa. Joppe de Ree and Eleonora Nillesen, "Aiding Violence or Peace? The Impact of Foreign Aid on the Risk of Civil Conflict in Sub-Saharan Africa," *Journal of Development Economics* 88, no. 2 (2009): 301–13.

54. Oeindrila Dube and Suresh Naidu, "Bases, Bullets and Ballots: The Effect of US Military Aid on Political Conflict in Colombia," *Journal of Politics* 77, no. 1 (2015): 249–67.

55. Benjamin Crost, Joseph Felter, and Patrick Johnston, "Aid Under Fire: Development Projects and Civil Conflict," *American Economic Review* 104, no. 6 (2014): 1833–56; Reed M. Wood and Christopher Sullivan, "Doing Harm by Doing Good? The Negative Externalities of Humanitarian Aid Provision During Civil Conflict," *Journal of Politics* 77, no. 3 (2015): 736–48.

CHAPTER 2

1. Morgenthau, "Political Theory of Foreign Aid."

2. Edward T. Rowe, "Aid and Coups d'Etat: Aspect of the Impact of American Military Assistance Programs in the Less Developed Countries," *International Studies Quarterly* 18, no. 2 (1974): 239–55. For an overview of the Mali 2012 coup, see Moyar, *Aid for Elites*, 1–4; Joshua E. Keating, "Trained in the USA," *Foreign Policy*, March 28, 2012, http://www.foreignpolicy.com/articles/2012/03/28/trained_in_the_usa.

3. USAID, *US Overseas Loans and Grants: Obligations and Loan Authorizations, July 1, 1945–September 30, 2016*, accessed March 31, 2018, https://explorer.usaid.gov/reports.html. Aid allocations are logged in order to correct for the skewed distribution. 1 is added to the total amount of aid to avoid losing zeros as observations.

4. Ben Kiernan, *Blood and Soil: A World History of Genocide and Extermination from Sparta to Darfur* (New Haven, CT: Yale University Press, 2007); Barbara Harff, "No Lessons Learned from the Holocaust? Assessing Risks of Genocide and Political Mass Murder Since 1955," *American Political Science Review* 97, no. 1 (2003): 57–73; Barbara Harff and Ted Robert Gurr, "Toward Empirical Theory of Genocides and Politicides: Identification and Measurement of Cases Since 1945," *International Studies Quarterly* 32, no. 3 (1988): 359–71.

5. Valentino and colleagues set a lower bound of 50,000 fatalities incurred over a period of less than five years and identify thirty-one episodes of mass killings during wartime for the period 1945 to 2000. Alternatively, Querido employs a limit of 1,000 or more civilians killed in the course of combat during an intrastate conflict. Benjamin Valentino, Paul Huth, and Dylan Balch-Lindsay, "'Draining the Sea': Mass Killing and Guerrilla Warfare," *International Organization* 58, no. 2 (2004): 375–407. See also Joan M. Esteban, Massimo Morelli, and Dominic Rohner, "Strategic Mass Killings," *Journal of Political Economy* 123, no. 5 (2015): 1087–132; Chyanda M. Querido, "State-Sponsored Mass Killing in African Wars—Greed or Grievance?" *International Advances in Economic Research* 15, no. 3 (2009): 351–61.

6. For this measure, I use the Uppsala Conflict Data Project's One-Sided Violence Dataset (1989–2016), which captures the intentional and direct killings of civilians as a result of armed force. This dataset is based on over 350,000 news reports that were individually coded into an events dataset and subsequently aggregated into annual measures. For a country to be included, more than twenty-five civilians must have been killed by state forces in a given year. I also use the Political Instability Task Force (PITF) Worldwide Atrocities Dataset and the PITF GenoPoliticides Dataset to generate a comprehensive estimate of the number of state-caused civilian fatalities. See Kristine Eck and Lisa Hultman, "One-Sided Violence Against Civilians in War: Insights from New Fatality Data," *Journal of Peace Research* 44,

no. 2 (2007): 233–46; Philip A. Schrodt and Jay Ulfelder, *Political Instability Task Force World-wide Atrocities Dataset*, version 1.1b (September 12, 2016).

7. See Reed M. Wood and Mark Gibney, "The Political Terror Scale (PTS): A Re-introduction and a Comparison to CIRI," *Human Rights Quarterly* 32, no. 2 (2010): 367–400; Mark Gibney et al., *The Political Terror Scale, 1976–2016*, October 11, 2017, http://www.political terrorscale.org.

8. United Nations, "Convention Against Torture and Other Cruel, Inhuman or Degrad-ing Treatment or Punishment" in *United Nations Treaty Series*, vol. 1465 (New York: United Nations, 1984): 85.

9. David L. Cingranelli, David L. Richards, and K. Chad Clay, "The CIRI Human Rights Dataset," version 2014.04.14, http://www.humanrightsdata.com.

10. Faisal Z. Ahmed, "Does Foreign Aid Harm Political Rights? Evidence from U.S. Aid," *Quarterly Journal of Political Science* 11, no. 2 (2016): 183–217.

11. Moyar, *Aid for Elites*.

12. Mariya Omelicheva, Brittnee Carter, and Luke B. Campbell, "Military Aid and Human Rights: Assessing the Impact of U.S. Security Assistance Programs," *Political Science Quarterly* 132, no. 1 (2017): 140–41.

13. Omelicheva, Carter, and Campbell, "Military Aid and Human Rights," 138, 141.

14. See Carol Atkinson, *Military Soft Power: Public Diplomacy Through Military Educa-tional Exchanges* (Lanham, MD: Rowman and Littlefield, 2014).

15. Omelicheva, Carter, and Campbell, "Military Aid and Human Rights," 128.

16. In a direct test of the cooption hypothesis, Taydas and Peksen find that only social welfare spending, not general government spending or military expenditure, decreases the likelihood of civil war onset. See Zaynep Taydas and Dursen Peksen, "Can States Buy Peace? Social Welfare Spending and Civil Conflicts," *Journal of Peace Research* 49, no. 2 (2012): 273–87.

17. See Christian Davenport, "The Weight of the Past: Exploring Lagged Determinants of Political Repression," *Political Research Quarterly* 49, no. 2 (1996): 377–403.

CHAPTER 3

1. Mari Alkatiri, "Statement Submitted by Mari Alkatiri," in *East Timor: Five Years After the Indonesian Invasion, Testimony Presented at the Decolonization Committee of the United Nations' General Assembly, October 1980*, ed. James W. Clay (Cambridge, MA: Cultural Sur-vival, 1980), 9.

2. Robert Cribb, "How Many Deaths? Problems in the Statistics of Massacre in Indone-sia (1965–1966) and East Timor (1975–1980)," in *Violence in Indonesia*, ed. Ingrid Wessel and Georgia Wimhöfer (Hamburg: Abera, 2001); Central Intelligence Agency, Center for the Study of Intelligence, "The Lessons of the September 30 Affair," July 2, 1996, https://www .cia.gov/library/center-for-the-study-of-intelligence/kent-csi/vol14no2/html/v14i2a02p _0001.htm; Kai Thaler, "Foreshadowing Future Slaughter: From the Indonesian Killings of 1965–1966 to the 1974–1999 Genocide in East Timor," *Genocide Studies and Prevention* 7, no. 2/3 (2012): 204–22.

3. Central Intelligence Agency, "The Situation in Indonesia," August 15, 1966, https://www .cia.gov/library/readingroom/docs/CIA-RDP79T00826A001100010028-3.pdf.

4. This unprecedented development foreshadowed U.S. support for Pakistan in its crack-down in East Pakistan (now Bangladesh) in 1971. U.S. Department of State, "Editorial Note," in *FRUS, 1964–1968*, vol. XXVI, *Indonesia; Malaysia-Singapore; Philippines*, ed. Edward C.

Keefer (Washington, DC: Government Printing Office, 2000), Document 162; Central Intelligence Agency, Center for the Study of Intelligence, "Lessons of the September 30 Affair." On Pakistan, see Gary J. Bass, *The Blood Telegram: Nixon, Kissinger, and a Forgotten Genocide* (New York: Alfred A. Knopf, 2013).

5. Until 1999, when the police became institutionally separate from the military, the armed forces of Indonesia were known as the Angkatan Bersenjata Republik Indonesia. I use the more recent designation as the Tentara Nasional Indonesia for the entire period.

6. Ben Kiernan, *Genocide and Resistance in Southeast Asia: Documentation, Denial, and Justice in Cambodia and East Timor* (New York: Routledge, 2008); Ben Kiernan, "The Demography of Genocide in Southeast Asia: The Death Tolls in Cambodia, 1975–1979 and East Timor, 1975–1980," *Critical Asian Studies* 35, no. 4 (2003): 585–97; Thaler, "Foreshadowing Future Slaughter."

7. R. William Liddle, "Polity and Economy in Suharto's Indonesia," *Crossroads: An Interdisciplinary Journal of Southeast Asian Studies* 1, no. 3 (1983): 39.

8. See M. C. Ricklefs, *A History of Modern Indonesia, c. 1300 to the Present* (Bloomington: Indiana University Press, 1981).

9. For further details, see Leonard C. Sebastian, *Realpolitik Ideology: Indonesia's Use of Military Force* (Singapore: Utopia Press, 2006) and Salim Said, *Legitimizing Military Rule: Indonesian Armed Forces Ideology, 1958–2000*, trans. Toenggoel P. Siagian (Jakarta: Pustaka Sinar Harapan, 2006).

10. See John Roosa, *Pretext for Mass Murder: The September 30th Movement and Suharto's Coup d'Etat in Indonesia* (Madison: University of Wisconsin Press, 2006).

11. Central Intelligence Agency, Directorate of Intelligence, "Weekly Summary Special Report: The New Order in Indonesia," No. 0302/67A, August 11, 1967, https://www.cia.gov /library/readingroom/docs/CIA-RDP79-00927A005900080002-0.pdf.

12. Ikrar Nusa Bhakti, Sri Yanuarti, and Mochamad Nurhasim, "Military Politics, Ethnicity and Conflict in Indonesia" (CRISE Working Paper No. 62, Centre for Research on Inequality, Human Security and Ethnicity, University of Oxford, Oxford, UK, 2009), 9.

13. Central Intelligence Agency, Directorate of Intelligence, "Weekly Summary Special Report: Suharto's Indonesia," May 15, 1970, https://www.cia.gov/library/readingroom/docs /CIA-RDP85T00875R001500020025-3.pdf.

14. U.S. Department of State, "Note to the National Security Council by the Executive Secretary (Lay)," in *FRUS, 1952–1954, East Asia and the Pacific*, vol. XII, part 1, ed. David W. Mabon (Washington, DC: Government Publishing Office, 1984), Document 428; U.S. Department of State, "Draft Position Paper Prepared in the Department of State," in *FRUS, 1952–1954*, vol. XII, part 1, Document 432.

15. Donald Hindley, "Foreign Aid to Indonesia and Its Political Implications," *Pacific Affairs* 36, no. 2 (1963): 112.

16. Amount reported in constant 2016 dollars, as per USAID, *US Overseas Loans and Grants*. See U.S. Department of State, "The Secretary of State to the Embassy in Indonesia," in *FRUS, 1952–1954, East Asia and the Pacific*, vol. XII, part 2, ed. Carl N. Raether and Harriet D. Schwar (Washington, DC: Government Printing Office, 1987), Document 203; Mutual Defense Assistance Act of 1949, 22 U.S.C. § 1571 et seq. (1949).

17. U.S. Department of State, "The Ambassador in Indonesia (Cochran) to the Department of State," in *FRUS, 1952–1954*, vol. XII, part 2, Document 193.

18. This section was amended in 1973. See Dianne E. Rennack, "Foreign Assistance Act of 1961: Authorizations and Corresponding Appropriations," CRS Report for Congress R40089 (Washington, DC: Congressional Research Service, 2010).

19. USAID, *US Overseas Loans and Grants*, constant 2016 dollars.

20. U.S. Department of State, "Telegram from the Embassy in Indonesia to the Department of State," in *FRUS, 1961–1963*, vol. XXIII, *Southeast Asia* (Washington, DC: Government Printing Office, 1994), Document 143.

21. Bradley R. Simpson, *Economists with Guns: Authoritarian Development and U.S.-Indonesian Relations, 1960–1968* (Stanford, CA: Stanford University Press, 2008), 97.

22. U.S. Department of State, "Memorandum from the Joint Chiefs of Staff to Secretary of Defense McNamara," in *FRUS, 1961–1963*, vol. XXIII, Document 288; Ricklefs, *History of Modern Indonesia*, 264.

23. U.S. Department of State, "Memorandum from the Under Secretary of State (Ball) to President Kennedy," in *FRUS, 1961–1963*, vol. XXIII, Document 291.

24. U.S. Department of State, "Memorandum from Michael V. Forrestal of the National Security Council Staff to President Kennedy," in *FRUS, 1961–1963*, vol. XXIII, Document 296.

25. U.S. Department of State, "Memorandum from the Assistant Administrator for the Far East, Agency for International Development (Janow) to Michael V. Forrestal of the National Security Council Staff," in *FRUS, 1961–1963*, vol. XXIII, Document 313.

26. U.S. Department of State, "Summary of President Kennedy's Remarks to the 496th Meeting of the National Security Council," in *FRUS, 1961–1963*, vol. VIII, *National Security Policy*, ed. David W. Mabon (Washington, DC: Government Printing Office, 1996), Document 69.

27. Simpson, *Economists with Guns*, 97.

28. U.S. Department of State, "Memorandum from Robert W. Komer of the National Security Council Staff to President Kennedy," in *FRUS, 1961–1963*, vol. XXIII, Document 312.

29. Franklin D. Roosevelt, "Executive Order 6581 Creating the Export-Import Bank of Washington," February 2, 1934; U.S. Congress, Export-Import Bank Act of 1945, 12 U.S.C. § 635 (1945).

30. Ricklefs, *History of Modern Indonesia*, 268.

31. This loan, agreed to in September 1956 but not ratified by the Indonesian parliament until February 1958, featured a 2.5 percent interest rate and a twelve-year term. Guy J. Pauker, "The Soviet Challenge in Indonesia," *Foreign Affairs*, July 1962, https://www.foreignaffairs .com/articles/asia/1962-07-01/soviet-challenge-indonesia; Ragna Boden, "Cold War Economics: Soviet Aid to Indonesia," *Journal of Cold War Studies* 10, no. 3 (2008): 115.

32. Hindley, "Foreign Aid to Indonesia," 108–9; Pauker, "Soviet Challenge in Indonesia," 613–14; Ricklefs, *History of Modern Indonesia*, 257.

33. Boden, "Cold War Economics," 120.

34. Central Intelligence Agency, Directorate of National Intelligence, "Intelligence Memorandum: Possible Resumption of Soviet Aid to Indonesia," ER IM 71–190, October 1970, https://www.cia.gov/library/readingroom/docs/CIA-RDP85T00875R00170002 0044-0.pdf.

35. U.S. Department of State, "Memorandum from the Joint Chiefs of Staff to Secretary of Defense McNamara," in *FRUS, 1961–1963*, vol. XXIII, Document 198.

36. U.S. Department of Defense, Department of the Air Force, Office of the Director, "Soviet Military Buildup in Indonesia," November 9, 1962, https://www.cia.gov/library /readingroom/docs/CIA-RDP80B01676R000100140018-9.pdf.

37. U.S. Department of State, "Summary of President Kennedy's Remarks," Document 69.

38. U.S. Department of State, "Memorandum of Conversation," in *FRUS, 1961–1963*, vol. XXIII, Document 145.

39. Hindley, "Foreign Aid to Indonesia," 111; Pauker, "Soviet Challenge in Indonesia," 616.

40. Central Intelligence Agency, Directorate of National Intelligence, "Intelligence Memorandum."

41. Hindley, "Foreign Aid to Indonesia," 114.

42. Hindley, "Foreign Aid to Indonesia," 114.

43. William N. Mott, *Soviet Military Assistance: An Empirical Perspective* (Westport, CT: Praeger, 2001).

44. U.S. Department of State, "Memorandum of Conversation," in *FRUS, 1961–1963*, vol. XXIII, Document 258; U.S. Department of State, "Memorandum from Attorney General Kennedy to the President's Special Assistant for National Security Affairs (Bundy)," in *FRUS, 1961–1963*, vol. XXIII, Document 277; Ricklefs, *History of Modern Indonesia*, 258.

45. U.S. Department of State, "Memorandum from the Assistant Secretary of State for Far Eastern Affairs (Parsons) to the Deputy Under Secretary of State for Political Affairs (Hare)," in *FRUS, 1961–1963*, vol. XXIII, Document 146; U.S. Department of State, "Memorandum of Conversation," in *FRUS, 1961–1963*, vol. XXIII, Document 172; U.S. Department of State, "Telegram from the Department of State to the Embassy in Indonesia," in *FRUS, 1961–1963*, vol. XXIII, Document 209; U.S. Department of State, "Telegram from the Department of State to the Embassy in Indonesia," in *FRUS, 1961–1963*, vol. XXIII, Document 210.

46. U.S. Department of State, "Summary of President Kennedy's Remarks," Document 69.

47. U.S. Department of State, "Memorandum from the Director of Central Intelligence's Assistant (Knoche) to Director of Central Intelligence McCone," in *FRUS, 1961–1963*, vol. XXIII, Document 269.

48. Central Intelligence Agency, Office of the Director, "Executive Memorandum: U.S. Policy Toward Indonesia," ER 62-5895, August 17, 1962, https://www.cia.gov/library/readingroom/docs/CIA-RDP80M01048A000100100071-9.pdf.

49. According to the UCDP/PRIO Armed Conflict Dataset, civil war between the TNI and the Free Papua Movement occurred in 1967–1969, 1976–1978, 1981, and 1984. See Lotta Themnér and Peter Wallensteen, "Armed Conflict, 1946–2011," *Journal of Peace Research* 49, no. 4 (2012): 565–75.

50. Unless flown along with, and below, the Indonesian flag.

51. Central Intelligence Agency, Office of National Estimates, "Memorandum for the Director: Probable Repercussions of US Aid Cuts to Indonesia," January 7, 1964, https://www.cia.gov/library/readingroom/docs/CIA-RDP79R00904A001000050036-9.pdf.

52. Central Intelligence Agency, Office of National Estimates, "Memorandum for the Director."

53. U.S. Department of State, "Memorandum from President Nixon to his Assistant for National Security Affairs (Kissinger)," in *FRUS, 1969–1976*, vol. XX, *Southeast Asia, 1969–1972*, ed. Daniel J. Lawler (Washington, DC: Government Printing Office, 2006), Document 290.

54. USAID, *US Overseas Loans and Grants*, constant 2016 dollars.

55. U.S. Department of State, "Memorandum for the President's File," in *FRUS, 1969–1976*, vol. XX, Document 321.

56. U.S. Department of State, "Telegram from the Embassy in Indonesia to the Department of State," in *FRUS, 1969–1976*, vol. XX, Document 329.

57. U.S. Department of State, "Memorandum of Conversation," in *FRUS, 1969–1976*, vol. XX, Document 308.

58. See U.S. Department of State, "Memorandum of Conversation," in *FRUS, 1969–1976*, vol. XX, Document 310; U.S. Department of State, "Memorandum for the Record," in *FRUS, 1969–1976*, vol. XX, Document 281; U.S. Department of State, "Memorandum of Conversation," in *FRUS, 1969–1976*, vol. XX, Document 288.

59. U.S. Department of State, "Telegram from the Embassy in Indonesia to the Department of State"; U.S. Department of State, "Memorandum of Conversation, Washington, May 15, 1973, 4:30 P.M.," in *FRUS, 1969–1976*, vol. E-12, *Documents on East and Southeast Asia, 1973–1976*, ed. Bradley Lynn Coleman, David Goldman, and David Nickles (Washington, DC: Government Printing Office, 2010), Document 97; U.S. Department of State, "Letter from President Nixon to Indonesian President Suharto, Washington, July 12, 1973," in *FRUS, 1969–1976*, vol. E-12, Document 98.

60. U.S. Department of State, "Memorandum of Conversation," in *FRUS, 1969–1976*, vol. XX, Document 303.

61. In historical (1970) dollars, the increase was from around $4.5 million to $18 million. See U.S. Department of State, "Memorandum from John H. Holdridge and Richard T. Kennedy of the National Security Council Staff to the President's Assistant for National Security Affairs (Kissinger)," in *FRUS, 1969–1976*, vol. XX, Document 314.

62. U.S. Department of State, "Memorandum from the Executive Secretary of the Department of State (Eliot) to the President's Assistant for National Security Affairs (Kissinger)," in *FRUS, 1969–1976*, vol. XX, Document 318.

63. U.S. Department of State, "Memorandum of Conversation, Washington, January 22, 1974, 1100–1130," in *FRUS, 1969–1976*, vol. E-12, Document 104.

64. U.S. Department of State, "Backchannel Message 179 from the Ambassador to Indonesia (Newsom) to W. R. Smyser of the National Security Council Staff, Jakarta, January 13, 1975, 1139Z," in *FRUS, 1969–1976*, vol. E-12, Document 116.

65. U.S. Department of State, "Memorandum from the President's Assistant for National Security Affairs (Kissinger) to President Nixon, Washington, undated," in *FRUS, 1969–1976*, vol. E-12, Document 110. For more details, see also Department of State, "Memorandum from Charles A. Cooper of the National Security Council Staff to Secretary of State Kissinger, Washington, November 24, 1973," in *FRUS, 1969–1976*, vol. E-12, Document 101; U.S. Department of State, "Memorandum from Charles A. Cooper of the National Security Council Staff to Secretary of State Kissinger, Washington, December 4, 1973," in *FRUS, 1969–1976*, vol. E-12, Document 102; U.S. Department of State, "Telegram 47882 from the Department of State to the Embassy in Indonesia, March 9, 1974, 0010Z," in *FRUS, 1969–1976*, vol. E-12, Document 107.

66. U.S. Embassy Jakarta to Department of State, Telegram 16378, December 20, 1976, D760470-0565, Central Foreign Policy Files, 1973-79/D-Reel Microfilm, Record Group 59: General Records of the Department of State, U.S. National Archives.

67. U.S. Department of State, "Memorandum from the President's Assistant for National Security Affairs (Kissinger) to President Ford, Washington, May 7, 1975," in *FRUS, 1969–1976*, vol. E-12, Document 122.

68. "Ex-Im Bank Approves Loan of $292.5 Million for Indonesia Refinery," *Wall Street Journal*, October 1, 1982, 43.

69. "Ex-Im Bank Approves Loan."

70. "Ex-Im Bank Sets Loan to Indonesia for Parts Supplied by Boeing Unit," *Wall Street Journal*, March 9, 1984, 15.

71. USAID, *US Overseas Loans and Grants*; U.S. Department of State, "Memorandum from the President's Assistant for National Security Affairs (Kissinger) to President Nixon," in *FRUS, 1969–1976*, vol. XX, Document 317.

72. U.S. Department of State, "Backchannel Message 179," Document 116. See also U.S. Department of State, "Telegram 026805 from the Department of State to the Embassy in Indonesia, February 6, 1975, 0006Z," in *FRUS, 1969–1976*, vol. E-12, Document 117; U.S. Department of State, "Telegram 194779 from the Department of State to the Embassies in Indonesia and Australia, August 16, 1975, 0028Z," in *FRUS, 1969–1976*, vol. E-12, Document 128; U.S. Department of State, "Telegram 2022 from the Embassy in Jakarta to the Department of State, February 19, 1975, 0001Z," in *FRUS, 1969–1976*, vol. E-12, Document 119.

73. U.S. Department of State, "Memorandum of Conversation, Washington, June 29, 1976," in *FRUS, 1969–1976*, vol. E-12, Document 160.

74. U.S. Embassy Jakarta to Department of State, Telegram 06757, May 21, 1976, D760198-0367, Central Foreign Policy Files, 1973-79/D-Reel Microfilm, Record Group 59: General Records of the Department of State, U.S. National Archives.

75. Amounts reported in historical (1976) dollars. See U.S. Embassy Jakarta to Department of State, Telegram 01308, January 29, 1976, D760034-0019, Central Foreign Policy Files, 1973-79/D-Reel Microfilm, Record Group 59: General Records of the Department of State, U.S. National Archives.

76. Bradley R. Simpson, "Denying the 'First Right': The United States, Indonesia, and the Ranking of Human Rights by the Carter Administration, 1976–1980," *International History Review* 32, no. 4 (2009): 809.

77. Simpson, "Denying the 'First Right,'" 807.

78. Geoffrey Robinson, *"If You Leave Us Here, We Will Die": How Genocide Was Stopped in East Timor* (Princeton, NJ: Princeton University Press, 2010), 62.

79. Jacques Bertrand, *Nationalism and Ethnic Conflict in Indonesia* (Cambridge: Cambridge University Press, 2004), 149.

80. Robinson, *"If You Leave Us Here,"* 59.

81. U.S. Department of State, "Minutes of the Secretary of State's Staff Meeting, Washington, December 23, 1975, 8:12 A.M.," in *FRUS, 1969–1976*, vol. E-12, Document 147.

82. U.S. Department of State, "Memorandum from Thomas J. Barnes of the National Security Council Staff to the President's Assistant for National Security Affairs (Scowcroft), Washington, December 9, 1975," in *FRUS, 1969–1976*, vol. E-12, Document 143.

83. Ben Kiernan, "War, Genocide, and Resistance in East Timor, 1975–99: Comparative Reflections on Cambodia," in *War and State Terror: The United States, Japan, and the Asia-Pacific in the Long Twentieth Century*, ed. Mark Selden and Alvin Y. So (Lanham, MD: Rowman and Littlefield, 2003), 210.

84. Bertrand, *Nationalism and Ethnic Conflict*, 138.

85. Michele Turner, *Telling East Timor: Personal Testimonies, 1942–1992* (Kensington, Australia: New South Wales University Press, 1992).

86. U.S. Embassy Jakarta to Department of State, Telegram 13695, January 29, 1976, D760393-0209, Central Foreign Policy Files, 1973-79/D-Reel Microfilm, Record Group 59: General Records of the Department of State, U.S. National Archives.

87. Comissão de Acolhimento, Verdade e Reconciliação de Timor-Leste, *Chega! The Final Report of the Commission for Reception, Truth and Reconciliation in Timor-Leste* (Dili, Timor-Leste: Comissão de Acolhimento, Verdade e Reconciliação de Timor-Leste, 2005).

88. Kiernan, "War, Genocide, and Resistance," 221; Robinson, *"If You Leave Us Here,"* 57.

89. Amembassy Jakarta to the Secstate, "[Redacted] Views on East Timor Developments," Jakarta, cable 14397, September 9, 1983, in *Suharto: A Declassified Documentary Obit*, ed. Bradley Simpson (Washington, DC: National Security Archive, 2008); Amembassy to Secstate, "Current Developments in East Timor," Jakarta, cable 15303, September 23, 1983, in Simpson, *Suharto*, https://nsarchive2.gwu.edu/NSAEBB/NSAEBB242/index.htm.

90. Robinson, *"If You Leave Us Here,"* 69.

91. Bertrand, *Nationalism and Ethnic Conflict*, 150.

92. Robinson, *"If You Leave Us Here,"* 66–68; Centre for Strategic and International Studies, *Kliping Tentang Peristiwa Dili, Timor Timur, November 12, 1991* (Jakarta: Centre for Strategic and International Studies, 1992).

93. East Timor Action Network, "The Santa Cruz Massacre: 12 November 1991," ETAN .org, 2012, http://www.etan.org/timor/SntaCRUZ.htm.

94. Bertrand, *Nationalism and Ethnic Conflict*, 150.

95. The reemergence of the Free Aceh Movement, which previously had been active around the 1977 elections, was attributed to economic dislocation in the region as well as government attempts to crack down on the local marijuana trade.

96. Human Rights Watch, "Indonesia: Human Rights Abuses in Aceh," December 27, 1990, https://www.hrw.org/report/1990/12/27/indonesia-human-rights-abuses-aceh.

97. Kirsten E. Schulze, "Insurgency and Counter-insurgency: Strategy in the Aceh Conflict," in *Verandah of Violence: Aceh's Contested Place in Indonesia*, ed. Anthony Reid (Singapore: Singapore University Press, 2006), 257.

98. Patrick Barron, Samuel Clark, and Muslahuddin Daud, *Conflict and Recovery in Aceh: An Assessment of Conflict Dynamics and Options for Supporting the Peace Process* (Washington, DC: World Bank, 2005), 58.

99. USAID, *US Overseas Loans and Grants*, constant 2016 dollars.

100. Sebastian, *Realpolitik Ideology*, 121.

101. Hamish McDonald et al., eds., *Masters of Terror: Indonesia's Military and Violence in East Timor in 1999* (Canberra: Australian National University, 2002), 9.

102. Robinson, *"If You Leave Us Here,"* 104.

103. Kiernan, "War, Genocide, and Resistance," 223.

104. McDonald et al., *Masters of Terror*, 8.

105. Komisi Penyelidik Pelanggaran Hak Asasi Manusia di Timor Timur (Commission of Inquiry into Human Rights Violations in East Timor), "Full Report of the Investigative Commission into Human Rights Violations in East Timor," in McDonald et al., *Masters of Terror* (Canberra: Australian National University, 2002), 15–59.

106. "Governor Jailed for East Timor Violence," CNN, August 14, 2002, http://www.cnn .com/2002/WORLD/asiapcf/southeast/08/14/timor.soares.trial/index.html.

107. Human Rights Watch, "Justice Denied for East Timor," December 20, 2002, https:// www.hrw.org/legacy/backgrounder/asia/timor/etimor1202bg.htm.

108. USAID, *US Overseas Loans and Grants*, constant 2016 dollars.

109. Themnér and Wallensteen, "Armed Conflict, 1946–2011."

110. Marzuki, Nashrun, and Adi Warsidi, eds., *Fakta Bicara: Mengungkap Pelanggaran HAM di Aceh 1989–2005* (Banda Aceh, Indonesia: Koalisi NGO HAM Aceh, 2011).

111. Bruce Vaughn, "Papua, Indonesia: Issues for Congress," CRS Report No. RL33260 (Washington, DC: Congressional Research Service, 2006); University of Maryland Center for International Development and Conflict Management, "Chronology for Papuans in Indonesia," Minorities at Risk Project, last modified July 16, 2010, http://www.mar.umd.edu /chronology.asp?groupId=85005.

112. USAID's Tsunami Recovery and Reconstruction Fund provided funds from 2005 to 2011 totaling more than $398 million. USAID, *US Overseas Loans and Grants*, constant 2016 dollars.

113. USAID, *US Overseas Loans and Grants*, constant 2016 dollars.

114. "Aceh Rebels Sign Peace Agreement," BBC News, August 15, 2005, http://news.bbc .co.uk/2/hi/asia-pacific/4151980.stm.

115. Amnesty International, "Indonesia," in *Amnesty International Report 2006: The State of the World's Human Rights* (London: Amnesty International, 2006).

116. See Human Rights Watch, *Prosecuting Political Aspiration: Indonesia's Political Prisoners* (New York: Human Rights Watch, 2010); Jeff Waters, "Torture in West Papua: The Video Verdict Is In," ABC, October 27, 2010, https://www.abc.net.au/news/2010-10-27 /torture-in-west-papua-the-video-verdict-is-in/2313438; Karishma Vaswani, "Indonesia Confirms Papua Torture," BBC News, October 22, 2010, http://www.bbc.co.uk/news /world-asia-pacific-11604361.

117. Amnesty International, "Indonesia," in *Amnesty International Report 2008: The State of the World's Human Rights* (London: Amnesty International, 2008).

118. In a summary of a congressional hearing on Indonesia held in April 1976, Secretary Kissinger notes that Professor Don Emerson stated that "cutting military aid . . . will not free political prisoners." See Congressional Hearing on Indonesia, April 14, 1976, Central Foreign Policy Files, 7/1/1973-12/31/1979; Electronic Telegrams, 1976, General Records of the Department of State, Record Group 59, National Archives at College Park, MD.

119. Christopher J. Coyne and Abigail R. Hall, *Tyranny Comes Home: The Domestic Fate of U.S. Militarism* (Stanford, CA: Stanford University Press, 2018).

120. Alex Horton, "Secretary Mattis Seeks Ties with Once-Brutal Indonesia Special Forces Unit, with an Eye on China," *Washington Post*, January 23, 2018, https://www.washingtonpost .com/news/checkpoint/wp/2018/01/23/secretary-mattis-seeks-ties-with-once-brutal -indonesia-special-forces-unit-with-an-eye-on-china/.

CHAPTER 4

1. Michael McClintock, *The American Connection*, vol. 1, *State Terror and Popular Resistance in El Salvador* (London: Zed Books, 1985), 112–16; William Stanley, *The Protection Racket State: Elite Politics, Military Extortion, and Civil War in El Salvador* (Philadelphia: Temple University Press, 1996), 43–55.

2. Charles D. Brockett, "Sources of State Terrorism in Rural Central America," in *State Organized Terror: The Case of Violent Internal Repression*, ed. P. Timothy Bushnall et al. (Boulder, CO: Westview Press, 1991), 59–76.

3. Erik Ching, *Authoritarian El Salvador: Politics and the Origins of the Military Regimes, 1880–1940* (Notre Dame, IN: University of Notre Dame Press, 2014), 246–47.

4. Ching, *Authoritarian El Salvador*, 257, 259.

5. Ching, *Authoritarian El Salvador*, 346–47.

6. Stanley, *Protection Racket State*, 3.

7. The Center for Justice and Accountability claims that over 75,000 civilians died at the hands of government forces during the civil war in El Salvador (1980–1992). Center for Jus-

tice and Accountability, "El Salvador," accessed January 10, 2018, http://cja.org/article.php ?list=type&type=199.

8. Belisario Betancur and Reinaldo Figueredo Planchart, *From Madness to Hope: The 12-Year War in El Salvador: Report of the Commission on the Truth for El Salvador* (Washington, DC: United States Institute of Peace Library, 2001).

9. Russell Crandall, *The Salvador Option: The United States in El Salvador, 1977–1992* (New York: Cambridge University Press, 2016), 461–64.

10. World Bank, *World Development Indicators*, accessed March 31, 2018, http://data .worldbank.org/data-catalog/world-development-indicators.

11. World Bank, *World Development Indicators*.

12. Carlos Acevedo and Maynor Cabrera, "Social Policies or Private Solidarity? The Equalizing Role of Migration and Remittances in El Salvador," Working Paper No. 2012/13, United Nations University-World Institute for Development Economics Research, Helsinki, Finland, 2012, 16, https://www.wider.unu.edu/sites/default/files/wp2012-013.pdf.

13. Nelson Renteria, "Gang Warfare in El Salvador Pushes Death Rate to Record," Reuters, January 21, 2016, https://www.reuters.com/article/us-el-salvador-violence-widerimage/gang -warfare-in-el-salvador-pushes-death-rate-to-record-idUSKCN0UZ1FK.

14. In April 2019, President Trump directed his administration to end aid to El Salvador as well as neighboring Guatemala and Honduras because of their inability to deter migration to the United States. See Camilo Montoya-Galvez, "Trump's Move to Cut Aid to Central America Will Spur More Migration, Aid Workers Warn," *CBS News*, April 4, 2019, https:// www.cbsnews.com/news/trumps-move-to-cut-aid-to-central-america-will-spur-more -migration-aid-workers-warn.

15. USAID, *US Overseas Loans and Grants*, constant 2016 dollars.

16. U.S. Department of State, "The Ambassador in El Salvador (McDermott) to the Department of State," in *FRUS, 1952–1954*, vol. IV, ed. N. Stephen Kane and William F. Sanford Jr. (Washington, DC: Government Printing Office, 1983), Document 395.

17. U.S. Department of State, "Ambassador in El Salvador (McDermott)," Document 395.

18. U.S. Department of State, "The Secretary of State to the Secretary of Defense (Wilson)," in *FRUS, 1952–1954*, vol. IV, Document 26; U.S. Department of State, "The Ambassador in El Salvador (McDermott) to the Assistant Secretary of State for Inter-American Affairs (Holland)," in *FRUS, 1952–1954*, vol. IV, Document 403.

19. McClintock, *American Connection*, 61.

20. Stanley, *Protection Racket State*, 82.

21. U.S. Department of State, "Intelligence Note No. 548 From the Director of the Bureau of Intelligence and Research (Hughes) to Secretary of State Rogers, Washington, July 18, 1969," in *FRUS, 1969–1976*, vol. E-10, *Documents on American Republics, 1969–1972*, ed. Douglas Kraft and James Siekmeier (Washington, DC: Government Printing Office, 2009), Document 646.

22. U.S. Department of State, "Airgram A-21 from the Embassy in El Salvador to the Department of State," in *FRUS, 1969–1976*, vol. E-11, *Documents on Mexico; Central America; and the Caribbean, 1973–1976*, ed. Halbert Jones (Washington, DC: Government Printing Office, 2015), Document 157.

23. U.S. Department of State, "Telegram 37 from the Embassy in El Salvador to the Department of State," in *FRUS, 1969–1976*, vol. E-11, Document 154.

24. U.S. Department of State, "Airgram A-21 from the Embassy in El Salvador," Document 157.

25. U.S. Department of State, "Airgram A-108 from the Embassy in El Salvador to the Department of State," in *FRUS, 1969–1976*, vol. E-11, Document 160.

26. USAID, *US Overseas Loans and Grants*, constant 2016 dollars.

27. U.S. Department of State, "Airgram A-108 from the Embassy in El Salvador," Document 160.

28. U.S. Department of State, "Memorandum from Robert Pastor of the National Security Council Staff to the President's Assistant for National Security Affairs (Brezinski) and the President's Deputy Assistant for National Security Affairs (Aaron)," in *FRUS, 1977–1980*, vol. I, *Foundations of Foreign Policy*, ed. Kristin L. Ahlberg (Washington, DC: Government Printing Office, 2014), Document 98.

29. Department of State, "Memorandum from Secretary of Defense Brown to President Carter," in *FRUS, 1977–1980*, vol. XV, *Central America, 1977–1980*, ed. Nathaniel L. Smith (Washington, DC: Government Publishing Office, 2016), Document 471.

30. U.S. Department of State, "Paper Prepared in the Department of State," in *FRUS, 1977–1980;* vol. XV, Document 364.

31. U.S. Department of State, "Tab 1: Memorandum From Robert Pastor of the National Security Council Staff to the President's Assistant for National Security Affairs (Brzezinski) and the President's Deputy Assistant for National Security Affairs (Aaron)," in *FRUS, 1977–1980*, vol. XV, Document 395.

32. U.S. Department of State, "Telegram from the Embassy in El Salvador to the Department of State," in *FRUS, 1977–1980*, vol. XV, Document 400.

33. U.S. Department of State, "Presidential Finding," in *FRUS 1977–1980*, vol. XV, Document 398, https://history.state.gov/historicaldocuments/frus1977-80v15/d398; U.S. Department of State, "Telegram from the Department of State to the Embassy in El Salvador," in *FRUS, 1977–1980*, vol. XV, Document 393.

34. U.S. Department of State, "The Ambassador in El Salvador (McDermott) to the Assistant Secretary of State for Inter-American Affairs (Holland)," Document 403.

35. U.S. Department of State, "Summary of Conclusions of a Special Coordination Committee (Intelligence) Meeting," in *FRUS, 1977–1980*, vol. XV, Document 396.

36. U.S. Department of State, "Summary of Conclusions of a Policy Review Committee Meeting," in *FRUS, 1977–1980*, vol. XV, Document 475; U.S. Department of State, "Telegram from the Department of State to the Embassy in El Salvador," in *FRUS, 1977–1980*, vol. XV, Document 379.

37. U.S. Department of State, "Telegram from the Embassy in El Salvador to the Department of State," in *FRUS, 1977–1980*, vol. XV, Document 397.

38. U.S. Department of State, "Telegram from the Embassy in El Salvador," Document 397.

39. U.S. Department of State, "Minutes of a Special Coordination Committee (Intelligence) Meeting," in *FRUS, 1977–1980*, vol. XV, Document 412; U.S. Department of State, "Memorandum from the President's Assistant for National Security Affairs (Brzezinski) to President Carter," in *FRUS, 1977–1980*, vol. XV, Document 433.

40. U.S. Department of State, "Memorandum from the President's Assistant," Document 433; U.S. Department of State, "Memorandum from Secretary of State Vance to President Carter," in *FRUS, 1977–1980*, vol. XV, Document 421.

41. U.S. Department of State, "Memorandum from the National Intelligence Officer for Latin America (Davis) to Director of Central Intelligence Turner and the Deputy Director of the Central Intelligence Agency (Carlucci)," in *FRUS, 1977–1980*, vol. XV, Document 404.

42. U.S. Department of State, "Memorandum from Robert Pastor of the National Security Council Staff to the President's Assistant for National Security Affairs (Brzezinski) and the President's Special Representative for Economic Summits (Owen)," in *FRUS, 1977–1980*, vol. XV, Document 401.

43. "20 Die as Gun Battle Ends Demonstration in El Salvador," *Washington Post*, January 23, 1980, p. A26 quoted in U.S. Department of State, "Minutes of a Special Coordination Committee Meeting," in *FRUS, 1977–1980*, vol. XV, Document 406.

44. Karen DeYoung, "Carter Decides to Resume Military Aid to El Salvador," *Washington Post*, January 14, 1981, https://www.washingtonpost.com/archive/politics/1981/01/14 /carter-decides-to-resume-military-aid-to-el-salvador/16084fe6-8174-49dc-be5f -a5a147566f96/.

45. U.S. Department of State, "Telegram from the Embassy in El Salvador to the Department of State," in *FRUS, 1977–1980*, vol. XV, Document 435.

46. U.S. Department of State, "Memorandum from Robert Pastor of the National Security Council Staff to the President's Assistant for National Security Affairs (Brzezinski)," in *FRUS, 1977–1980*, vol. XV, Document 443.

47. U.S. Department of State, "Memorandum from Robert Pastor of the National Security Council Staff to the President's Assistant for National Security Affairs (Brzezinski) and the President's Deputy Assistant for National Security Affairs (Aaron)," in *FRUS, 1977–1980*, vol. XV, Document 448; U.S. Department of State, "Minutes of a Special Coordination Committee Meeting," in *FRUS, 1977–1980*, vol. XV, Document 449.

48. U.S. government documents report a figure of 9,000 deaths but acknowledge that the number's accuracy is difficult to establish. See U.S. Department of State, "Memorandum of Conversation," in *FRUS, 1977–1980*, vol. XV, Document 450; Socorro Juridico Cristiano (Christian Legal Aid), "Sobre los Refugiados Salvadorenos," San Salvador, 1981. Cited in Stanley, *Protection Racket State*, 206.

49. U.S. Department of State, "Memorandum of Conversation," Document 450.

50. U.S. Department of State, "Memorandum from the President's Assistant for National Security Affairs (Brzezinski) to President Carter," in *FRUS, 1977–1980*, vol. XV, Document 459.

51. Juan de Onis, "U.S. Giving Salvador Combat Equipment," *New York Times*, January 19, 1981, http://www.nytimes.com/1981/01/19/world/us-giving-salvador-combat-equipment .html.

52. U.S. Department of State, "Memorandum from the President's Assistant," Document 459.

53. U.S. Department of State, "Minutes of a National Security Council Meeting," in *FRUS, 1981–1988*, vol. III, *Soviet Union, January 1981–January 1983*, ed. James Graham Wilson (Washington, DC: Government Publishing Office, 2016), Document 15. Brands notes that Reagan initially considered Guatemala, but its abominable human rights record meant that it would be difficult to expand U.S. foreign assistance there. Hal Brands, *Latin America's Cold War* (Cambridge, MA: Harvard University Press, 2010), 199.

54. William Chapman, "U.S. to Send More Aid to El Salvador," *Washington Post*, February 2, 1982, https://www.cia.gov/library/readingroom/docs/CIA-RDP84B00049 R000902300020-1.pdf.

55. John M. Goshko, "Haig Cautions Hill Against Ending Aid to El Salvador," *Washington Post*, March 11, 1982, https://www.cia.gov/library/readingroom/docs/CIA-RDP90 -00552R000100390023-5.pdf.

56. World Bank, *World Development Indicators*.

57. Brands, *Latin America's Cold War*, 199.

58. Americas Watch and the American Civil Liberties Union, *Report on Human Rights in El Salvador, Second Supplemental*, January 1983, 87, cited in U.S. Congress, Arms Control and Foreign Policy Caucus, *U.S. Aid to El Salvador: An Evaluation of the Past, a Proposal for*

the Future; A Report to the Arms Control and Foreign Policy Caucus from Rep. Jim Leach, Rep. George Miller and Sen. Mark O. Hatfield (Washington, DC: Arms Control and Foreign Policy Caucus, 1985), 11. See also Lesley Gill, *The School of the Americas: Military Training and Political Violence in the Americas* (Durham, NC: Duke University Press, 2004).

59. *El Salvador Assistance Act of 1981*, H.R. 3009, 97th Cong. (1981), https://www.congress .gov/bill/97th-congress/house-bill/3009.

60. Americas Watch, *El Salvador's Decade of Terror: Human Rights Since the Assassination of Archbishop Romero* (New Haven, CT: Yale University Press, 1991), 118, 120.

61. Bernard Weinraub, "Reagan Certifies Salvador for Aid," *New York Times*, July 28, 1982, http://www.nytimes.com/1982/07/28/world/reagan-certifies-salvador-for-aid.html.

62. William M. LeoGrande, *Our Own Backyard: The United States in Central America, 1977–1992* (Chapel Hill, NC: University of North Carolina Press, 1998), 153–54.

63. LeoGrande, *Our Own Backyard*, 151.

64. U.S. Congress, Arms Control and Foreign Policy Caucus, *U.S. Aid to El Salvador*, 23.

65. Ian Urbina, "O.A.S. to Reopen Inquiry into Massacre in El Salvador in 1981," *New York Times*, March 5, 2005, http://www.nytimes.com/2005/03/08/international/americas /08salvador.html; Shirley Christian, "Salvador Battalion Ends in Praise and Protest," *New York Times*, December 9, 1992, http://www.nytimes.com/1992/12/09/world/salvador-battalion -ends-in-praise-and-protest.html; Raymond Bonner, "Massacre of Hundreds Reported in Salvador Village," *New York Times*, January 27, 1982, http://www.nytimes.com/1982/01/27 /world/massacre-of-hundreds-reported-in-salvador-village.html. See also Mark Danner, *The Massacre at El Mozote* (New York: Vintage Books, 1994).

66. Bonner, "Massacre of Hundreds."

67. LeoGrande, *Our Own Backyard*, 171.

68. These estimates likely underreport violence in rural areas. Socorro Jurídico Cristiano (Christian Legal Aid), *Informe No. 11, Años IX* (San Salvador: Arzobispado de San Salvador, 1984); Stanley, *Protection Racket State*, 222–24. The ACLU claimed 12,501 were killed in El Salvador in 1981; John M. Goshko, "Record on Rights Entitles Salvador to Aid, US Says," *Washington Post*, January 29, 1982, https://www.cia.gov/library/readingroom/docs/CIA -RDP90-00965R000302450038-0.pdf.

69. Bonner, "Massacre of Hundreds."

70. Bonner, "Massacre of Hundreds."

71. Stanley, *Protection Racket State*, 2.

72. For example, a military campaign in San Vicente resulted in the deaths of 300 to 400 peasants. "Archbishop Oscar Romero: Timeline," Kellogg Institute for International Studies, University of Notre Dame, accessed January 15, 2018, https://kellogg.nd.edu/archbishop -oscar-romero#tab-1491.

73. Americas Watch, *El Salvador's Decade of Terror*, 121.

74. Stanley, *Protection Racket State*, 120–21.

75. Ronald Reagan, "Remarks on Central America and El Salvador at the Annual Meeting of the National Association of Manufacturers" (speech), March 10, 1983.

76. USAID, *US Overseas Loans and Grants*, constant 2016 dollars.

77. Ronald Reagan, "Address Before a Joint Session of the Congress on Central America" (speech), April 27, 1983.

78. Lydia Chavez, "In Salvador, Bush Assails Death Squads," *New York Times*, December 12, 1983, https://www.nytimes.com/1983/12/12/world/in-salvador-bush-assails-death -squads.html.

79. U.S. Congress, Arms Control and Foreign Policy Caucus, *U.S. Aid to El Salvador*, 12.

80. Stanley, *Protection Racket State*, 229.

81. Brands, *Latin America's Cold War*, 203.

82. Henry Kissinger, *Report of the National Bipartisan Commission on Central America* (Washington, DC: Government Printing Office, 1984). For critiques of the commission's report, see Arthur Schlesinger Jr., "Failings of the Kissinger Report," *New York Times*, January 17, 1984, https://www.nytimes.com/1984/01/17/opinion/failings-of-the-kissinger-report.html; and Richard E. Feinberg, "The Kissinger Commission Report: A Critique," *World Development* 12, no. 8 (1984): 867–76.

83. Alfonso Chardy, "House OKs Military Aid for Salvador," *Philadelphia Inquirer*, May 25, 1984, https://www.cia.gov/library/readingroom/docs/CIA-RDP90-00965R000201090020-1.pdf; Alfonso Chardy, "Military Aid for Salvador, Contras OKd," *Miami Herald*, March 15, 1984, https://www.cia.gov/library/readingroom/docs/CIA-RDP90-00965R000201090027-4.pdf. Subsequent congressional investigations determined that there was no emergency in supply. Data supplied by the Defense Security Assistance Agency also demonstrated that the majority of the supplemental aid was used to expand the Salvadoran Army by building new units rather than resupplying existing units in the field. U.S. Congress, Arms Control and Foreign Policy Caucus, *U.S. Aid to El Salvador*, 4–5.

84. For details on the appropriations process, see K. Larry Storrs, "Kissinger Commission Implementation: Action by the Congress Through 1986 on the Recommendations of the National Bipartisan Commission on Central America," CRS Report No. 87–291 F (Washington, DC: Congressional Research Service, 1987).

85. Joanne Omang, "Duarte Conquers Congress on Aid to El Salvador," *Washington Post*, May 23, 1984, https://www.cia.gov/library/readingroom/docs/CIA-RDP90-00552R000100980003-2.pdf.

86. A federal jury in Memphis found Carranza guilty of crimes against humanity in 2005 and ordered him to pay $6 million in damages to four plaintiffs who recounted stories of torture and murder. Attempts to strip Carranza of his U.S. citizenship stalled and in 2017 he died in Memphis at the age of 84. Other Salvadoran military officials accused of torture and extrajudicial killings—including the former defense minister General Carlos Eugenio Vides Casanova—have been successfully deported or extradited. See Philip Taubman, "Top Salvador Police Official Said to Be a CIA Informant," *New York Times*, March 22, 1984, http://www.nytimes.com/1984/03/22/world/top-salvador-police-official-said-to-be-a-cia-informant.html; Nina Lakhani, "An American Sanctuary Ends For Salvadoran General," *Al Jazeera*, April 8, 2015, https://www.aljazeera.com/indepth/features/2015/04/american-sanctuary-ends-salvadoran-general-150406210929299.html.

87. U.S. Congress, Arms Control and Foreign Policy Caucus, *U.S. Aid to El Salvador*, 1–7.

88. Joanne Omang and Michael J. Weisskopf, "Reagan to Push Aid for Duarte's Military," *Washington Post*, June 21, 1985, https://www.cia.gov/library/readingroom/docs/CIA-RDP90-00965R000807300020-5.pdf; USAID, *US Overseas Loans and Grants*, constant 2016 dollars.

89. According to Human Rights Watch, there were 1,900 political killings and disappearances in 1985, of which 90 percent can be attributed to the government. Americas Watch, *El Salvador's Decade of Terror*, 126.

90. Lou Cannon, "Reagan Appeals for Extra Aid to El Salvador," *Washington Post*, May 10, 1984, https://www.cia.gov/library/readingroom/docs/CIA-RDP90-00965R000201020009-1.pdf.

91. USAID, *US Overseas Loans and Grants*, constant 2016 dollars.

92. World Bank, *World Development Indicators*.

93. Author's calculations based on World Bank, *World Development Indicators* and USAID, *US Overseas Loans and Grants*.

94. U.S. Congress, Arms Control and Foreign Policy Caucus, *U.S. Aid to El Salvador*, ii. Emphasis in the original.

95. Neil A. Lewis, "Congress Says El Salvador Misuses U.S. Aid," *New York Times*, November 16, 1987, https://www.nytimes.com/1987/11/16/world/congress-says-el-salvador -misuses-us-aid.html.

96. U.S. Congress, Arms Control and Foreign Policy Caucus, *U.S. Aid to El Salvador*, 17–18.

97. U.S. General Accounting Office, *El Salvador: Accountability for U.S. Military and Economic Aid* (Washington, DC: General Accounting Office, 1990).

98. U.S. General Accounting Office, *El Salvador: Transfers of Military Assistance Fuels* (Washington, DC: General Accounting Office, 1989), 6.

99. U.S. General Accounting Office, *El Salvador: Accountability*, 24.

100. U.S. General Accounting Office, *El Salvador: Accountability*, 25–26.

101. U.S. General Accounting Office, *El Salvador: Accountability*, 35.

102. Christian, "Salvador Battalion Ends in Praise and Protest."

103. Lindsey Gruson, "6 Priests Killed in a Campus Raid in San Salvador," *New York Times*, November 17, 1989, http://www.nytimes.com/1989/11/17/world/6-priests-killed-in-a -campus-raid-in-san-salvador.html.

104. "El Salvador Court Quashes Arrest Order for Soldiers over 1989 Murders," Reuters, August 22, 2017, https://www.reuters.com/article/us-elsalvador-killings-spain-idUSKCN 1B307I.

105. Brands, *Latin America's Cold War*, 205.

106. Stanley, *Protection Racket State*, 3.

107. Brands, *Latin America's Cold War*, 201.

108. U.S. General Accounting Office, *Central America: Impact of U.S. Assistance in the 1980s* (Washington, DC: General Accounting Office, 1989), 41.

109. U.S. Congress, Arms Control and Foreign Policy Caucus, *U.S. Aid to El Salvador*, 41.

CHAPTER 5

1. World Bank, *World Development Indicators*.

2. Bruce Cummings, *Korea's Place in the Sun: A Modern History* (New York: W. W. Norton, 2005), 147.

3. Cummings, *Korea's Place in the Sun*, 147.

4. See Timothy L. Savage, "The American Response to the Korean Independence Movement, 1910–1945," *Korean Studies* 20 (1996): 189–231.

5. Cummings reports these figures as coming from "Korean nationalist sources" and cites an official Japanese figure of 553 killed and over 12,000 arrested. Cummings, *Korea's Place in the Sun*, 155.

6. George Hicks, *The Comfort Women: Japan's Brutal Regime of Enforced Prostitution in the Second World War* (New York: W. W. Norton, 1997).

7. Cummings, *Korea's Place in the Sun*, 175.

8. Charles R. Frank Jr., Kwang Suk Kim, and Larry E. Westphal, "Economic Growth in South Korea Since World War II," in *Foreign Trade Regimes and Economic Development: South Korea* (Cambridge, MA: National Bureau of Economic Research, 1975), 6–24.

9. Richard Allen, "President Chun of Korea," memorandum, January 29, 1981, in *Seeing Human Rights in the "Proper Manner,"* ed. Robert Wampler (Washington, DC: National Security Archive, 2010).

10. Cummings, *Korea's Place in the Sun*, 192.

11. Hak-Kyu Sohn, *Authoritarianism and Opposition in South Korea* (London: Routledge, 1989), 16–17.

12. Carter J. Eckert et al., *Korea Old and New: A History* (Cambridge, MA: Harvard University Press, 1990), 348–49.

13. Central Intelligence Agency, "South Korea," *National Intelligence Survey*, October 1973, 11, https://www.cia.gov/library/readingroom/docs/CIA-RDP01-00707R000200080007-0 .pdf.

14. Eckert et al., *Korea Old and New*, 358.

15. U.S. Department of State, "Memorandum by the Assistant Secretary of State for Far Eastern Affairs (Allison) to the Secretary of State," in *FRUS, 1952–1954, Korea*, vol. XV, part 1, ed. Edward C. Keefer (Washington, DC: Government Publishing Office, 1984), Document 386.

16. U.S. Department of State, "Note by the Executive Secretary (Lay) to the National Security Council," in *FRUS, 1952–1954, Korea*, vol. XV, part 2, ed. Edward C. Keefer (Washington, DC: Government Publishing Office, 1984), Document 632.

17. U.S. Department of State, "Memorandum by the Assistant Secretary of State," Document 386.

18. Lee Kye Woo, "The Role of Aid in Korea's Development," in *Korea's Economy*, vol. 30, ed. Troy Stangarone (Washington, DC: Korea Economic Institute of America, 2015), 7–25.

19. Woo, "Role of Aid," 15.

20. U.S. Department of State, "Note by the Executive Secretary (Lay)," Document 632.

21. U.S. Department of State, "Strengthening the Korean Economy: Report by the National Security Council Planning Board to the National Security Council," in *FRUS, 1952–1954, Korea*, vol. XV, part 2, 1384, Document 775.

22. Sung Chul Yang, "Student Political Activism: The Case of the 1960 April Revolution in South Korea," *Youth and Society* 5, no. 1 (1973): 57.

23. Eckert et al., *Korea Old and New*, 355.

24. Sohn, *Authoritarianism and Opposition*, 18.

25. Central Intelligence Agency, Senior Research Staff on International Communism, "Proposal for U.S. Action in South Korea," April 21, 1960, 3, https://www.cia.gov/library /readingroom/docs/CIA-RDP80-01446R000100060004-7.pdf.

26. Sohn, *Authoritarianism and Opposition*, 20.

27. Central Intelligence Agency, "Proposal for U.S. Action in South Korea," 3–4.

28. Eckert et al., *Korea Old and New*, 361–62.

29. Central Intelligence Agency, "Update of South Korea Handbook," No. 0539, November 1970, https://www.cia.gov/library/readingroom/docs/CIA-RDP79-00891A000700020001 -4.pdf.

30. Central Intelligence Agency, "Update of South Korea Handbook."

31. Richard Nixon, "Informal Remarks in Guam with Newsmen" (speech), July 25, 1969.

32. Memo, Talks Between President Nixon and President Pak, August 21, 1969, folder Memoranda for the President: Beginning August 17, 1969, box 79, White House Special Files: President's Office Files, Richard Nixon Presidential Library and Museum, Yorba Linda, CA.

33. Sohn, *Authoritarianism and Opposition*, 35; Sheena Chestnut Greitens, *Dictators and Their Secret Police: Coercive Institutions and State Violence* (Cambridge: Cambridge University Press, 2016), 161.

34. Sohn, *Authoritarianism and Opposition*, 40.

35. Paul Y. Chang, *Protest Dialectics: State Repression and South Korea's Democracy Movement, 1970–1979* (Stanford, CA: Stanford University Press, 2015), 66.

36. Central Intelligence Agency, "South Korea: The Outlook for the Pak Government," September 17, 1974, 4, https://www.cia.gov/library/readingroom/docs/CIA-RDP79R01099 A001600040003-4.pdf.

37. Central Intelligence Agency, "South Korea: Outlook," 7.

38. Central Intelligence Agency, "South Korea: Outlook," 2–3; Richard Halloran, "With President's Grip Ever Tighter, Seoul Is Jumpy and Confused," *New York Times,* June 8, 1974, https://www.nytimes.com/1974/06/08/archives/with-presidents-grip-ever-tighter-seoul-is -jumpy-and-confused.html.

39. Yong-Jick Kim, "The Security, Political, and Human Rights Conundrum, 1974–1979," in *The Park Chung Hee Era: The Transformation of South Korea,* ed. Byung-Kook Kim and Ezra F. Vogel (Cambridge MA: Harvard University Press, 2011), 462.

40. Richard Halloran, "Seoul to Release All Foes in Prison but 'Communists,'" *New York Times,* February 15, 1975.

41. Richard Halloran, "Seoul Silences Opponents in Campaign for Vote on Constitution," *New York Times,* February 1, 1975, https://www.nytimes.com/1975/02/01/archives/seoul -silences-opponents-in-campaign-for-vote-on-constitution.html.

42. Kim, "Security, Political, and Human Rights Conundrum," 465.

43. U.S. Department of State, *Country Reports on Human Rights Practices: Report Submitted to the Committee on Foreign Relations, U.S. Senate and Committee on Foreign Affairs, U.S. House of Representatives* (Washington, DC: Government Printing Office, 1978), microform, 247.

44. Jimmy Carter, "Universal Declaration of Human Rights Remarks at a White House Meeting Commemorating the 30th Anniversary of the Declaration's Signing" (speech), December 6, 1978.

45. Richard Halloran, "Hoover Memos Told Nixon Aides of Korea," *New York Times,* March 22, 1978, https://www.cia.gov/library/readingroom/docs/CIA-RDP81M00980 R000600200007-7.pdf.

46. Charles R. Babcock, "Koreagate: Bringing Forth a Mouse, but an Honest One," *Washington Post,* October 9, 1978, https://www.washingtonpost.com/archive/politics/1978/10/09 /koreagate-bringing-forth-a-mouse-but-an-honest-one/3329ce7e-095f-4bb3-9cd1 -f909a158183a/.

47. U.S. Congress, Committee on International Relations and Committee on Foreign Relations, *Investigation of Korean-American Relations,* 95th Cong., 2d sess., 1978 (Washington, DC: Government Printing Office, 1978).

48. Ron Sarro, "House Upholds Korea Aid," *Washington Star,* n.d., accessed January 15, 2019, https://www.cia.gov/library/readingroom/docs/CIA-RDP81M00980R000600170018-9 .pdf.

49. Central Intelligence Agency, Directorate of Intelligence, Office of East Asian Analysis, "South Korea: Chun's Growing Political Confidence," EA 83–10091, June 1983, https:// www.cia.gov/library/readingroom/docs/CIA-RDP84S00553R000200040003-1.pdf.

50. Linda S. Lewis, *Laying Claim to the Memory of May: A Look Back at the 1980 Kwangju Uprising* (Honolulu: University of Hawai'i Press, 2002), 23.

51. Lewis, *Laying Claim*, 69–70.

52. "South Korea Apologises for Rapes During 1980 Gwangju Protest Crackdown," BBC News, November 7, 2018, https://www.bbc.com/news/world-asia-46123548.

53. Central Intelligence Agency, Foreign Broadcast Information Service, "Korea Affairs Report," August 6, 1980, 4, https://www.cia.gov/library/readingroom/docs/CIA-RDP82 -00850R000300020007-9.pdf.

54. Alexander Haig to the President, "Your Meeting with Chun Doo-Hwan, President of the Republic of Korea," memorandum, February 1–3, 1981, in Wampler, *Seeing Human Rights.*

55. Richard V. Allen to the President, "Your Meeting with President Chun of Korea," memorandum, February 6, 1981, in Wampler, *Seeing Human Rights.*

56. Greitens, *Dictators and Their Secret Police*, 261.

CHAPTER 6

1. Boschini and Olofsgård, "Foreign Aid."

2. Stephane Courtois et al., *The Black Book of Communism: Crimes, Terror, Repression* (Cambridge, MA: Harvard University Press, 1999).

3. David Dollar and Victoria Levin, "The Increasing Selectivity of Foreign Aid, 1984– 2003," *World Development* 34, no. 12 (2006): 2034–46; Seonjou Kang and James Meernik, "Determinants of Post-Conflict Economic Assistance," *Journal of Peace Research* 41, no. 2 (2004): 149–66; Mark McGillivray, "What Determines African Bilateral Aid Receipts," *Journal of International Development* 17, no. 8 (2005): 1003–18.

4. Daniel Yuichi Kono and Gabriella R. Montinola, "Does Foreign Aid Support Autocrats, Democrats, or Both?," *Journal of Politics* 71, no. 2 (2009): 704–18.

5. Sarah Blodgett Bermeo, "Aid Is Not Oil: Donor Utility, Heterogeneous Aid, and the Aid-Democratization Relationship," *International Organization* 70, no. 1 (2016): 1–32.

6. "The 1992 Campaign; Transcript of 2d TV Debate between Bush, Clinton and Perot," *New York Times*, October 16, 1992, http://www.nytimes.com/1992/10/16/us/the-1992 -campaign-transcript-of-2d-tv-debate-between-bush-clinton-and-perot.html.

7. See Todd Moss, David Roodman, and Scott Standley, "The Global War on Terror and US Development Assistance: USAID Allocation by Country, 1998–2005" (Working Paper No. 62, Center for Global Development, Washington, DC, 2005); Robert K. Fleck and Christopher Kilby, "Changing Aid Regimes? US Foreign Aid from the Cold War to the War on Terror," *Journal of Development Economics* 91, no. 2 (2010): 185–97.

8. Meernik, Krueger, and Poe, "Testing Models"; Steven W. Hook, "'Building Democracy' Through Foreign Aid: The Limitations of United States Political Conditionalities, 1992– 96," *Democratization* 5, no. 3 (1998): 156–80; Brian Lai, "Examining the Goals of U.S. Foreign Assistance in the Post–Cold War Period, 1991–96," *Journal of Peace Research* 40, no. 1 (2003): 103–28.

9. Thomas Lum, "U.S. Foreign Aid to East and South Asia: Selected Recipients," CRS Report for Congress RL31362 (Washington, DC: Congressional Research Service, 2008).

10. Tarnoff and Lawson, "Foreign Aid," 10.

11. Tarnoff and Lawson, "Foreign Aid," 14.

12. Lum, "U.S. Foreign Aid."

13. Though the two samples are roughly comparable in terms of their temporal span, the latter sample features the inclusion of new countries (panels) due to the breakup of the Soviet Union, Yugoslavia, and Czechoslovakia.

14. George W. Bush, *The National Security Strategy for the United States of America* (Washington, DC: White House, 2002).

15. Jessica N. Trisko, "Coping with the Islamist Threat: Analysing Repression in Kazakhstan, Kyrgyzstan and Uzbekistan," *Central Asian Survey* 24, no. 4 (2005): 373–89.

16. Simon Denyer, "Former Inmates of China's Muslim 'Reeducation' Camps Tell of Brainwashing, Torture," *Washington Post*, May 17, 2018, https://www.washingtonpost.com /world/asia_pacific/former-inmates-of-chinas-muslim-re-education-camps-tell-of -brainwashing-torture/2018/05/16/32b330e8-5850-11e8-8b92-45fdd7aaef3c_story.html.

17. Extraordinary rendition is defined as "a hybrid human rights violation, combining elements of arbitrary arrest, enforced disappearance, forcible transfer, torture, denial of access to consular officials, and denial of impartial tribunals. It involves the state-sponsored abduction of a person in one country, with or without the cooperation of the government of that country, and the subsequent transfer of that person to another country for detention and interrogation." See David Weissbrodt and Amy Bergquist, "Extraordinary Rendition: A Human Rights Analysis," *Harvard Human Rights Journal* 19 (2006): 127; Leila Nadya Sadat, "Ghost Prisoners and Black Sites: Extraordinary Rendition Under International Law," *Case Western Reserve Journal of International Law* 37, no. 2 (2006): 309–42.

18. An analysis covering 1976 to 2016 and including a dummy variable for the years 2002 to 2016 indicated that the period was systematically different (results not reported).

19. Alex de Waal, "When Kleptocracy Becomes Insolvent: Brute Causes of the Civil War in South Sudan," *African Affairs* 113, no. 452 (2014): 352.

20. John Prendergast, *Frontline Diplomacy: Humanitarian Aid and Conflict in Africa* (Boulder, CO: Lynne Riener, 1996), 23.

21. De Waal, "When Kelptocracy Becomes Insolvent," 355.

22. De Waal, "When Kelptocracy Becomes Insolvent," 356.

23. On March 15, 2019, the UN Security Council voted to extend UNMISS's mission for another year.

24. United Nations, United Nations Peacekeeping, "UNMISS Fact Sheet: United Nations Mission in the Republic of South Sudan," accessed January 23, 2019, https://peacekeeping .un.org/en/mission/unmiss.

25. U.S. Department of State, *United States Contributions to International Organizations: Sixty-Sixth Annual Report to the Congress; Fiscal Year 2017* (Washington, DC: Department of State, 2017).

26. "South Sudan Waives Registration Fees for Aid Groups for a Year," Reuters, January 27, 2018, https://www.reuters.com/article/southsudan-aid/south-sudan-waives-registration-fees -for-aid-groups-for-a-year-idUSL8N1PM0B9.

27. Jane Ayeko-Kümmeth, "UNICEF: 'Child Soldiers Want to Continue Their Education,'" *Deutsche Welle*, February 12, 2018, https://www.dw.com/en/unicef-child-soldiers-want -to-continue-their-education/a-42554038.

28. Humanitarian assistance is not restricted by the Child Soldiers Prevention Act.

29. "U.S. Military Aid to South Sudan Government Criticized by Opposition Faction," *Sudan Tribune*, October 9, 2016, http://www.sudantribune.com/spip.php?article60476.

30. Colum Lynch, Dan de Luce, and Paul McLeary, "The U.S. Helped Birth South Sudan. Now Americans Are Being Beaten and Targeted by Its Troops," *Foreign Policy*, August 16, 2016, http://foreignpolicy.com/2016/08/16/the-u-s-helped-birth-south-sudan-now-americans -are-being-beaten-and-targeted-by-its-troops/; Associated Press in Nairobi, "UN Peacekeepers in South Sudan 'Ignored Rape and Assault of Aid Workers,'" *Guardian*, August 15, 2016,

https://www.theguardian.com/world/2016/aug/15/south-sudan-aid-worker-rape-attack
-united-nations-un.

31. Jason Burke and Ed Pilkington, "UN Under Pressure over 'Failure to Act' During
South Sudan Rampage," *Guardian*, August 17, 2016, https://www.theguardian.com/world
/2016/aug/17/un-under-pressure-over-failure-to-act-during-south-sudan-rampage.

32. Associated Press in Nairobi, "UN Peacekeepers in South Sudan."

33. Between January 2016 and March 2017, 106 aid workers were victims of attacks in
South Sudan. This number does not include UN personnel. U.S. Department of State, "Attacks on Aid Workers: Countries with Ten or More Victims, Jan. 2016–Mar. 2017," *Humanitarian Information Unit*, accessed April 25, 2018, https://hiu.state.gov/#global,U1567.

34. Jason Burke, "South Sudan Soldiers Jailed for Murder and Rape in Hotel Attack,"
Guardian, September 6, 2018, https://www.theguardian.com/world/2018/sep/06/south-sudan
-soldiers-jailed-for-and-in-hotel-attack.

35. United Nations, General Assembly, Human Rights Council, *Report of the Commission on Human Rights in South Sudan*, A/HRC/37/71 (New York: United Nations, 2018).

36. USAID, "South Sudan—Crisis: Fact Sheet #5, Fiscal Year (FY) 2019," April 8, 2019,
https://www.usaid.gov/sites/default/files/documents/1866/south_sudan_cr_fs05_04-08
-2019.pdf.

37. Nikki Haley, "Remarks at the U.S. Holocaust Memorial Museum Program: 'Our
Walls Bear Witness: South Sudan—Where Do We Go from Here?'" (speech), November 15,
2017.

CONCLUSION

1. U.S. Department of State, "Memorandum from the Deputy Secretary of State," Document 54.

2. Louisa Loveluck, "What's Non-Lethal About Aid to the Syrian Opposition?" *Foreign
Policy*, September 20, 2012, https://foreignpolicy.com/2012/09/20/whats-non-lethal-about-aid
-to-the-syrian-opposition/.

3. Emily Stephenson and Roberta Rampton, "U.S. to Send $70 Million in Non-Lethal
Aid to Syrian Opposition," Reuters, March 13, 2015, https://www.reuters.com/article/us-usa
-syria-aid/u-s-to-send-70-million-in-non-lethal-aid-to-syrian-opposition
-idUSKBN0M91WF20150313; "U.S. Admits Supplying Lethal Aid to Syrian Rebels," *Haaretz*,
June 7, 2014, https://www.haaretz.com/u-s-supplying-lethal-aid-to-syrian-rebels-1.5250990.
See also, Fiona Terry, *Condemned to Repeat? The Paradox of Humanitarian Action* (Ithaca,
NY: Cornell University Press, 2002).

4. Susan B. Epstein, Marian L. Lawson, and Cory R. Gill, "Department of State, Foreign
Operations and Related Programs: FY2019 Budget and Appropriations," CRS Report No.
R45168 (Washington, DC: Congressional Research Service, 2018), 14.

5. Nina Lakhani, "'We Fear Soldiers More Than Gangsters': El Salvador's 'Iron Fist' Policy Turns Deadly," *Guardian*, February 6, 2017, https://www.theguardian.com/world/2017
/feb/06/el-salvador-gangs-police-violence-distrito-italia.

6. Moyar, *Aid for Elites*, 111.

7. U.S. Department of State, "Memorandum from the President's Assistant," Document
122.

8. Chris Barrett and Erin Lentz, "U.S. Monetization Policy: Recommendations for Improvement" (Policy Development Studies Series, Chicago Council on Global Affairs, Chicago, 2009).

9. Annie Sparrow, "How UN Humanitarian Aid Has Propped Up Assad," *Foreign Affairs*, September 20, 2018, https://www.foreignaffairs.com/articles/syria/2018-09-20/how-un-humanitarian-aid-has-propped-assad; Robert Ford and Mark Ward, "Assad's Syria Plays Dirty with US Humanitarian Aid," *The Hill*, February 12, 2018, https://thehill.com/opinion/national-security/373449-assads-syria-plays-dirty-with-us-humanitarian-aid.

10. Samuel Okiror, "'They Exaggerated Figures': Ugandan Aid Officials Suspended over Alleged Fraud," *Guardian*, February 8, 2018, https://www.theguardian.com/global-development/2018/feb/08/they-exaggerated-figures-uganda-aid-officials-suspended-over-alleged-fraud; "Ugandans Suspended over 'Refugee Scam,'" BBC News, February 9, 2018, https://www.bbc.com/news/world-africa-43002680.

11. Susanne Jaspars, *Food Aid in Sudan: A History of Power, Politics and Profit* (London: Zed Books, 2018).

12. Simone Dietrich, "Bypass or Engage? Explaining Donor Delivery Tactics in Foreign Aid Allocation," *International Studies Quarterly* 57, no. 4 (2013): 698–712; Martin Acht, Toman Omar Mahmoud, and Rainer Thiele, "Corrupt Governments Do Not Receive More State-to-State Aid: Governance and the Delivery of Foreign Aid Through Non-State Actors," *Journal of Development Economics* 114 (May 2015): 20–33.

13. Susanna Campbell, Matthew DiGiuseppe, and Amanda Murdie, "International Development NGOs and Bureaucratic Capacity: Facilitator or Destroyer?" *Political Research Quarterly* 72, no. 1 (2019): 3–18.

14. Laura Zanotti, "Cacophonies of Aid, Failed State Building and NGOs in Haiti: Setting the Stage for Disaster, Envisioning the Future," *Third World Quarterly* 31, no. 5 (2010): 755–71; Coyne, *Doing Bad by Doing Good*; Amanda Murdie, *Help or Harm: The Human Security Effects of International NGOs* (Stanford, CA: Stanford University Press, 2014).

15. Dean Chahim and Aseem Prakash, "NGOization, Foreign Funding, and the Nicaraguan Civil Society," *Voluntas* 25, no. 2 (2014): 487–513.

16. Darin Christensen and Jeremy M. Weinstein, "Defunding Dissent: Restrictions on Aid to NGOs," *Journal of Democracy* 24, no. 2 (2013): 77–91; Kendra Dupuy, James Ron, and Aseem Prakash, "Hands Off My Regime! Governments' Restrictions on Foreign Aid to Non-Governmental Organizations in Poor and Middle-Income Countries," *World Development* 84 (August 2016): 299–311.

17. Murdie and Bhasin, "Aiding and Abetting."

18. Dupuy, Ron, and Prakash, "Hands Off My Regime!," 299.

19. Peter Moore, "Foreign Aid: Most People Think America Gives Too Much Away," YouGov, March 11, 2016, https://today.yougov.com/news/2016/03/11/foreign-aid/.

20. "Most See U.S. Foreign Aid as a Bad Deal for America," *Rasmussen Reports*, March 20, 2017, http://www.rasmussenreports.com/public_content/politics/general_politics/march_2017/most_see_u_s_foreign_aid_as_a_bad_deal_for_america.

21. Committee for Responsible Foreign Policy, "Committee for Responsible Foreign Policy Releases Research That Shows Americans Are Ready for Decreased U.S. Military Intervention and Increased Congressional Oversight," PR Newswire, January 3, 2018, https://www.prnewswire.com/news-releases/committee-for-responsible-foreign-policy-releases-research-that-shows-americans-are-ready-for-decreased-us-military-intervention-and-increased-congressional-oversight-300577145.html.

22. "Most Still Question the Value of Foreign Aid," *Rasmussen Reports*, January 8, 2018, http://www.rasmussenreports.com/public_content/politics/general_politics/january_2018/most_still_question_the_value_of_foreign_aid.

23. Thomas J. Scotto et al., "We Spend How Much? Misperceptions, Innumeracy, and Support for the Foreign Aid in the United States and Great Britain," *Journal of Experimental Political Science* 4, no. 2 (2017): 119–28.

24. U.S. Office of Management and Budget, *America First: A Budget Blueprint to Make America Great Again, Budget of the United States Government, Fiscal Year 2018* (Washington, DC: Government Publishing Office, 2017).

25. U.S. Department of State, "Minutes of a National Security Council Meeting," Document 15.

26. Deborah Brautigam, *The Dragon's Gift: The Real Story of China in Africa* (Oxford: Oxford University Press, 2010); Dambisa Moyo, *Winner Take All: China's Race for Resources and What It Means for the World* (Toronto: HarperCollins, 2012).

27. Naohiro Kitano and Yukinori Harada, "Estimating China's Foreign Aid 2001–2013," *Journal of International Development* 28, no. 7 (2016): 1050–74.

28. AidData, "China's Global Development Footprint: The Clearest Look Yet at Chinese Official Finance Worldwide," accessed November 30, 2018, https://www.aiddata.org/china -official-finance.

29. Sarah Blodgett Bermeo, "Foreign Aid and Regime Change: A Role for Donor Intent," *World Development* 39, no. 11 (2011): 2021–31.

30. Organisation for Economic Cooperation and Development, "Turkey's Official Development Assistance (ODA)," accessed January 17, 2019, http://www.oecd.org/dac/stats /turkeys-official-development-assistanceoda.htm; Saudi Aid Platform, "Financial Statistics," accessed January 17, 2019, https://data.ksrelief.org/en/FinancialStatistics.aspx.

31. Chithra Purushothaman, "Why Is the Philippines Turning Away Foreign Aid?" *Diplomat*, May 25, 2017, http://thediplomat.com/2017/05/why-is-the-philippines-turning-away -foreign-aid/.

32. Pia Ranada, "China Gives P370M in Guns, Ammunition to PH," *Rappler*, June 28, 2017, https://www.rappler.com/nation/174190-china-military-aid-guns-ammunition-phili ppines-marawi-terrorism.

33. See, for example, Sophal Ear, *Aid Dependence in Cambodia: How Foreign Assistance Undermines Democracy* (New York: Columbia University Press, 2012).

34. Siobhan O'Grady, "A New Report Estimates that More Than 380,000 People Have Died in South Sudan's Civil War," *Washington Post*, September 26, 2018, https://www .washingtonpost.com/world/africa/a-new-report-estimates-more-than-380000-people-have -died-in-south-sudans-civil-war/2018/09/25/e41fcb84-c0e7-11e8-9f4f-a1b7af255aa5_story .html.

35. Carter, "Universal Declaration of Human Rights."

36. Jimmy Carter, "Inaugural Address" (speech), January 20, 1977.

References

Abouharb, M. Rodwan, and David L. Cingranelli. "The Human Rights Effects of World Bank Structural Adjustment, 1981–2000." *International Studies Quarterly* 50, no. 2 (2006): 233–62.

Aboulenein, Ahmed. "Egypt Issues NGO Law, Cracking Down on Dissent." Reuters, May 29, 2017. http://www.reuters.com/article/us-egypt-rights-idUSKBN18P1OL.

Acevedo, Carlos, and Maynor Cabrera. "Social Policies or Private Solidarity? The Equalizing Role of Migration and Remittances in El Salvador." Working Paper No. 2012/13, United Nations University-World Institute for Development Economics Research, Helsinki, Finland, 2012. https://www.wider.unu.edu/sites/default/files/wp2012-013.pdf.

Acht, Martin, Toman Omar Mahmoud, and Rainer Thiele. "Corrupt Governments Do Not Receive More State-to-State Aid: Governance and the Delivery of Foreign Aid Through Non-State Actors." *Journal of Development Economics* 114 (May 2015): 20–33.

Ahmed, Faisal Z. "Does Foreign Aid Harm Political Rights? Evidence from U.S. Aid." *Quarterly Journal of Political Science* 11, no. 2 (2016): 183–217.

Ahmed, Faisal Z., and Eric D. Werker. "Aid and the Rise and Fall of Conflict in the Muslim World." *Quarterly Journal of Political Science* 10, no. 2 (2015): 155–86.

Ahn, Daniel P., and Rodney D. Ludema. "Measuring Smartness: Understanding the Economic Impact of Targeted Sanctions." U.S. Department of State, Office of the Chief Economist Working Paper 2017–01, Department of State, Washington, DC, 2016. https://www.state.gov/documents/organization/267590.pdf.

AidData. "China's Global Development Footprint: The Clearest Look Yet at Chinese Official Finance Worldwide." Accessed November 30, 2018. https://www.aiddata.org/china-official-finance.

Alkatiri, Mari. "Statement Submitted by Mari Alkatiri." In *East Timor: Five Years After the Indonesian Invasion, Testimony Presented at the Decolonization Committee of the United Nations' General Assembly, October 1980*, edited by James W. Clay, 5–10. Cambridge, MA: Cultural Survival, 1980.

Americas Watch. *El Salvador's Decade of Terror: Human Rights Since the Assassination of Archbishop Romero*. New Haven, CT: Yale University Press, 1991.

Amnesty International. "Hungary: Plan to Brand NGOs Has Somber Echoes of Russia's 'Foreign Agents Law.'" April 7, 2017. https://www.amnesty.org/en/latest/news/2017/04/hungary-plan-to-brand-ngos-has-sombre-echoes-of-russias-foreign-agents-law/.

———. "Indonesia." In *Amnesty International Report 2006: The State of the World's Human Rights*. London: Amnesty International, 2006. https://www.amnesty.org/download/Documents/POL1000012006ENGLISH.PDF.

———. "Indonesia." In *Amnesty International Report 2008: The State of the World's Human Rights*. London: Amnesty International, 2008. https://www.amnesty.org/download /Documents/POL100012008ENGLISH.PDF.

———. "Indonesia: Kopassus Conviction Small Step Towards Ending Impunity." September 5, 2013. https://www.amnesty.org/en/latest/news/2013/09/indonesia-kopassus -conviction-small-step-towards-ending-impunity/.

———. "Russia: Four Years of Putin's 'Foreign Agents' Law to Shackle and Silence NGOs." November 18, 2016. https://www.amnesty.org/en/latest/news/2016/11/russia -four-years-of-putins-foreign-agents-law-to-shackle-and-silence-ngos/.

Anderson, Christopher J., Patrick M. Regan, and Robert L. Ostergard. "Political Repression and Public Perceptions of Human Rights." *Political Research Quarterly* 55, no. 2 (2002): 439–56.

Anderson, Mary B. *Do No Harm: How Aid Can Support Peace—or War*. Boulder, CO: Lynne Rienner, 1999.

Apodaca, Clair, and Michael Stohl. "United States Human Rights Policy and Foreign Assistance." *International Studies Quarterly* 43, no. 1 (1999): 185–98.

Arendt, Hannah. *The Origins of Totalitarianism*. New York: Schocken Books, 1951.

Associated Press. "UN Operating Budget Cut by $285M; US Claims Credit for It." December 26, 2017. https://www.apnews.com/6558eea166404e769df6a93ccdb10240.

Associated Press in Nairobi. "UN Peacekeepers in South Sudan 'Ignored Rape and Assault of Aid Workers.'" *Guardian*, August 15, 2016. https://www.theguardian.com/world /2016/aug/15/south-sudan-aid-worker-rape-attack-united-nations-un.

Atkinson, Carol. *Military Soft Power: Public Diplomacy Through Military Educational Exchanges*. Lanham, MD: Rowman and Littlefield, 2014.

Ausderan, Jacob. "How Naming and Shaming Affects Human Rights Perceptions in the Shamed Country." *Journal of Peace Research* 51, no. 1 (2014): 81–95.

Ayeko-Kümmeth, Jane. "UNICEF: 'Child Soldiers Want to Continue Their Education.'" *Deutsche Welle*, February 12, 2018. https://www.dw.com/en/unicef-child-soldiers-want -to-continue-their-education/a-42554038.

Azam, Jean-Paul. "How to Pay for the Peace? A Theoretical Framework with References to African Countries." *Public Choice* 83, no. 1/2 (1995): 173–84.

Babcock, Charles R. "Koreagate: Bringing Forth a Mouse, but an Honest One." *Washington Post*, October 9, 1978. https://www.washingtonpost.com/archive/politics/1978/10 /09/koreagate-bringing-forth-a-mouse-but-an-honest-one/3329ce7e-095f-4bb3-9cd1 -f909a158183a/.

Balla, Eliana, and Gina Yannitell Reinhardt. "Giving and Receiving Foreign Aid: Does Conflict Count?" *World Development* 36, no. 12 (2008): 2566–85.

Barratt, Bethany. *Human Rights and Foreign Aid: For Love or Money?* New York: Routledge, 2008.

Barrett, Chris, and Erin Lentz. "U.S. Monetization Policy: Recommendations for Improvement." Policy Development Studies Series, Chicago Council on Global Affairs, Chicago, 2009.

Barron, Patrick, Samuel Clark, and Muslahuddin Daud. *Conflict and Recovery in Aceh: An Assessment of Conflict Dynamics and Options for Supporting the Peace Process*. Washington, DC: World Bank, 2005.

Bass, Gary J. *The Blood Telegram: Nixon, Kissinger, and a Forgotten Genocide*. New York: Alfred A. Knopf, 2013.

BBC News. "Aceh Rebels Sign Peace Agreement." August 15, 2005. http://news.bbc.co.uk
/2/hi/asia-pacific/4151980.stm.

———. "Sergei Lavrov: Russia Rejects Use of Force in Syria." June 9, 2012. http://www
.bbc.co.uk/news/world-middle-east-18384519.

———. "South Korea Apologises for Rapes During 1980 Gwangju Protest Crackdown."
November 7, 2018. https://www.bbc.com/news/world-asia-46123548.

———. "Ugandans Suspended over 'Refugee Scam.'" February 9, 2018. https://www.bbc
.com/news/world-africa-43002680.

Bell, Sam R., and Amanda Murdie. "The Apparatus for Violence: Repression, Violent Protest, and Civil War in a Cross-National Framework." *Conflict Management and Peace
Science* 35, no. 4 (2016): 336–54.

Berlin, Isaiah. "A Message to the Twenty-First Century." Speech, University of Toronto,
Toronto, ON, Canada, November 25, 1994.

Bermeo, Sarah Blodgett. "Aid Is Not Oil: Donor Utility, Heterogeneous Aid, and the Aid-
Democratization Relationship." *International Organization* 70, no. 1 (2016): 1–32.

———. "Foreign Aid and Regime Change: A Role for Donor Intent." *World Development*
39, no. 11 (2011): 2021–31.

Bertrand, Jacques. *Nationalism and Ethnic Conflict in Indonesia.* Cambridge: Cambridge
University Press, 2004.

Betancur, Belisario, and Reinaldo Figueredo Planchart. *From Madness to Hope: The 12-Year
War in El Salvador: Report of the Commission on the Truth for El Salvador.* Washington,
DC: United States Institute of Peace Library, 2001.

Bhakti, Ikrar Nusa, Sri Yanuarti, and Mochamad Nurhasim. "Military Politics, Ethnicity
and Conflict in Indonesia." CRISE Working Paper No. 62, Centre for Research on
Inequality, Human Security and Ethnicity, University of Oxford, Oxford, UK, 2009.
https://assets.publishing.service.gov.uk/media/57a08b7bed915d3cfd000d4a/wp62.pdf.

Bhalla, Nita. "India Uses Foreign Funding Law to Harass Charities: Rights Groups."
Reuters, November 8, 2016. http://www.reuters.com/article/us-india-ngos-crackdown
-idUSKBN134056.

Boden, Ragna. "Cold War Economics: Soviet Aid to Indonesia." *Journal of Cold War Studies* 10, no. 3 (2008): 110–28.

Böhnke, Jan Rasmus, and Christoph Zürcher. "Aid, Minds and Hearts: The Impact of
Aid in Conflict Zones." *Conflict Management and Peace Science* 30, no. 5 (2013):
411–32.

Bonner, Raymond. "Massacre of Hundreds Reported in Salvador Village." *New York Times*,
January 27, 1982. http://www.nytimes.com/1982/01/27/world/massacre-of-hundreds
-reported-in-salvador-village.html.

Boschini, Anne, and Anders Olofsgård. "Foreign Aid: An Instrument for Communism?"
Journal of Development Studies 43, no. 4 (2007): 622–48.

Brands, Hal. *Latin America's Cold War.* Cambridge, MA: Harvard University Press,
2010.

Brautigam, Deborah. *The Dragon's Gift: The Real Story of China in Africa.* Oxford: Oxford
University Press, 2010.

Brockett, Charles D. "Sources of State Terrorism in Rural Central America." In *State Or-
ganized Terror: The Case of Violent Internal Repression*, edited by P. Timothy Bushnall,
Vladimir Shlapentokh, Christopher K. Vanderpool, and Jeyaratnam Sundram, 59–76.
Boulder, CO: Westview Press, 1991.

Bueno de Mesquita, Bruce, James D. Morrow, Randolph M. Siverson, and Alastair Smith. "An Institutional Explanation of the Democratic Peace." *American Political Science Review* 93, no. 4 (1999): 791–807.

Bueno de Mesquita, Bruce, and Alastair Smith. "Foreign Aid and Policy Concessions." *Journal of Conflict Resolution* 51, no. 2 (2007): 251–84.

Burke, Jason. "South Sudan Soldiers Jailed for Murder and Rape in Hotel Attack." *Guardian*, September 6, 2018. https://www.theguardian.com/world/2018/sep/06/south-sudan -soldiers-jailed-for-and-in-hotel-attack.

Burke, Jason, and Ed Pilkington. "UN Under Pressure over 'Failure to Act' During South Sudan Rampage." *Guardian*, August 17, 2016. https://www.theguardian.com/world /2016/aug/17/un-under-pressure-over-failure-to-act-during-south-sudan-rampage.

Burnside, Craig, and David Dollar. "Aid, Policies, and Growth." *American Economic Review* 90, no. 4 (2000): 847–68.

Bush, George W. "George W. Bush: PEPFAR Saves Millions of Lives in Africa. Keep It Fully Funded." *Washington Post*, April 7, 2017. https://www.washingtonpost.com/opinions /george-w-bush-pepfar-saves-millions-of-lives-in-africa-keep-it-fully-funded/2017/04 /07/2089fa46-1ba7-11e7-9887-1a5314b56a08_story.html.

———. *The National Security Strategy for the United States of America.* Washington, DC: White House, 2002. https://www.state.gov/documents/organization/63562.pdf.

Bush, Sarah Sunn. *The Taming of Democracy Assistance: Why Democracy Promotion Does Not Confront Dictators.* Cambridge: Cambridge University Press, 2015.

Callaway, Rhonda L., and Elizabeth G. Matthews. *Strategic US Foreign Assistance: The Battle Between Human Rights and National Security.* Burlington, VT: Ashgate, 2008.

Campbell, Susanna, Matthew DiGiuseppe, and Amanda Murdie. "International Development NGOs and Bureaucratic Capacity: Facilitator or Destroyer?" *Political Research Quarterly* 72, no. 1 (2019): 3–18.

Cannon, Lou. "Reagan Appeals for Extra Aid to El Salvador." *Washington Post*, May 10, 1984. https://www.cia.gov/library/readingroom/docs/CIA-RDP90-00965R000201020009-1.pdf.

Cardenas, Sonia. "Norm Collision: Explaining the Effects of International Human Rights Pressure on State Behavior." *International Studies Review* 6, no. 2 (2004): 213–31.

Carey, Sabine C. "The Use of Repression as Response to Domestic Dissent." *Political Studies* 58, no. 1 (2010): 167–86.

Carothers, Thomas. *Aiding Democracy Abroad: The Learning Curve.* Washington, DC: Carnegie Endowment for International Peace, 1999.

Carter, Jimmy. "Inaugural Address." January 20, 1977. Avalon Project, Yale Law School. http://avalon.law.yale.edu/20th_century/carter.asp. Transcript.

———. "Universal Declaration of Human Rights Remarks at a White House Meeting Commemorating the 30th Anniversary of the Declaration's Signing." December 6, 1978. American Presidency Project, University of California–Santa Barbara. https:// www.presidency.ucsb.edu/documents/universal-declaration-human-rights-remarks -white-house-meeting-commemorating-the-30th. Transcript.

Cederman, Lars-Erik, Simon Hug, and Lutz F. Krebs. "Democratization and Civil War: Empirical Evidence." *Journal of Peace Research* 47, no. 4 (2010): 377–94.

Center for Justice and Accountability. "El Salvador." Accessed January 10, 2018. http://cja .org/article.php?list=type&type=199.

Central Intelligence Agency. "The Situation in Indonesia." August 15, 1966. https://www .cia.gov/library/readingroom/docs/CIA-RDP79T00826A001100010028-3.pdf.

———. "South Korea." *National Intelligence Survey*, October 1973. https://www.cia.gov /library/readingroom/docs/CIA-RDP01-00707R000200080007-0.pdf.

———. "South Korea: The Outlook for the Pak Government." September 17, 1974. https://www.cia.gov/library/readingroom/docs/CIA-RDP79R01099A001600040003 -4.pdf.

———. "Update of South Korea Handbook." No. 0539. November 1970. https://www.cia .gov/library/readingroom/docs/CIA-RDP79-00891A000700020001-4.pdf.

Central Intelligence Agency. Center for the Study of Intelligence. "The Lessons of the September 30 Affair." July 2, 1996. https://www.cia.gov/library/center-for-the-study-of -intelligence/kent-csi/vol14no2/html/v14i2a02p_0001.htm.

Central Intelligence Agency. Directorate of Intelligence. "Weekly Summary Special Report: Suharto's Indonesia." No. 0370/70A. May 15, 1970. https://www.cia.gov/library /readingroom/docs/CIA-RDP85T00875R001500020025-3.pdf.

———. "Weekly Summary Special Report: The New Order in Indonesia." No. 0302/67A. August 11, 1967. https://www.cia.gov/library/readingroom/docs/CIA-RDP79-00927 A005900080002-0.pdf.

Central Intelligence Agency. Directorate of Intelligence. Office of African and Latin American Analysis. "Ethiopia: Political and Security Impact of the Drought." ALA 85-10039. April 3, 1985. https://www.cia.gov/library/readingroom/docs/CIA-RDP86T00589R000200160004 -5.pdf.

Central Intelligence Agency. Directorate of Intelligence. Office of East Asian Analysis. "South Korea: Chun's Growing Political Confidence." EA 83-10091. June 1983. https:// www.cia.gov/library/readingroom/docs/CIA-RDP84S00553R000200040003-1.pdf.

Central Intelligence Agency. Directorate of National Intelligence. "Intelligence Memorandum: Possible Resumption of Soviet Aid to Indonesia." ER IM 71–190. October 1970. https:// www.cia.gov/library/readingroom/docs/CIA-RDP85T00875R001700020044-0.pdf.

Central Intelligence Agency. Foreign Broadcast Information Service. "Korea Affairs Report." August 6, 1980, 4. https://www.cia.gov/library/readingroom/docs/CIA-RDP82 -00850R000300020007-9.pdf.

Central Intelligence Agency. Office of the Director. "Executive Memorandum: U.S. Policy Toward Indonesia." ER 62–5895. August 17, 1962. https://www.cia.gov/library /readingroom/docs/CIA-RDP80M01048A001500100071-9.pdf.

Central Intelligence Agency. Office of National Estimates. "Memorandum for the Director: Probable Repercussions of US Aid Cuts to Indonesia." January 7, 1964. https:// www.cia.gov/library/readingroom/docs/CIA-RDP79R00904A001000050036-9.pdf.

Central Intelligence Agency. Senior Research Staff on International Communism. "Proposal for U.S. Action in South Korea." April 21, 1960. https://www.cia.gov/library /readingroom/docs/CIA-RDP80-01446R000100060004-7.pdf.

Centre for Strategic and International Studies. *Kliping Tentang Peristiwa Dili, Timor Timur, November 12, 1991*. Jakarta: Centre for Strategic and International Studies, 1992.

Chahim, Dean, and Aseem Prakash. "NGOization, Foreign Funding, and the Nicaraguan Civil Society." *Voluntas* 25, no. 2 (2014): 487–513.

Chang, Paul Y. *Protest Dialectics: State Repression and South Korea's Democracy Movement, 1970–1979*. Stanford, CA: Stanford University Press, 2015.

Chapman, William. "U.S. to Send More Aid to El Salvador." *Washington Post*, February 2, 1982. https://www.cia.gov/library/readingroom/docs/CIA-RDP84B00049R000902300020 -1.pdf.

Chardy, Alfonso. "House OKs Military Aid for Salvador." *Philadelphia Inquirer*, May 25, 1984. https://www.cia.gov/library/readingroom/docs/CIA-RDP90-00965R000201090020 -1.pdf.

———. "Military Aid for Salvador, Contras OKd." *Miami Herald*, March 15, 1984. https:// www.cia.gov/library/readingroom/docs/CIA-RDP90-00965R000201090027-4.pdf.

Chavez, Lydia. "In Salvador, Bush Assails Death Squads." *New York Times*, December 12, 1983. https://www.nytimes.com/1983/12/12/world/in-salvador-bush-assails-death-squads .html.

Chicago Tribune Press Service. "House Committee Votes to Cut Off Aid to Indonesia." *Spokesman-Review* (Spokane, WA), July 26, 1963.

Ching, Erik. *Authoritarian El Salvador: Politics and the Origins of the Military Regimes, 1880–1940*. Notre Dame, IN: University of Notre Dame Press, 2014.

Christensen, Darin, and Jeremy M. Weinstein. "Defunding Dissent: Restrictions on Aid to NGOs." *Journal of Democracy* 24, no. 2 (2013): 77–91.

Christian, Shirley. "Salvador Battalion Ends in Praise and Protest." *New York Times*, December 9, 1992. http://www.nytimes.com/1992/12/09/world/salvador-battalion-ends-in -praise-and-protest.html.

Cingranelli, David L., and Thomas E. Pasquarello. "Human Rights Practices and the Distribution of US Foreign Aid to Latin American Countries." *American Journal of Political Science* 29, no. 3 (1985): 539–63.

Cingranelli, David L., David L. Richards, and K. Chad Clay. "The CIRI Human Rights Dataset." Version 2014.04.14. Distributed by the CIRI Human Rights Data Project. Accessed March 31, 2018. http://www.humanrightsdata.com.

Clinton, William J. "Inaugural Address." January 20, 1993. American Presidency Project, University of California–Santa Barbara. https://www.presidency.ucsb.edu/documents /inaugural-address-51. Transcript.

CNN. "Governor Jailed for East Timor Violence." August 14, 2002, http://www.cnn.com /2002/WORLD/asiapcf/southeast/08/14/timor.soares.trial/index.html.

Collier, Paul. *The Bottom Billion: Why the Poorest Countries Are Failing and What Can Be Done About It*. Oxford: Oxford University Press, 2007.

Collier, Paul, and Anke Hoeffler. "Aid, Policy and Peace: Reducing the Risks of Civil Conflict." *Defence and Peace Economics* 13, no. 6 (2002): 435–50.

———. "Unintended Consequences: Does Aid Promote Arms Races?" *Oxford Bulletin of Economics and Statistics* 69, no. 1 (2007): 1–27.

Collier, Paul, and Nicholas Sambanis, eds. *Understanding Civil War: Evidence and Analysis*. Washington, DC: World Bank, 2005.

Comer, Charles "Ken." "Leahy in Indonesia: Damned If You Do (and Even If You Don't)." *Asian Affairs: An American Review* 37, no. 2 (2010): 53–70.

Comissão de Acolhimento, Verdade e Reconciliação de Timor-Leste. *Chega! The Final Report of the Commission for Reception, Truth and Reconciliation in Timor-Leste*. Dili, Timor-Leste: Comissão de Acolhimento, Verdade e Reconciliação de Timor-Leste, 2005.

Committee for Responsible Foreign Policy. "Committee for Responsible Foreign Policy Releases Research That Shows Americans Are Ready for Decreased U.S. Military Intervention and Increased Congressional Oversight." PR Newswire, January 3, 2018. https:// www.prnewswire.com/news-releases/committee-for-responsible-foreign-policy-releases -research-that-shows-americans-are-ready-for-decreased-us-military-intervention-and -increased-congressional-oversight-300577145.html.

Cortright, David, and George A. Lopez, eds. *Smart Sanctions: Targeting Economic Statecraft.* New York: Rowman and Littlefield, 2002.

Courtois, Stephane, Nicolas Werth, Jean-Louis Panne, Andrzej Paczkowski, Karel Bartosek, and Jean-Louis Margolin. *The Black Book of Communism: Crimes, Terror, Repression.* Cambridge, MA: Harvard University Press, 1999.

Coyne, Christopher J. *After War: The Political Economy of Exporting Democracy.* Stanford, CA: Stanford University Press, 2007.

———. *Doing Bad by Doing Good: Why Humanitarian Action Fails.* Stanford, CA: Stanford University Press, 2013.

Coyne, Christopher J., and Abigail R. Hall. *Tyranny Comes Home: The Domestic Fate of U.S. Militarism.* Stanford, CA: Stanford University Press, 2018.

Cramer, Christopher. "Does Inequality Cause Conflict?" *Journal of International Development* 15, no. 4 (2003): 397–412.

Crandall, Russell. *The Salvador Option: The United States in El Salvador, 1977–1992.* New York: Cambridge University Press, 2016.

Cribb, Robert. "How Many Deaths? Problems in the Statistics of Massacre in Indonesia (1965–1966) and East Timor (1975–1980)." In *Violence in Indonesia,* edited by Ingrid Wessel and Georgia Wimhöfer, 82–98. Hamburg: Abera, 2001.

Crost, Benjamin, Joseph Felter, and Patrick Johnston. "Aid Under Fire: Development Projects and Civil Conflict." *American Economic Review* 104, no. 6 (2014): 1833–56.

Cummings, Bruce. *Korea's Place in the Sun: A Modern History.* New York: W. W. Norton, 2005.

Danner, Mark. *The Massacre at El Mozote.* New York: Vintage Books, 1994.

Davenport, Christian. "Assessing the Military's Influence on Political Repression." *Journal of Political and Military Sociology* 23, no. 1 (1995): 119–44.

———. "Multi-Dimensional Threat Perception and State Repression: An Inquiry into Why States Apply Negative Sanctions." *American Journal of Political Science* 39, no. 3 (1995): 683–713.

———. "State Repression and Political Order." *Annual Review of Political Science* 10, no. 1 (2007): 1–23.

———. *State Repression and the Domestic Democratic Peace.* Cambridge: Cambridge University Press, 2007.

———. "State Repression and the Tyrannical Peace." *Journal of Peace Research* 44, no. 4 (2007): 485–504.

———. "The Weight of the Past: Exploring Lagged Determinants of Political Repression." *Political Research Quarterly* 49, no. 2 (1996): 377–403.

Davenport, Christian, and David A. Armstrong. "Democracy and the Violation of Human Rights: A Statistical Analysis from 1976 to 1996." *American Journal of Political Science* 48, no. 3 (2004): 538–54.

Davenport, Christian, David A. Armstrong, and Mark I. Lichbach. "From Mountains to Movements: Dissent, Repression and Escalation to Civil War." Unpublished Manuscript, 2006. https://christiandavenportphd.weebly.com/uploads/1/8/3/5/18359923/movements andmountains040406.pdf.

Deger, Saadet, and Somnath Sen. "Military Expenditure, Aid, and Economic Development." In *Proceedings of the Annual Conference on Development Economics 1991,* edited by Lawrence H. Summers and Shekhar Shah, 159–86. Washington, DC: World Bank, 1992.

————. "Military Expenditure and Developing Countries." In *Handbook of Defense Economics*, vol. 1, edited by Keith Hartley and Todd Sandler, 276–307. Amsterdam: Elsevier Science BV, 1995.

Denyer, Simon. "Former Inmates of China's Muslim 'Reeducation' Camps Tell of Brainwashing, Torture." *Washington Post*, May 17, 2018. https://www.washingtonpost.com /world/asia_pacific/former-inmates-of-chinas-muslim-re-education-camps-tell-of -brainwashing-torture/2018/05/16/32b330e8-5850-11e8-8b92-45fdd7aaef3c_story.html.

De Onis, Juan. "U.S. Giving Salvador Combat Equipment." *New York Times*, January 19, 1981. http://www.nytimes.com/1981/01/19/world/us-giving-salvador-combat-equipment .html.

De Ree, Joppe, and Eleonora Nillesen. "Aiding Violence or Peace? The Impact of Foreign Aid on the Risk of Civil Conflict in Sub-Saharan Africa." *Journal of Development Economics* 88, no. 2 (2009): 301–13.

De Waal, Alex. "When Kleptocracy Becomes Insolvent: Brute Causes of the Civil War in South Sudan." *African Affairs* 113, no. 452 (2014): 347–69.

DeYoung, Karen. "Carter Decides to Resume Military Aid to El Salvador." *Washington Post*, January 14, 1981. https://www.washingtonpost.com/archive/politics/1981/01/14 /carter-decides-to-resume-military-aid-to-el-salvador/16084fe6-8174-49dc-be5f -a5a147566f96/.

————. "How the U.S. Came to Abstain on a U.N. Resolution Condemning Israeli Settlements." *Washington Post*, December 28, 2016. https://www.washingtonpost.com /world/national-security/how-the-us-came-to-abstain-on-a-un-resolution-condemning -israeli-settlements/2016/12/28/fed102ee-cd38-11e6-b8a2-8c2a61b0436f_story.html.

Dietrich, Simone. "Bypass or Engage? Explaining Donor Delivery Tactics in Foreign Aid Allocation." *International Studies Quarterly* 57, no. 4 (2013): 698–712.

Djankov, Simeon, and Marta Reynal-Querol. "Poverty and Civil War: Revisiting the Evidence." *Review of Economics and Statistics* 92, no. 4 (2010): 1035–41.

Dollar, David, and Victoria Levin. "The Increasing Selectivity of Foreign Aid, 1984–2003." *World Development* 34, no. 12 (2006): 2034–46.

Dollar, David, and Lant Pritchett. *Assessing Aid: What Works, What Doesn't, and Why*. New York: Oxford University Press, 1998.

Drezner, Daniel W. "The Hidden Hand of Economic Coercion." *International Organization* 57, no. 3 (2003): 643–59.

————. *The Sanctions Paradox: Economic Statecraft and International Relations*. Cambridge: Cambridge University Press, 1999.

————. "Sanctions Sometimes Smart: Targeted Sanctions in Theory and Practice." *International Studies Review* 13, no. 1 (2011): 96–108.

Dube, Oeindrila, and Suresh Naidu. "Bases, Bullets and Ballots: The Effect of US Military Aid on Political Conflict in Colombia." *Journal of Politics* 77, no. 1 (2015): 249–67.

Dupuy, Kendra, James Ron, and Aseem Prakash. "Hands Off My Regime! Governments' Restrictions on Foreign Aid to Non-Governmental Organizations in Poor and Middle-Income Countries." *World Development* 84 (August 2016): 299–311.

Ear, Sophal. *Aid Dependence in Cambodia: How Foreign Assistance Undermines Democracy*. New York: Columbia University Press, 2012.

Easterly, William. *The White Man's Burden: Why the West's Efforts to Aid the Rest Have Done So Much Ill and So Little Good*. New York: Penguin, 2006.

East Timor Action Network. "The Santa Cruz Massacre: November 12, 1991." ETAN.org, 2012. http://www.etan.org/timor/SntaCRUZ.htm.

Eck, Kristine, and Lisa Hultman. "One-Sided Violence Against Civilians in War: Insights from New Fatality Data." *Journal of Peace Research* 44, no. 2 (2007): 233–46.

Eckert, Carter J., Ki-baik Lee, Young Ick Lew, Michael Robinson, and Edward W. Wagner. *Korea Old and New: A History.* Cambridge, MA: Harvard University Press, 1990.

Economist. "What Fuels, Bread and Water Reveal About How Egypt Is Mismanaged." February 10, 2018. https://www.economist.com/news/middle-east-and-africa/21736552 -egyptians-are-addicted-subsidies-make-them-poorer-what-fuel-bread-and.

Ekbladh, David. "Harry S. Truman, Development Aid, and American Foreign Policy." In *Foreign Aid and the Legacy of Harry S. Truman,* edited by Raymond H. Gezelbracht, 61–72. Kirksville, MO: Truman State University Press, 2015.

Elbadawi, Ibrahim, and Nicholas Sambanis. "How Much War Will We See? Explaining the Prevalence of Civil War." *Journal of Conflict Resolution* 46, no. 3 (2002): 307–34.

Enterline, Andrew J., and J. Michael Greig. "Perfect Storms? Political Instability in Imposed Polities and the Futures of Iraq and Afghanistan." *Journal of Conflict Resolution* 52, no. 6 (2008): 880–915.

Epstein, Susan B., Marian L. Lawson, and Cory R. Gill. "Department of State, Foreign Operations and Related Programs: FY2019 Budget and Appropriations." CRS Report No. R45168. Washington, DC: Congressional Research Service, 2018. https://fas.org /sgp/crs/row/R45168.pdf.

Esarey, Justin, and Jacqueline H. R. DeMeritt, "Political Context and the Consequences of Naming and Shaming for Human Rights Abuse." *International Interactions* 43, no. 4 (2017): 589–618.

Esteban, Joan M., Massimo Morelli, and Dominic Rohner. "Strategic Mass Killings." *Journal of Political Economy* 123, no. 5 (2015): 1087–132.

Fearon, James D., and David D. Laitin. "Ethnicity, Insurgency, and Civil War." *American Political Science Review* 97, no. 1 (2003): 75–90.

Fein, Helen. "More Murder in the Middle: Life-Integrity Violations and Democracy in the World, 1987." *Human Rights Quarterly* 17, no. 1 (1995): 170–91.

Feinberg, Richard E. "The Kissinger Commission Report: A Critique." *World Development* 12, no. 8 (1984): 867–76.

Feyzioglu, Tarhan, Vinaya Swaroop, and Min Zhu. "A Panel Data Analysis of the Fungibility of Foreign Aid." *World Bank Economic Review* 12, no. 1 (1998): 29–58.

Fleck, Robert K., and Christopher Kilby. "Changing Aid Regimes? US Foreign Aid from the Cold War to the War on Terror." *Journal of Development Economics* 91, no. 2 (2010): 185–97.

Flynn, Michael E. "Before the Dominos Fall: Regional Conflict, Donor Interests, and US Foreign Aid." *Conflict Management and Peace Science,* June 16, 2017, 1–19.

Ford, Robert, and Mark Ward. "Assad's Syria Plays Dirty with US Humanitarian Aid." *The Hill,* February 12, 2018. https://thehill.com/opinion/national-security/373449-assads -syria-plays-dirty-with-us-humanitarian-aid.

Frank, Charles R., Jr., Kwang Suk Kim, and Larry E. Westphal. "Economic Growth in South Korea Since World War II." In *Foreign Trade Regimes and Economic Development: South Korea,* 6–24. Cambridge, MA: National Bureau of Economic Research, 1975.

Franklin, James C. "IMF Conditionality, Threat Perception, and Political Repression: A Cross-National Analysis." *Comparative Political Studies* 30, no. 5 (1997): 576–606.

———. "Shame on You: The Impact of Human Rights Criticism on Political Repression in Latin America." *International Studies Quarterly* 52, no. 1 (2008): 187–211.

Friman, H. Richard, ed. *The Politics of Leverage in International Relations: Name, Shame, and Sanction*. New York: Palgrave Macmillan, 2015.

Gartner, Scott Sigmund, and Patrick M. Regan. "Threat and Repression: The Non-Linear Relationship Between Government and Opposition Violence." *Journal of Peace Research* 33, no. 3 (1996): 273–87.

Gerth, H. H., and C. Wright Mills, eds. and trans. *From Max Weber: Essays in Sociology*. New York: Oxford University Press, 1946.

Gibney, Mark, Linda Cornett, Reed Wood, Peter Haschke, Daniel Arnon, and Attilio Pisano. *The Political Terror Scale*. October 11, 2017. http://www.politicalterrorscale.org.

Gill, Lesley. *The School of the Americas: Military Training and Political Violence in the Americas*. Durham, NC: Duke University Press, 2004.

Gill, Peter. *Famine and Foreigners: Ethiopia Since Live Aid*. Oxford: Oxford University Press, 2010.

Gilligan, Michael J., and Nathaniel H. Nesbitt. "Do Norms Reduce Torture?" *Journal of Legal Studies* 38, no. 2 (2009): 445–70.

Goshko, John M. "Haig Cautions Hill Against Ending Aid to El Salvador." *Washington Post*, March 11, 1982. https://www.cia.gov/library/readingroom/docs/CIA-RDP90 -00552R000100390023-5.pdf.

———. "Record on Rights Entitles Salvador to Aid, US Says." *Washington Post*, January 29, 1982. https://www.cia.gov/library/readingroom/docs/CIA-RDP90-00965R0003024 50038-0.pdf.

Greitens, Sheena Chestnut. *Dictators and Their Secret Police: Coercive Institutions and State Violence*. Cambridge: Cambridge University Press, 2016.

Gruson, Lindsey. "6 Priests Killed in a Campus Raid in San Salvador." *New York Times*, November 17, 1989. http://www.nytimes.com/1989/11/17/world/6-priests-killed-in-a -campus-raid-in-san-salvador.html.

Gurr, Ted Robert. *Why Men Rebel*. Princeton, NJ: Princeton University Press, 1970.

Haaretz. "U.S. Admits Supplying Lethal Aid to Syrian Rebels." June 7, 2014. https://www .haaretz.com/u-s-supplying-lethal-aid-to-syrian-rebels-1.5250990.

Hafner-Burton, Emilie M. "Right or Robust? The Sensitive Nature of Repression to Globalization." *Journal of Peace Research* 42, no. 6 (2005): 679–98.

———. "Sticks and Stones: Naming and Shaming the Human Rights Enforcement Problem." *International Organization* 62, no. 4 (2008): 689–716.

———. "Trading Human Rights: How Preferential Trade Agreements Influence Government Repression." *International Organization* 59, no. 3 (2005): 593–629.

Hafner-Burton, Emilie M., and James Ron. "Seeing Double: Human Rights Impact Through Qualitative and Quantitative Eyes." *World Politics* 61, no. 2 (2009): 360–401.

Hafner-Burton, Emilie M., and Kiyoteru Tsutsui. "Human Rights in a Globalizing World: The Paradox of Empty Promises." *American Journal of Sociology* 110, no. 5 (2005): 1373–411.

Haley, Nikki. "Remarks at the U.S. Holocaust Memorial Museum Program: 'Our Walls Bear Witness: South Sudan—Where Do We Go from Here?'" November 15, 2017. United States Mission to the United Nations. https://usun.state.gov/remarks/8121. Transcript.

Halloran, Richard. "Hoover Memos Told Nixon Aides of Korea." *New York Times*, March 22, 1978. https://www.cia.gov/library/readingroom/docs/CIA-RDP81M00980 R000600200007-7.pdf.

———. "Seoul Silences Opponents in Campaign for Vote on Constitution." *New York Times*, February 1, 1975. https://www.nytimes.com/1975/02/01/archives/seoul-silences-opponents-in-campaign-for-vote-on-constitution.html.

———. "Seoul to Release All Foes in Prison but 'Communists.'" *New York Times*, February 15, 1975.

———. "With President's Grip Ever Tighter, Seoul Is Jumpy and Confused." *New York Times*, June 8, 1974. https://www.nytimes.com/1974/06/08/archives/with-presidents-grip-ever-tighter-seoul-is-jumpy-and-confused.html.

Harff, Barbara. "No Lessons Learned from the Holocaust? Assessing Risks of Genocide and Political Mass Murder Since 1955." *American Political Science Review* 97, no. 1 (2003): 57–73.

Harff, Barbara, and Ted Robert Gurr. "Toward Empirical Theory of Genocides and Politicides: Identification and Measurement of Cases Since 1945." *International Studies Quarterly* 32, no. 3 (1988): 359–71.

Hathaway, Oona A. "Do Human Rights Treaties Make a Difference?" *Yale Law Journal* 111, no. 8 (2002): 1935–2042.

———. "Why Do Countries Commit to Human Rights Treaties?" *Journal of Conflict Resolution* 51, no. 4 (2007): 588–621.

Hegre, Håvard, Tanja Ellingsen, Scott Gates, and Nils Petter Gleditsch. "Towards a Democratic Civil Peace? Democracy, Political Change, and Civil War, 1816–1992." *American Political Science Review* 95, no. 1 (2001): 33–48.

Hicks, George. *The Comfort Women: Japan's Brutal Regime of Enforced Prostitution in the Second World War*. New York: W. W. Norton, 1997.

Hindley, Donald. "Foreign Aid to Indonesia and Its Political Implications." *Pacific Affairs* 36, no. 2 (1963): 107–19.

Hook, Steven W. "'Building Democracy' Through Foreign Aid: The Limitations of United States Political Conditionalities, 1992–96." *Democratization* 5, no. 3 (1998): 156–80.

Hopkins, Nick, and Emma Beals. "How Assad Regime Controls UN Aid Intended for Syria's Children." *Guardian*, August 29, 2016. https://www.theguardian.com/world/2016/aug/29/how-assad-regime-controls-un-aid-intended-for-syrias-children.

Horton, Alex. "Secretary Mattis Seeks Ties with Once-Brutal Indonesia Special Forces Unit, with an Eye on China." *Washington Post*, January 23, 2018. https://www.washingtonpost.com/news/checkpoint/wp/2018/01/23/secretary-mattis-seeks-ties-with-once-brutal-indonesia-special-forces-unit-with-an-eye-on-china/.

Human Rights Watch. "India: Events of 2016." December 19, 2016. https://www.hrw.org/world-report/2017/country-chapters/india.

———. "Indonesia: Human Rights Abuses in Aceh." December 27, 1990. https://www.hrw.org/report/1990/12/27/indonesia-human-rights-abuses-aceh.

———. "Justice Denied for East Timor." December 20, 2002. https://www.hrw.org/legacy/backgrounder/asia/timor/etimor1202bg.htm.

———. *Prosecuting Political Aspiration: Indonesia's Political Prisoners*. New York: Human Rights Watch, 2010.

Jaspars, Susanne. *Food Aid in Sudan: A History of Power, Politics and Profit*. London: Zed Books, 2018.

Johnson, Doug, and Tristan Zajonc. "Can Foreign Aid Create an Incentive for Good Governance? Evidence from the Millennium Challenge Corporation." CID Working Paper No. 11, Center for International Development, Harvard Kennedy School of Government, Harvard University, Cambridge, MA, 2006. https://www.hks.harvard.edu/sites/default/files/centers/cid/files/publications/fellow_graduate_student_working_papers/011-2.pdf.

Kalyvas, Stathis N. *The Logic of Violence in Civil War.* Cambridge: Cambridge University Press, 2006.

Kang, Seonjou, and James Meernik. "Determinants of Post-Conflict Economic Assistance." *Journal of Peace Research* 41, no. 2 (2004): 149–66.

Keating, Joshua E. "Trained in the USA." *Foreign Policy*, March 28, 2012. https://foreignpolicy.com/2012/03/28/trained-in-the-u-s-a/.

Kennedy, John F. "Inaugural Address." January 20, 1961. John F. Kennedy Presidential Library and Museum. https://www.jfklibrary.org/Research/Research-Aids/Ready-Reference/JFK-Quotations/Inaugural-Address.aspx. Transcript.

———. "Remarks upon Signing the Foreign Assistance Act." August 1, 1962. American Presidency Project, University of California–Santa Barbara. https://www.presidency.ucsb.edu/documents/remarks-upon-signing-the-foreign-assistance-act. Transcript.

———. "Special Message to the Congress on Foreign Aid." March 22, 1961. American Presidency Project, University of California–Santa Barbara. https://www.presidency.ucsb.edu/documents/special-message-the-congress-foreign-aid-1. Transcript.

Khilji, Nasir M., and Ernest M. Zampelli. "The Fungibility of US Military and Non-Military Assistance and the Impacts on Expenditures of Major Aid Recipients." *Journal of Development Economics* 43, no. 2 (1994): 345–62.

Kiernan, Ben. *Blood and Soil: A World History of Genocide and Extermination from Sparta to Darfur.* New Haven, CT: Yale University Press, 2007.

———. "The Demography of Genocide in Southeast Asia: The Death Tolls in Cambodia, 1975–1979 and East Timor, 1975–1980." *Critical Asian Studies* 35, no. 4 (2003): 585–97.

———. *Genocide and Resistance in Southeast Asia: Documentation, Denial, and Justice in Cambodia and East Timor.* New York: Routledge, 2008.

———. "War, Genocide, and Resistance in East Timor, 1975–99: Comparative Reflections on Cambodia." In *War and State Terror: The United States, Japan, and the Asia-Pacific in the Long Twentieth Century*, edited by Mark Selden and Alvin Y. So, 199–233. Lanham, MD: Rowman and Littlefield, 2003.

Kim, Yong-Jick. "The Security, Political, and Human Rights Conundrum, 1974–1979." In *The Park Chung Hee Era: The Transformation of South Korea*, edited by Byung-Kook Kim and Ezra F. Vogel, 457–82. Cambridge, MA: Harvard University Press, 2011.

Kissinger, Henry. *Report of the National Bipartisan Commission on Central America.* Washington, DC: Government Printing Office, 1984.

Kitano, Naohiro, and Yukinori Harada. "Estimating China's Foreign Aid 2001–2013." *Journal of International Development* 28, no. 7 (2016): 1050–74.

Knack, Stephen. "Aid Dependence and the Quality of Governance: Cross-Country Empirical Tests." *Southern Economic Journal* 68, no. 2 (2001): 310–29.

———. "Does Foreign Aid Promote Democracy?" *International Studies Quarterly* 48, no. 1 (2004): 251–66.

Komisi Penyelidik Pelanggaran Hak Asasi Manusia di Timor Timur [Commission of Inquiry into Human Rights Violations in East Timor]. "Full Report of the Investigative Commission into Human Rights Violations in East Timor." In *Masters of Terror: Indonesia's Military and Violence in East Timor in 1999*, edited by Hamish McDonald, Desmond Ball, James Dinn, Gerry van Klinken, David Bourchier, Douglas Kammen, and Richard Tanter, 15–59. Canberra: Australian National University, 2002.

Kono, Daniel Yuichi, and Gabriella R. Montinola. "Does Foreign Aid Support Autocrats, Democrats, or Both?" *Journal of Politics* 71, no. 2 (2009): 704–18.

———. "The Uses and Abuses of Foreign Aid: Development Aid and Military Spending." *Political Research Quarterly* 66, no. 3 (2012): 615–29.

Kye Woo, Lee. "The Role of Aid in Korea's Development." In *Korea's Economy*, vol. 30, edited by Troy Stangarone, 7–25. Washington, DC: Korea Economic Institute of America, 2015. http://keia.org/sites/default/files/publications/kei_koreaseconomy_lee _0.pdf.

Lai, Brian. "Examining the Goals of US Foreign Assistance in the Post–Cold War Period, 1991–96." *Journal of Peace Research* 40, no. 1 (2003): 103–28.

Lakhani, Nina. "'We Fear Soldiers More Than Gangsters': El Salvador's 'Iron Fist' Policy Turns Deadly." *Guardian*, February 6, 2017. https://www.theguardian.com/world/2017 /feb/06/el-salvador-gangs-police-violence-distrito-italia.

———. "An American Sanctuary Ends For Salvadoran General." *Al Jazeera*. April 8, 2015. https://www.aljazeera.com/indepth/features/2015/04/american-sanctuary-ends -salvadoran-general-150406210929299.html.

Lancaster, Carol. *Foreign Aid: Diplomacy, Development, Domestic Politics*. Chicago: University of Chicago Press, 2007.

Landman, Todd, and Marco Larizza. "Inequality and Human Rights: Who Controls What, When, and How." *International Studies Quarterly* 53, no. 3 (2009): 715–36.

Larson, Greg, Peter Biar Ajak, and Lant Pritchett. "South Sudan's Capability Trap: Building a State with Disruptive Innovation." CID Working Paper No. 268, Center for International Development, Harvard University Kennedy School of Government, Harvard University, Cambridge, MA, 2013.

Le Billon, Philippe. "Buying Peace or Fuelling War: The Role of Corruption in Armed Conflicts." *Journal of International Development* 15, no. 4 (2003): 413–26.

Lebovic, James H. "National Interests and US Foreign Aid: The Carter and Reagan Years." *Journal of Peace Research* 25, no. 2 (1988): 115–35.

Lebovic, James H., and Erik Voeten. "The Cost of Shame: International Organizations and Foreign Aid in the Punishing of Human Rights Violators." *Journal of Peace Research* 46, no. 1 (2009): 79–97.

———. "The Politics of Shame: The Condemnation of Country Human Rights Practices in the UNCHR." *International Studies Quarterly* 50, no. 4 (2006): 861–88.

Leenders, Reinoud, and Kholoud Mansour. "Humanitarianism, State Sovereignty, and Authoritarian Regime Maintenance in the Syrian War." *Political Science Quarterly* 133, no. 2 (2018): 225–57.

Lentz, Erin C., Stephanie Mercier, and Christopher B. Barrett. *Food Aid and Assistance Programs and the Next Farm Bill*. Washington, DC: American Enterprise Institute, 2017.

LeoGrande, William M. *Our Own Backyard: The United States in Central America, 1977–1992*. Chapel Hill: University of North Carolina Press, 1998.

Leonard, Andrew M. "Getting the Leahy Law Right: How to Improve U.S. Funding of Foreign Forces." *Foreign Affairs*, June 29, 2017. https://www.foreignaffairs.com/articles /2017-06-29/getting-leahy-law-right.

Lewis, Linda S. *Laying Claim to the Memory of May: A Look Back at the 1980 Kwangju Uprising*. Honolulu: University of Hawai'i Press, 2002.

Lewis, Neil A. "Congress Says El Salvador Misuses U.S. Aid." *New York Times*, November 16, 1987. https://www.nytimes.com/1987/11/16/world/congress-says-el-salvador-misuses-us -aid.html.

Lichbach, Mark Irving. "An Evaluation of 'Does Economic Inequality Breed Political Conflict?' Studies." *World Politics* 41, no. 4 (1989): 431–70.

Liddle, R. William. "Polity and Economy in Suharto's Indonesia." *Crossroads: An Interdisciplinary Journal of Southeast Asian Studies* 1, no. 3 (1983): 35–46.

Linz, Juan J. *Totalitarian and Authoritarian Regimes.* Boulder, CO: Lynne Rienner, 2000.

Lipset, Seymour Martin. "Some Social Requisites of Democracy: Economic Development and Political Legitimacy." *American Political Science Review* 53, no. 1 (1959): 69–105.

Lischer, Sarah Kenyon. "Collateral Damage: Humanitarian Assistance as a Cause of Conflict." *International Security* 28, no. 1 (2003): 79–109.

Loveluck, Louisa "What's Non-Lethal About Aid to the Syrian Opposition?" *Foreign Policy,* September 20, 2012. https://foreignpolicy.com/2012/09/20/whats-non-lethal-about -aid-to-the-syrian-opposition/.

Lum, Thomas. "U.S. Foreign Aid to East and South Asia: Selected Recipients." CRS Report No. RL31362. Washington, DC: Congressional Research Service, 2008.

Lynch, Colum, Dan de Luce, and Paul McLeary. "The U.S. Helped Birth South Sudan. Now Americans Are Being Beaten and Targeted by Its Troops." *Foreign Policy,* August 16, 2016. http://foreignpolicy.com/2016/08/16/the-u-s-helped-birth-south-sudan -now-americans-are-being-beaten-and-targeted-by-its-troops/.

Malkin, Elizabeth, and Azam Ahmed. "U.S. Withholds $5 Million in Antidrug Aid to Mexico as Human Rights Rebuke." *New York Times,* October 19, 2015. https://www .nytimes.com/2015/10/20/world/americas/us-withholds-5-million-in-antidrug-aid-to -mexico-over-human-rights.html.

Mansfield, Edward, and Jack Snyder. "Democratic Transitions, Institutional Strength, and War." *International Organization* 56, no. 2 (2002): 297–337.

Maoz, Zeev, and Bruce Russett. "Normative and Structural Causes of Democratic Peace, 1946–1986." *American Political Science Review* 87, no. 3 (1993): 624–38.

Marshall, Monty G. *Major Episodes of Political Violence (MEPV) and Conflict Regions, 1946–2016.* July 25, 2017. Accessed March 31, 2018. Distributed by the Center for Systemic Peace. http://www.systemicpeace.org/inscrdata.html.

Marshall, Monty G., Ted Gurr, and Barbara Harff. *PITF-State Failure Problem Set: Internal Wars and Failures of Governance, 1955–2016.* June 21, 2017. Distributed by Societal-Systems Research Inc. http://www.systemicpeace.org/inscr/PITFProbSetCodebook2016.pdf.

Marshall, Monty G., Ted Robert Gurr, and Keith Jaggers. *Polity IV Project: Political Regime Characteristics and Transitions, 1800–2016.* July 25, 2017. Distributed by the Center for Systemic Peace. http://www.systemicpeace.org/polityproject.html.

Martins, Mark S. "The Commander's Emergency Response Program." *Joint Force Quarterly* 37 (2005): 46–52.

Marzuki, Nashrun, and Adi Warsidi, eds. *Fakta Bicara: Mengungkap Pelanggaran HAM di Aceh 1989–2005.* Banda Aceh, Indonesia: Koalisi NGO HAM Aceh, 2011.

Mason, T. David, and Dale A. Krane. "The Political Economy of Death Squads: Toward a Theory of the Impact of State-Sanctioned Terror." *International Studies Quarterly* 33, no. 2 (1989): 175–98.

McClintock, Michael. *The American Connection.* Vol. 1, *State Terror and Popular Resistance in El Salvador.* London: Zed Books, 1985.

McDonald, Hamish, Desmond Ball, James Dinn, Gerry van Klinken, David Bourchier, Douglas Kammen, and Richard Tanter. *Masters of Terror: Indonesia's Military and Violence in East Timor in 1999.* Canberra: Australian National University, 2002.

McFaul, Michael. "Democracy Promotion as a World Value." *Washington Quarterly* 28, no. 1 (2004): 147–63.

McGillivray, Mark. "What Determines African Bilateral Aid Receipts." *Journal of International Development* 17, no. 8 (2005): 1003–18.

McGillivray, Mark, and Oliver Morrissey. "Aid Fungibility in *Assessing Aid*: Red Herring or True Concern?" *Journal of International Development* 12, no. 3 (2000): 413–28.

McGuire, Martin C. "US Assistance, Israeli Allocation, and the Arms Race in the Middle East: An Analysis of Three Interdependent Resource Allocation Processes." *Journal of Conflict Resolution* 26, no. 2 (1982): 199–235.

McLaren, L. M. "The Effect of IMF Austerity Programs on Human Rights Violations: An Exploratory Analysis of Peru, Argentina, and Brazil." Paper presented at the 56th Annual Meeting of the Midwest Political Science Association, Chicago, IL, April 1998.

McVety, Amanda. *Enlightened Aid: U.S. Development as Foreign Policy in Ethiopia*. Oxford: Oxford University Press, 2012.

Meernik, James, Eric. L. Krueger, and Steven C. Poe. "Testing Models of US Foreign Policy: Foreign Aid During and After the Cold War." *Journal of Politics* 60, no. 1 (1998): 63–85.

Meernik, James, and Steven C. Poe. "US Foreign Aid in the Domestic and International Environments." *International Interactions* 22, no. 1 (1996): 21–40.

Menon, Rajan. *The Conceit of Humanitarian Intervention*. Oxford: Oxford University Press, 2016.

Meyer, William H. *Human Rights and International Political Economy in Third World Nations: Multinational Corporations, Foreign Aid, and Repression*. Westport, CT: Praeger, 1998.

——. "Human Rights and MNCs: Theory Versus Quantitative Analysis." *Human Rights Quarterly* 18, no. 2 (1996): 368–97.

Michaelson, Ruth. "'We Want Bread': Subsidy Cut Sparks Protests Across Egypt." *Guardian*, March 8, 2017. https://www.theguardian.com/world/2017/mar/08/egypt-protests -we-want-bread-subsidy-cut.

Midlarsky, Manus I. "Rulers and the Ruled: Patterned Inequality and the Onset of Mass Political Violence." *American Political Science Review* 82, no. 2 (1988): 491–509.

Montoya-Galvez, Camilo. "Trump's Move to Cut Aid to Central America Will Spur More Migration, Aid Workers Warn." *CBS News*, April 4, 2019. https://www.cbsnews.com /news/trumps-move-to-cut-aid-to-central-america-will-spur-more-migration-aid -workers-warn.

Moore, Peter. "Foreign Aid: Most People Think America Gives Too Much Away." YouGov, March 11, 2016. https://today.yougov.com/news/2016/03/11/foreign-aid/.

Morgenthau, Hans. "A Political Theory of Foreign Aid." *American Political Science Review* 56, no. 2 (1962): 301–9.

Moss, Todd, David Roodman, and Scott Standley. "The Global War on Terror and US Development Assistance: USAID Allocation by Country, 1998–2005." Working Paper No. 62, Center for Global Development, Washington, DC, 2005.

Mott, William N. *Soviet Military Assistance: An Empirical Perspective*. Westport, CT: Praeger, 2001.

Moyar, Mark. *Aid for Elites: Building Partner Nations and Ending Poverty Through Human Capital*. New York: Cambridge University Press, 2016.

Moyo, Dambisa. *Winner Take All: China's Race for Resources and What It Means for the World*. Toronto: HarperCollins, 2012.

Muller, Edward N. "Income Inequality, Regime Repressiveness, and Political Violence." *American Sociological Review* 50, no. 1 (1985): 47–61.

Muller, Edward N., and Mitchell A. Seligson. "Inequality and Insurgency." *American Political Science Review* 81, no. 2 (1987): 425–52.

Murdie, Amanda. *Help or Harm: The Human Security Effects of International NGOs.* Stanford, CA: Stanford University Press, 2014.

Murdie, Amanda, and Tavishi Bhasin. "Aiding and Abetting: Human Rights INGOs and Domestic Protest." *Journal of Conflict Resolution* 55, no. 2 (2011): 163–91.

Murdie, Amanda, and Simone Dietrich. "Human Rights Shaming Through INGOs and Foreign Aid Delivery." *Review of International Organizations* 12, no. 1 (2017): 95–120.

Murdie, Amanda, and Dursun Peksen. "The Impact of Human Rights INGO Shaming on Humanitarian Intervention." *Journal of Politics* 76, no. 1 (2014): 215–28.

———. "Women's Rights INGO Shaming and the Government Respect for Women's Rights." *Review of International Organizations* 10, no. 1 (2015): 1–22.

Murshed, Syed Mansoob, and Somnath Sen. "Aid Conditionality and Military Expenditure Reduction in Developing Countries: Models of Asymmetric Information." *Economic Journal* 105, no. 429 (1995): 498–509.

Narang, Neil. "Assisting Uncertainty: How Humanitarian Aid Can Inadvertently Prolong Civil War." *International Studies Quarterly* 59, no. 1 (2015): 184–95.

Neumayer, Eric. "Do International Human Rights Treaties Improve Respect for Human Rights?" *Journal of Conflict Resolution* 49, no. 6 (2005): 925–53.

———. "Self-Interest, Foreign Need, and Good Governance: Are Bilateral Investment Treaty Programs Similar to Aid Allocation?" *Foreign Policy Analysis* 2, no. 3 (2006): 245–67.

Neumayer, Eric, and Laura Spess. "Do Bilateral Investment Treaties Increase Foreign Direct Investment to Developing Countries?" *World Development* 33, no. 10 (2005): 1567–85.

New York Times. "The 1992 Campaign; Transcript of 2d TV Debate Between Bush, Clinton and Perot." October 16, 1992. http://www.nytimes.com/1992/10/16/us/the-1992 -campaign-transcript-of-2d-tv-debate-between-bush-clinton-and-perot.html.

Nixon, Richard. "Informal Remarks in Guam with Newsmen." July 25, 1969. American Presidency Project, University of California–Santa Barbara. https://www.presidency .ucsb.edu/documents/informal-remarks-guam-with-newsmen. Transcript.

———. "Special Message to the Congress on Foreign Aid." May 28, 1969. American Presidency Project, University of California–Santa Barbara. https://www.presidency.ucsb .edu/documents/special-message-the-congress-foreign-aid. Transcript.

Nunn, Nathan, and Nancy Qian. "U.S. Food Aid and Civil Conflict." *American Economic Review* 104, no. 6 (2014): 1630–66.

Obama, Barack. *National Security Strategy.* Washington, DC: White House, 2010. http:// nssarchive.us/NSSR/2010.pdf.

O'Grady, Siobhan. "A New Report Estimates That More Than 380,000 People Have Died in South Sudan's Civil War." *Washington Post,* September 26, 2018. https://www .washingtonpost.com/world/africa/a-new-report-estimates-more-than-380000-people -have-died-in-south-sudans-civil-war/2018/09/25/e41fcb84-c0e7-11e8-9f4f-a1b7af255aa5 _story.html.

Okiror, Samuel. "'They Exaggerated Figures': Ugandan Aid Officials Suspended over Alleged Fraud." *Guardian,* February 8, 2018. https://www.theguardian.com/global

-development/2018/feb/08/they-exaggerated-figures-uganda-aid-officials-suspended -over-alleged-fraud.

Omang, Joanne. "Duarte Conquers Congress on Aid to El Salvador." *Washington Post,* May 23, 1984. https://www.cia.gov/library/readingroom/docs/CIA-RDP90-00552R000 100980003-2.pdf.

Omang, Joanne, and Michael J. Weisskopf. "Reagan to Push Aid for Duarte's Military." *Washington Post,* June 21, 1985. https://www.cia.gov/library/readingroom/docs/CIA -RDP90-00965R000807300020-5.pdf.

Omelicheva, Mariya, Brittnee Carter, and Luke B. Campbell. "Military Aid and Human Rights: Assessing the Impact of U.S. Security Assistance Programs." *Political Science Quarterly* 132, no. 1 (2017): 119–44.

Organisation for Economic Co-operation and Development. "Net ODA." Accessed January 3, 2018. https://data.oecd.org/oda/net-oda.htm.

———. OECD.Stat. Accessed December 7, 2018. http://stats.oecd.org/.

———. "Turkey's Official Development Assistance (ODA)." Accessed January 17, 2019, http://www.oecd.org/dac/stats/turkeys-official-development-assistanceoda.htm.

Ottaway, Marina, and Thomas Carothers, eds. *Funding Virtue: Civil Society Aid and Democracy Promotion.* Washington, DC: Carnegie Endowment for International Peace, 2000.

Pack, Howard, and Janet Rothenberg Pack. "Foreign Aid and the Question of Fungibility." *Review of Economics and Statistics* 75, no. 2 (1993): 258–65.

Palda, Filip. "Can Repressive Regimes Be Moderated Through Foreign Aid?" *Public Choice* 77, no. 3 (1993): 535–50.

Pauker, Guy J. "The Soviet Challenge in Indonesia." *Foreign Affairs,* July 1962. https://www.foreignaffairs.com/articles/asia/1962-07-01/soviet-challenge-indonesia.

Peksen, Dursun. "Better or Worse? The Effect of Economic Sanctions on Human Rights." *Journal of Peace Research* 46, no. 1 (2009): 59–77.

Peksen Dursun, and A. Cooper Drury. "Coercive or Corrosive: The Negative Impact of Economic Sanctions on Democracy." *International Interactions* 36, no. 3 (2010): 240–64.

———. "Economic Sanctions and Political Repression: Assessing the Impact of Coercive Diplomacy on Political Freedoms." *Human Rights Review* 10, no. 3 (2009): 393–411.

Pettersson, Jan. "Foreign Sectoral Aid Fungibility, Growth and Poverty Reduction." *Journal of International Development* 19, no. 8 (2007): 1074–98.

Piazza, James A. "Incubators of Terror: Do Failed and Failing States Promote Transnational Terrorism?" *International Studies Quarterly* 52, no. 3 (2008): 469–88.

Pierskalla, Jan Henryk. "Protest, Deterrence, and Escalation: The Strategic Calculus of Government Repression." *Journal of Conflict Resolution* 54, no. 1 (2010): 117–45.

Prendergast, John. *Frontline Diplomacy: Humanitarian Aid and Conflict in Africa.* Boulder, CO: Lynne Rienner, 1996.

Purushothaman, Chithra. "Why Is the Philippines Turning Away Foreign Aid?" *Diplomat,* May 25, 2017. http://thediplomat.com/2017/05/why-is-the-philippines-turning -away-foreign-aid/.

Qian, Nancy, and David Yanagizawa-Drott. "Government Distortion in Independently Owned Media: Evidence from U.S. News Coverage of Human Rights." *Journal of the European Economic Association* 15, no. 2 (2017): 463–99.

———. "The Strategic Determinants of US Human Rights Reporting: Evidence from the Cold War." *Journal of the European Economic Association* 7, no. 2/3 (2009): 446–57.

Querido, Chyanda M. "State-Sponsored Mass Killing in African Wars—Greed or Grievance?" *International Advances in Economic Research* 15, no. 3 (2009): 351–61.

Radelet, Steven. *The Great Surge: The Ascent of the Developing World.* New York: Simon
and Schuster, 2015.

Ranada, Pia. "China Gives P370M in Guns, Ammunition to PH." *Rappler,* June 28, 2017.
https://www.rappler.com/nation/174190-china-military-aid-guns-ammunition
-philippines-marawi-terrorism.

Rasmussen Reports. "Most See U.S. Foreign Aid as a Bad Deal for America." March 20,
2017. http://www.rasmussenreports.com/public_content/politics/general_politics/march
_2017/most_see_u_s_foreign_aid_as_a_bad_deal_for_america.

———. "Most Still Question the Value of Foreign Aid." January 8, 2018. http://www
.rasmussenreports.com/public_content/politics/general_politics/january_2018/most
_still_question_the_value_of_foreign_aid.

Reagan, Ronald. "Address Before a Joint Session of the Congress on Central America."
April 27, 1983. Ronald Reagan Presidential Library. https://www.reaganlibrary.gov
/research/speeches/42783d. Transcript.

———. "Remarks at a White House Briefing for the Citizens Network for Foreign Affairs." October 21, 1987. Ronald Reagan Presidential Library. https://reaganlibrary
.archives.gov/archives/speeches/1987/102187a.htm. Transcript.

———. "Remarks on Central America and El Salvador at the Annual Meeting of the
National Association of Manufacturers." March 10, 1983. Ronald Reagan Presidential
Library. https://www.reaganlibrary.gov/research/speeches/31083a. Transcript.

Regan, Patrick M. "US Economic Aid and Political Repression: An Empirical Evaluation
of US Foreign Policy." *Political Research Quarterly* 48, no. 3 (1995): 613–28.

Regan, Patrick M., and Sam R. Bell. "Changing Lanes or Stuck in the Middle: Why Are
Anocracies More Prone to Civil Wars?" *Political Research Quarterly* 63, no. 4 (2010):
747–59.

Regan, Patrick M., and Errol A. Henderson. "Democracy, Threats and Political Repression
in Developing Countries: Are Democracies Internally Less Violent?" *Third World
Quarterly* 23, no. 1 (2002): 119–36.

Rennack, Dianne E. "Foreign Assistance Act of 1961: Authorizations and Corresponding
Appropriations." CRS Report No. R40089. Washington, DC: Congressional Research
Service, 2010.

Renteria, Nelson. "Gang Warfare in El Salvador Pushes Death Rate to Record." Reuters.
January 21, 2016. https://www.reuters.com/article/us-el-salvador-violence-widerimage
/gang-warfare-in-el-salvador-pushes-death-rate-to-record-idUSKCN0UZ1FK.

Reuters. "El Salvador Court Quashes Arrest Order for Soldiers over 1989 Murders."
August 22, 2017. https://www.reuters.com/article/us-elsalvador-killings-spain-idUSKCN
1B307I.

———. "South Sudan Waives Registration Fees for Aid Groups for a Year." January 27,
2018. https://www.reuters.com/article/southsudan-aid/south-sudan-waives-registration
-fees-for-aid-groups-for-a-year-idUSL8N1PM0B9.

Rich, Paul, and Richard Stubbs, eds. *The Counter-Insurgent State: Guerrilla Warfare and
State-Building in the Twentieth Century.* New York: St. Martin's Press, 1997.

Richards, David L., Ronald D. Gelleny, and David H. Sacko. "Money with a Mean Streak?
Foreign Economic Penetration and Government Respect for Human Rights in Developing Countries." *International Studies Quarterly* 45, no. 2 (2001): 219–39.

Ricklefs, M. C. *A History of Modern Indonesia, c. 1300 to the Present.* Bloomington: Indiana University Press, 1981.

Robinson, Geoffrey. *"If You Leave Us Here, We Will Die": How Genocide Was Stopped in East Timor.* Princeton, NJ: Princeton University Press, 2010.

Roosa, John. *Pretext for Mass Murder: The September 30th Movement and Suharto's Coup d'Etat in Indonesia.* Madison: University of Wisconsin Press, 2006.

Roosevelt, Franklin D. "Executive Order 6581 Creating the Export-Import Bank of Washington." February 2, 1934. American Presidency Project, University of California–Santa Barbara. https://www.presidency.ucsb.edu/documents/executive-order-6581-creating-the-export-import-bank-washington. Transcript.

Ross, Michael L. "Resources and Rebellion in Aceh, Indonesia." In *Understanding Civil War,* edited by Paul Collier and Nicholas Sambanis, 35–58. Washington, DC: World Bank, 2005.

Rotberg, Robert I., ed. *State Failure and State Weakness in a Time of Terror.* Washington, DC: Brookings Institution Press, 2003.

Rowe, Edward T. "Aid and Coups d'Etat: Aspect of the Impact of American Military Assistance Programs in the Less Developed Countries." *International Studies Quarterly* 18, no. 2 (1974): 239–55.

Sachs, Jeffrey D. *The End of Poverty: Economic Possibilities for Our Time.* New York: Penguin, 2005.

Sadat, Leila Nadya. "Ghost Prisoners and Black Sites: Extraordinary Rendition Under International Law." *Case Western Reserve Journal of International Law* 37, no. 2 (2006): 309–42.

Said, Salim. *Legitimizing Military Rule: Indonesian Armed Forces Ideology, 1958–2000.* Translated by Toenggoel P. Siagian. Jakarta: Pustaka Sinar Harapan, 2006.

Sambanis, Nicholas, and Annalisa Zinn. "From Protest to Violence: An Analysis of Conflict Escalation with an Application to Self-Determination Movements." Paper presented at the Annual Meeting of the American Political Science Association, Washington, DC, September 2005.

Sanchez, Thania. "After Ratification: The Domestic Politics of Treaty Implementation and Compliance." PhD diss., Columbia University, 2009.

Sarro, Ron. "House Upholds Korea Aid." *Washington Star,* n.d. Accessed January 15, 2019. https://www.cia.gov/library/readingroom/docs/CIA-RDP81M00980R000600170018-9.pdf.

Saudi Aid Platform. "Financial Statistics." Accessed January 17, 2019. https://data.ksrelief.org/en/FinancialStatistics.aspx.

Savage, Timothy L. "The American Response to the Korean Independence Movement, 1910–1945." *Korean Studies* 20 (1996): 189–231.

Schlesinger, Arthur, Jr. "Failings of the Kissinger Report." *New York Times,* January 17, 1984. https://www.nytimes.com/1984/01/17/opinion/failings-of-the-kissinger-report.html.

Schmitt, Eric. "Warnings of a 'Powder Keg' in Libya as ISIS Regroups." *New York Times,* March 12, 2017. https://www.nytimes.com/2017/03/21/world/africa/libya-isis.html.

Schrodt, Philip A., and Jay Ulfelder. *Political Instability Task Force Worldwide Atrocities Dataset.* Version 1.1b. September 12, 2016. Distributed by Computational Event Data System. http://eventdata.parusanalytics.com/data.dir/atrocities.html.

Schulze, Kirsten E. "Insurgency and Counter-insurgency: Strategy in the Aceh Conflict." In *Verandah of Violence: Aceh's Contested Place in Indonesia,* edited by Anthony Reid, 225–71. Singapore: Singapore University Press, 2006.

Schwartz, Felicia, and Jessica Donati. "U.S. Cuts Millions in Funding to U.N. Palestinian Agency." *Wall Street Journal*, August 31, 2018. https://www.wsj.com/articles/u-s-will -cut-millions-in-funding-to-u-n-palestinian-agency-1535739845.

Scott, James C. *Weapons of the Weak: Everyday Forms of Peasant Resistance.* New Haven, CT: Yale University Press, 1985.

Scotto, Thomas J., Jason Reifler, David Hudson, and Jennifer vanHeerde-Hudson. "We Spend How Much? Misperceptions, Innumeracy, and Support for the Foreign Aid in the United States and Great Britain." *Journal of Experimental Political Science* 4, no. 2 (2017): 119–28.

Sebastian, Leonard C. *Realpolitik Ideology: Indonesia's Use of Military Force.* Singapore: Utopia Press, 2006.

Serafino, Nina M., June S. Beittel, Lauren Ploch Blanchard, and Liana Rosen. "'Leahy Law' Human Rights Provisions and Security Assistance: Issue Overview." CRS Report No. 7-5700. Washington, DC: Congressional Research Service, 2014.

Shendruk, Amanda. "Many UN Agencies Are in a Precarious Position if the US Decides to Cut Foreign Aid." *Quartz*, September 29, 2018. https://qz.com/1405965/many-un -agencies-are-in-a-precarious-position-if-the-us-decides-to-cut-foreign-aid/.

Sigelman, Lee, and Miles Simpson. "A Cross-National Test of the Linkage Between Economic Inequality and Political Violence." *Journal of Conflict Resolution* 21, no. 1 (1977): 105–28.

Simpson, Bradley R. "Denying the 'First Right': The United States, Indonesia, and the Ranking of Human Rights by the Carter Administration, 1976–1980." *International History Review* 32, no. 4 (2009): 709–944.

———. *Economists with Guns: Authoritarian Development and U.S.-Indonesian Relations, 1960–1968.* Stanford, CA: Stanford University Press, 2008.

———, ed. *Suharto: A Declassified Documentary Obit.* Washington, DC: National Security Archive, 2008.

Snyder, Jack L. *From Voting to Violence: Democratization and Nationalist Conflict.* New York: Norton, 2000.

Socorro Juridico Cristiano (Christian Legal Aid). "Informe no. 11, ano IX." San Salvador, 1984.

———. "Sobre los Refugiados Salvadorenos." San Salvador, 1981.

Sohn, Hak-Kyu. *Authoritarianism and Opposition in South Korea.* London: Routledge, 1989.

Sparrow, Annie. "How UN Humanitarian Aid Has Propped Up Assad." *Foreign Affairs*, September 20, 2018. https://www.foreignaffairs.com/articles/syria/2018-09-20/how-un -humanitarian-aid-has-propped-assad.

Stanley, William. *The Protection Racket State: Elite Politics, Military Extortion, and Civil War in El Salvador.* Philadelphia: Temple University Press, 1996.

Stephenson, Emily, and Roberta Rampton. "U.S. to Send $70 Million in Non-Lethal Aid to Syrian Opposition." Reuters, March 13, 2015. https://www.reuters.com/article/us-usa -syria-aid/u-s-to-send-70-million-in-non-lethal-aid-to-syrian-opposition -idUSKBN0M91WF20150313.

Stohl, Michael, David Carleton, and Steven E. Johnson. "Human Rights and US Foreign Assistance from Nixon to Carter." *Journal of Peace Research* 21, no. 3 (1984): 215–26.

Storrs, K. Larry. "Kissinger Commission Implementation: Action by the Congress Through 1986 on the Recommendations of the National Bipartisan Commission on Central America." CRS Report No. 87–291 F. Washington, DC: Congressional Research Service, 1987.

Sudan Tribune. "U.S. Military Aid to South Sudan Government Criticized by Opposition Faction." October 9, 2016. http://www.sudantribune.com/spip.php?article60476.

Svensson, Jakob. "Aid, Growth and Democracy." *Economics and Politics* 11, no. 3 (1999): 275–97.

Swedlund, Haley. *The Development Dance: How Donors and Recipients Negotiate the Delivery of Foreign Aid.* Ithaca, NY: Cornell University Press, 2017.

Tarnoff, Curt, and Marian Leonardo Lawson. "Foreign Aid: An Introduction to US Programs and Policy." CRS Report No. R40213. Washington, DC: Congressional Research Service, 2018.

Taubman, Philip. "Top Salvador Police Official Said to Be a CIA Informant." *New York Times*, March 22, 1984. http://www.nytimes.com/1984/03/22/world/top-salvador-police -official-said-to-be-a-cia-informant.html.

Taydas, Zeynep, and Dursun Peksen. "Can States Buy Peace? Social Welfare Spending and Civil Conflicts." *Journal of Peace Research* 49, no. 2 (2012): 273–87.

Terry, Fiona. *Condemned to Repeat? The Paradox of Humanitarian Action.* Ithaca, NY: Cornell University Press, 2002.

Thaler, Kai. "Foreshadowing Future Slaughter: From the Indonesian Killings of 1965–1966 to the 1974–1999 Genocide in East Timor." *Genocide Studies and Prevention* 7, no. 2/3 (2012): 204–22.

Themnér, Lotta, and Peter Wallensteen. "Armed Conflict, 1946–2011." *Journal of Peace Research* 49, no. 4 (2012): 565–75.

Tilly, Charles. *From Mobilization to Revolution.* New York: Addison-Wesley, 1978.

Times of Israel. "UN Committees Adopt 10 Resolutions Against Israel in a Single Day." November 9, 2016. https://www.timesofisrael.com/un-committees-begin-voting-on-10 -resolutions-against-israel-in-a-single-day/.

Travis, Rick, and Nikolaos Zahariadis. "Aid for Arms: The Impact of Superpower Economic Assistance on Military Spending in Sub-Saharan Africa." *International Interactions* 17, no. 3 (1992): 233–43.

Trisko, Jessica N. "Coping with the Islamist Threat: Analysing Repression in Kazakhstan, Kyrgyzstan and Uzbekistan." *Central Asian Survey* 24, no. 4 (2005): 373–89.

Trisko Darden, Jessica. "Compounding Violent Extremism? When Efforts to Prevent Violence Backfire." *War on the Rocks*, June 6, 2018. https://warontherocks.com/2018/06 /compounding-violent-extremism-when-efforts-to-prevent-violence-backfire/.

Truman, Harry S. "Inaugural Address." January 20, 1949. Harry S. Truman Library and Museum. https://www.trumanlibrary.org/whistlestop/50yr_archive/inagural20jan1949 .htm. Transcript.

Tschirley, David, Cynthia Donovan, and Michael T. Weber. "Food Aid and Food Markets: Lessons from Mozambique." *Food Policy* 21, no. 2 (1996): 189–209.

Turner, Michele. *Telling East Timor: Personal Testimonies 1942–1992.* Kensington, Australia: New South Wales University Press, 1992.

United Nations. "Convention Against Torture and Other Cruel, Inhuman or Degrading Treatment or Punishment." In *United Nations Treaty Series*, vol. 1465, 85. New York: United Nations, 1984.

United Nations. General Assembly. *Universal Declaration of Human Rights.* A/RES/217. New York: United Nations, 1948. http://www.un.org/en/universal-declaration-human -rights/index.html.

United Nations. General Assembly. Human Rights Council. *Report of the Commission on Human Rights in South Sudan.* A/HRC/37/71. New York: United Nations, 2018.

United Nations. United Nations Peacekeeping. "UNMISS Fact Sheet: United Nations

Mission in the Republic of South Sudan." Accessed January 23, 2019. https://peacekeeping .un.org/en/mission/unmiss.

United Nations News. "UN Human Rights Chief Points to 'Textbook Example of Ethnic Cleansing' in Myanmar." September 11, 2017. https://news.un.org/en/story/2017 /09/564622-un-human-rights-chief-points-textbook-example-ethnic-cleansing -myanmar.

University of Maryland Center for International Development and Conflict Management. "Chronology for Papuans in Indonesia." Minorities at Risk Project. Last modified July 16, 2010. http://www.mar.umd.edu/chronology.asp?groupId=85005.

University of Washington. Institute for Health Metrics and Evaluation. *Financing Global Health 2010: Development Assistance and Country Spending in Economic Uncertainty.* Seattle, WA: Institute for Health Metrics and Evaluation, 2010. http://www.healthdata .org/sites/default/files/files/policy_report/2010/FGH2010/IHME_FGH2010 _FullReport.pdf.

Urbina, Ian. "O.A.S. to Reopen Inquiry into Massacre in El Salvador in 1981." *New York Times,* March 5, 2005. http://www.nytimes.com/2005/03/08/international/americas /08salvador.html.

USAID (U.S. Agency for International Development). *US Overseas Loans and Grants: Obligations and Loan Authorizations, July 1, 1945–September 30, 2016.* Accessed March 31, 2018. Distributed by the U.S. Agency for International Development. https://explorer .usaid.gov/reports.html.

———. "South Sudan—Crisis: Fact Sheet #5, Fiscal Year (FY) 2019." April 8, 2019. https://www.usaid.gov/sites/default/files/documents/1866/south_sudan_cr_fs05_04-08 -2019.pdf.

U.S. Congress. *Legislation on Foreign Relations Through 2002.* Vol. I-A. 108th Cong., 1st sess., July 2003. Washington, DC: Government Printing Office, 2003. https://www.usaid .gov/sites/default/files/documents/1868/faa.pdf.

U.S. Congress. Arms Control and Foreign Policy Caucus. *U.S. Aid to El Salvador: An Evaluation of the Past, a Proposal for the Future; A Report to the Arms Control and Foreign Policy Caucus from Rep. Jim Leach, Rep. George Miller and Sen. Mark O. Hatfield.* Washington, DC: Arms Control and Foreign Policy Caucus, 1985.

U.S. Congress. Committee on International Relations and Committee on Foreign Relations. *Investigation of Korean-American Relations.* 95th Cong., 2d sess., 1978. Washington, DC: Government Printing Office, 1978. https://archive.org/details/investigationofkoounit /page/n1.

U.S. Department of Defense. Department of the Air Force. Office of the Director. "Soviet Military Buildup in Indonesia." November 9, 1962. https://www.cia.gov/library/reading room/docs/CIA-RDP80B01676R000100140018-9.pdf.

U.S. Department of State. "Attacks on Aid Workers: Countries with Ten or More Victims, Jan. 2016–Mar. 2017." *Humanitarian Information Unit.* https://hiu.state.gov/#global,U1567.

———. *Country Reports on Human Rights Practices: Report Submitted to the Committee on Foreign Relations, U.S. Senate and Committee on Foreign Affairs, U.S. House of Representatives.* Washington, DC: Government Printing Office, 1978. Microform.

———. "Department of State & USAID Joint Strategy on Countering Violent Extremism." May 2016. https://www.usaid.gov/sites/default/files/documents/1866/FINAL%20 —%20State%20and%20USAID%20Joint%20Strategy%20on%20Countering%20Violent%20Extremism%20%28May%202016%29.pdf.

———. *Foreign Relations of the United States* (hereafter *FRUS*), *1952–1954.* Vol. IV, *The*

American Republics. Ed. N. Stephen Kane and William F. Sanford Jr. Washington, DC: Government Printing Office, 1983.

———. *FRUS, 1952–1954, East Asia and the Pacific*. Vol. XII, part 1. Ed. David W. Mabon. Washington, DC: Government Publishing Office, 1984.

———. *FRUS, 1952–1954, East Asia and the Pacific*. Vol. XII, part 2. Ed. Carl N. Raether and Harriet D. Schwar. Washington, DC: Government Printing Office, 1987.

———. *FRUS, 1952–1954, Korea*. Vol. XV, part 1. Ed. Edward C. Keefer. Washington, DC: Government Publishing Office, 1984.

———. *FRUS, 1952–1954, Korea*. Vol. XV, part 2. Ed. Edward C. Keefer. Washington, DC: Government Publishing Office, 1984.

———. *FRUS, 1961–1963*. Vol. VIII, *National Security Policy*. Ed. David W. Mabon. Washington, DC: Government Printing Office, 1996.

———. *FRUS, 1961–1963*. Vol. XXIII, *Southeast Asia*. Ed. Edward C. Keefer. Washington, DC: Government Printing Office, 1994.

———. *FRUS, 1964–1968*. Vol. XXVI, *Indonesia; Malaysia-Singapore; Philippines*. Ed. Edward C. Keefer. Washington, DC: Government Printing Office, 2000.

———. *FRUS, 1969–1976*. Vol. E-10, *Documents on American Republics, 1969–1972*. Ed. Douglas Kraft and James Siekmeier. Washington, DC: Government Printing Office, 2009.

———. *FRUS, 1969–1976*. Vol. E-12, *Documents on East and Southeast Asia, 1973–1976*. Ed. Bradley Lynn Coleman, David Goldman, and David Nickles. Washington, DC: Government Printing Office, 2010.

———. *FRUS, 1969–1976*. Vol. E-11, *Documents on Mexico; Central America; and the Caribbean, 1973–1976*. Ed. Halbert Jones. Washington, DC: Government Printing Office, 2015.

———. *FRUS, 1969–1976*. Vol. XX, *Southeast Asia, 1969–1972*. Ed. Daniel J. Lawler. Washington, DC: Government Printing Office, 2006.

———. *FRUS, 1977–1980*. Vol. XV, *Central America, 1977–1980*. Ed. Nathaniel L. Smith. Washington, DC: Government Publishing Office, 2016.

———. *FRUS, 1977–1980*. Vol. I, *Foundations of Foreign Policy*. Ed. Kristin L. Ahlberg. Washington, DC: Government Printing Office, 2014.

———. *FRUS, 1981–1988*. Vol. XLI, *Global Issues II*. Ed. Alexander O. Poster. Washington, DC: Government Publishing Office, 2017.

———. *FRUS, 1981–88*. Vol. III, *Soviet Union, January 1981–January 1983*. Ed. James Graham Wilson. Washington, DC: Government Publishing Office, 2016.

———. *Leading Through Civilian Power: The First Quadrennial Diplomacy and Development Review*. Washington, DC: Department of State, 2010.

———. *United States Contributions to International Organizations: Sixty-Sixth Annual Report to the Congress; Fiscal Year 2017*. Washington, DC: Department of State, 2017. https://www.state.gov/documents/organization/287307.pdf.

U.S. Department of State. Office of Inspector General. "Inspection of the Bureau of African Affairs' Foreign Assistance Program Management." ISP-I-18–02. Washington, DC: Department of State, 2017. https://www.oversight.gov/sites/default/files/oig-reports/ISP-I-18–02.pdf.

U.S. General Accounting Office. *Central America: Impact of U.S. Assistance in the 1980s*. Washington, DC: General Accounting Office, 1989. https://www.gao.gov/assets/150/147879.pdf.

———. *El Salvador: Accountability for U.S. Military and Economic Aid*. Washington, DC: General Accounting Office, 1990. https://www.gao.gov/assets/150/149630.pdf.

———. *El Salvador: Transfers of Military Assistance Fuels.* Washington, DC: General Accounting Office, 1989. https://www.gao.gov/assets/220/211593.pdf.

U.S. Government Accountability Office. "Human Rights: Additional Guidance, Monitoring, and Training Could Improve Implementation of the Leahy Laws." GAO-13–866. Washington, DC: Government Accountability Office, 2013. https://www.gao.gov/assets/660/658107.pdf.

U.S. Office of Management and Budget. *America First: A Budget Blueprint to Make America Great Again, Budget of the United States Government, Fiscal Year 2018.* Washington, DC: Government Publishing Office, 2017. https://www.govinfo.gov/content/pkg/BUDGET-2018-BLUEPRINT/pdf/BUDGET-2018-BLUEPRINT.pdf.

U.S. President's Emergency Plan for AIDS Relief. "PEPFAR Funding." July 2016. Accessed January 25, 2019. https://www.pepfar.gov/documents/organization/252516.pdf.

Valentino, Benjamin, Paul Huth, and Dylan Balch-Lindsay. "'Draining the Sea': Mass Killing and Guerrilla Warfare." *International Organization* 58, no. 2 (2004): 375–407.

Vaswani, Karishma. "Indonesia Confirms Papua Torture." BBC News, October 22, 2010. http://www.bbc.co.uk/news/world-asia-pacific-11604361.

Vaughn, Bruce. "Papua, Indonesia: Issues for Congress." CRS Report No. RL33260. Washington, DC: Congressional Research Service, 2006.

Vreeland, James Raymond. "The Effect of Political Regime on Civil War: Unpacking Anocracy." *Journal of Conflict Resolution* 52, no. 3 (2008): 401–25.

———. "Political Institutions and Human Rights: Why Dictatorships Enter into the United Nations Convention Against Torture." *International Organization* 62, no. 1 (2008): 65–101.

Wall Street Journal. "Ex-Im Bank Approves Loan of $292.5 Million for Indonesia Refinery." October 1, 1982. 43.

———. "Ex-Im Bank Sets Loan to Indonesia for Parts Supplied by Boeing Unit." March 9, 1984. 15.

Walsh, Declan, and Helen Pidd. "US to Cut Aid to Pakistan Military Units over Human Rights Abuses." *Guardian*, October 22, 2010. https://www.theguardian.com/world/2010/oct/22/us-cut-pakistan-military-aid.

Wampler, Robert, ed. *Seeing Human Rights in the "Proper Manner."* Washington, DC: National Security Archive, 2010.

Waters, Jeff. "Torture in West Papua: The Video Verdict Is In." ABC, October 27, 2010. https://www.abc.net.au/news/2010-10-27/torture-in-west-papua-the-video-verdict-is-in/2313438.

Weinraub, Bernard. "Reagan Certifies Salvador for Aid." *New York Times*, July 28, 1982. http://www.nytimes.com/1982/07/28/world/reagan-certifies-salvador-for-aid.html.

Weissbrodt, David, and Amy Bergquist. "Extraordinary Rendition: A Human Rights Analysis." *Harvard Human Rights Journal* 19 (2006): 123–60.

Wilson, Woodrow. "Address Delivered at Joint Session of the Two Houses of Congress." April 2, 1917. U.S. 65th Congress, 1st Session, Senate Document 5.

Wood, Reed M. "'A Hand upon the Throat of the Nation': Economic Sanctions and State Repression, 1976–2001." *International Studies Quarterly* 52, no. 3 (2008): 489–513.

Wood, Reed M., and Mark Gibney. "The Political Terror Scale (PTS): A Re-Introduction and a Comparison to CIRI." *Human Rights Quarterly* 32, no. 2 (2010): 367–400.

Wood, Reed M., and Christopher Sullivan. "Doing Harm by Doing Good? The Negative Externalities of Humanitarian Aid Provision During Civil Conflict." *Journal of Politics* 77, no. 3 (2015): 736–48.

World Bank. *World Development Indicators*. Accessed March 31, 2018. Distributed by the World Bank. http://data.worldbank.org/data-catalog/world-development-indicators.

Wright, Joseph. "How Foreign Aid Can Foster Democratization in Authoritarian Regimes." *American Journal of Political Science* 53, no. 3 (2009): 552–71.

Yamano, Takashi, Harold Alderman, and Luc Christiaensen. "Child Growth, Shocks, and Food Aid in Rural Ethiopia." *American Journal of Agricultural Economics* 87, no. 2 (2005): 273–88.

Yang, Sung Chul. "Student Political Activism: The Case of the 1960 April Revolution in South Korea." *Youth and Society* 5, no. 1 (1973): 47–60.

Zahariadis, Nikolaos, Rick Travis, and Paul F. Diehl. "Military Substitution Effects from Foreign Economic Aid: Buying Guns with Foreign Butter?" *Social Science Quarterly* 71, no. 4 (1990): 774–85.

Zanotti, Laura. "Cacophonies of Aid, Failed State Building and NGOs in Haiti: Setting the Stage for Disaster, Envisioning the Future." *Third World Quarterly* 31, no. 5 (2010): 755–71.

Zelin, Aaron. "The Islamic State of Iraq and Syria Has a Consumer Protection Office." *Atlantic*, June 13, 2014. https://www.theatlantic.com/international/archive/2014/06/the-isis-guide-to-building-an-islamic-state/372769/.

Zou, Heng-Fu. "A Dynamic Model of Capital and Arms Accumulation." *Journal of Economic Dynamics and Control* 19, no. 1/2 (1995): 371–93.

Index